L AMC GUIDE TO OUTDOOR EADERSHIP

ALEX KOSSEFF

Appalachian Mountain Club Books
Boston, Massachusetts

*To Mom, Dad, and my sister Lauren—who have
always had faith in me even when there were reasons to doubt.
Their support and assistance with this project were invaluable.*

Cover Design: Brandy Polay
Cover Photographs: Alex Kosseff, Katherine E. Jones, Holly Anderson, and
                  www.gettyimages.com
Interior Design: Kristin Camp
Interior Photographs: Alex Kosseff, Robert Kozlow, Katherine E. Jones, Mark Eis,
                  Bryan Courtois, Holly Anderson, and Marny Ashburne

Distributed by the Globe Pequot Press, Inc., Guilford, CT

LIBRARY OF CONGRESS CATALOGING-IN-PUBLICATION DATA

Kosseff, Alex, 1973-
AMC guide to outdoor leadership / Alex Kosseff.
     p.   cm.
Includes bibliographical references and index.
ISBN 1-929173-21-0 (paperback)
1. Recreation leadership. 2. Outdoor recreation.
I. Appalachian Mountain Club. II. Title.

GV181.4.K67 2003
796.5—dc21   2002154920

Please Note: Leading others in the outdoors is a complex and variable activity
that involves risk. No book can alert you to every hazard or provide appropriate
techniques for handling every situation. We recommend that this book be used
in conjunction with training to develop outdoor leadership skills. While this
book attempts to provide a guideline for outdoor leadership concepts, there are
no warranties regarding the usefulness and accuracy of the information here
within. Your use of this book indicates your assumption that it may contain
errors and is an acknowledgment of your own sole responsibility for your safety
and the safety of others for whom you are responsible.

The paper used in this publication meets the minimum requirements of the
American National Standard for Information Sciences—Permanence of Paper
for Printed Library Materials, ANSI Z39.48–1984.•

Printed on recycled paper using soy-based inks. ⊛

Printed in the United States of America.

10 9 8 7 6 5 4 3 2   04 05 06 07

Contents

Acknowledgments

Ultimately many people helped—both directly and indirectly—with the creation of this book. Some reviewed and commented on chapters. Others offered their insights or anecdotes. I greatly appreciate all of this assistance as well as the tremendous support I have received from friends, family, and housemates who have tolerated my diverted attention.

Numerous faculty members at Prescott College contributed their insights to the creation of this book, but three bear special mention. Laura Plaut and her Adventure Education students provided helpful input on several chapters. Though we only spent a short time together, Jim Miller's ideas were stimulating and his open enthusiasm for this undertaking was very welcome. When my computer was stolen and I had no place to stay my consistently amazing friend Erin Lotz rescued me and even helped nab the thief. Her assistance on this book, especially with chapter 1, was invaluable.

At the AMC, first thanks must go to Pat McCabe for her unwavering support on this project and all I have undertaken at the AMC. For working with me as I tried to juggle too many commitments and/or for their assistance with this book my friends Jeremy Johnson, Dara Houdek, Katherine Byers, Juliana Popper, and Faith Salter deserve special thanks. Working with the latter three members of that group—my department at the AMC—has been one of the great privileges of my life. One of the AMC's most incredible volunteers, Joe Kuzneski, provided valuable assistance just when it was most needed and helped shape several sections of this book.

At AMC Books I'd like to thank my editor, Blake Maher, for his insight, support, and most of all patience (it was tested). Publisher Beth Krusi has likewise been great to work with, and Belinda Thresher and Laurie O'Reilly have been helpful in every possible way. Thanks also to Mark Russell, former editor and publisher at AMC Books, who helped conceive this project three years ago.

Catherine Hansen-Stamp was a pleasure to work with on the legal issues section she contributed to this book. Scott Smalley and (in the final minutes) my longtime friend Brady Robinson also provided much-appreciated assistance.

Jed Williamson, President of Sterling College and Editor of Accidents in North American Mountaineering, provided late-breaking feedback that, regrettably, I was unable to acknowledge in the first printing. His editorial skills and insightful comments helped to polish the final product.

Finally, a big thank-you to all who have ventured out with me into the wild as mentors, co-leaders, participants, and friends. Each of those experiences we shared is reflected in some way in this book.

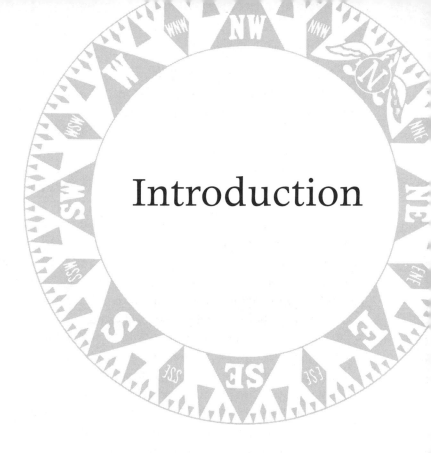

Introduction

It was only a hundred years ago that cities overtook small communities as home to the bulk of humanity. Aldo Leopold, one of America's great conservationists, wrote at a time when this great transformation had just taken place. Americans no longer lived in small towns and rural villages across the country, but in cities, and—increasingly—in suburbs. Outdoor work and play faded from many people's lives. When Leopold ran across some city boys on their first canoe camping trip he realized how little they and most other people knew of outdoor living. Regarding these boys he wrote: "The wilderness gave them their first taste of those rewards and penalties for wise and foolish acts which every outdoorsman faces daily, but against which civilization has built a thousand buffers."

Since Leopold's time the flow of people visiting, but not living in, America's wildlands has steadily increased. People go seeking rewards—a beautiful view, the spirit of adventure, or a greater understanding of themselves—but because many have limited experience in the outdoors, sometimes they instead suffer the consequences of their inexperience. The job of the outdoor leader is to try to ensure the rewards outweigh the penalties. From setting up a tent to working as a team to kayaking with the incoming tide, the outdoor leader makes the participants experience an enjoyable and educational one.

The outdoor leader evolved from origins in the frontier ideal into the Victorian model of the local guide for the elite. In the late 1800s and early 1900s, outdoor clubs such as the AMC, scouting programs, and summer camps emerged. From these origins sprang professional rafting guides, climbing guides, and adventure travel leaders, along with standard-bearing organizations such as Outward Bound and the National Outdoor Leadership School (NOLS). Over the past century, and particularly in the past thirty years, outdoor leadership has evolved from a casual pursuit into an activity that can be a professional career.

As outdoor leadership has evolved so has our understanding of what it takes to be a top-notch leader of people in the outdoors. Unfortunately, when I began leading I didn't know many of the helpful things others had already learned about effective outdoor leadership. The premise of this book is that you shouldn't have to reinvent the wheel. Whether you lead trips full time, for a season, occasionally as a volunteer, or are just interested in learning leadership skills, this book is intended to transfer some of what other leaders have learned to you. If you're just starting out it will give you a head start. If you are already an experienced leader you will gain new approaches to thinking about your work.

While experience and training remain critically important, the *AMC Guide to Outdoor Leadership* will always be there for you to consult. To the novice leader, reading this book will mean one thing, and parts may even be challenging to understand, but as you gain experience you will find new parts that resonate with you and help to build your skills. Refer back to this book, and reflect on your leadership experiences— used in combination this will maximize your growth as a leader.

Becoming an excellent outdoor leader requires patience and practice, training and tutelage, and reading that will reinforce and expand upon much of what you learn. To assist you in further reading, each chapter includes a recommended reading list. Most of the references contain additional information and ideas that supplement the text. Some references are marked with a diamond (♦) to indicate that the reference features material that is more advanced. Often these references focus on one narrow aspect of the chapter's material.

Finally, it is important to make a note on names used in this book. The *AMC Guide to Outdoor Leadership* relies extensively on stories or anecdotes relating actual events to illustrate many points. When a first and last name is used to identify the source of the story or a participant in it, the names of those involved are real. The stories in this book also involve many individuals who are identified only by first name. These first names are fictitious. The purpose of this book is to teach, not to glorify or cast blame.

My hope is that this book will help you and your groups enjoy more of the rewards Aldo Leopold mentions and suffer fewer of the penalties. Reading this book is not insurance against committing foolish acts, but it should aid you in making some wiser choices. Enjoy yourself and your leadership roles, and through this book, and otherwise, always keep learning!

CHAPTER I

Caring Leadership

S tanding out clearly in the fog of my childhood memories is my first recollection of outdoor leadership. My father, mother, little sister, and I set out to climb Mount Katahdin, Maine's highest peak. At least *I* recall setting out to scale the peak. My parents, I believe in retrospect, never truly had their hearts set on the summit. Contributing to their lack of commitment may have been my younger sister, who spent most of the trek in the child carrier on their backs.

With only minimal difficulty we reached Chimney Pond. From there we had a clear view of the stark ridges and rock walls leading up to the summit. It was a glorious sunny day. My parents off-loaded my sister on the shore and sat down for a snack. There was no indication that they planned to go any higher. I made my disappointment known. With the top of the mountain now in sight, I was quite clear that *this* was no time to sit down.

My parents tried to convince me the summit was still a long way off, but I was having none of that—I could, after all, see the top! Eventually they relented, and we decided that my mother and I would continue upward a short distance. We set off and soon came to a sign indicating that you had to be seven years old to proceed above that point. Being two months shy of that requirement, I was sure that this was the end of the road for me, but my mother kept climbing. Now this was adventure!

The trail, a veritable highway through the trees below, now headed up steep and jumbled boulders above the pond. It took assistance from my mother for me to overcome some of these obstacles. I didn't notice the clouds moving in until it began to snow. Snowing in the middle of summer! In my almost-seven-year-old mind this was extraordinarily exciting. Unfortunately the flurries lasted no more than a few minutes, and my fantasy of having enough for a snowball fight was dashed. Between the cold wind and the difficult climbing, I was ready to descend when my mother suggested it.

We rejoined my father and sister at Chimney Pond and began the hike down. It was late afternoon, and all I wanted to do was take a nap. I had never been this tired. As my parents encouraged me onward, I made it clear that I was not thrilled with my predicament. They mentioned that they had to switch off carrying my sister and the big backpack whereas I had nothing to carry; I should have plenty of energy. Logic didn't work. Nor did singing. We walked slowly, other hikers passing us, as the shadows grew longer and longer.

Suddenly my eye caught sight of a quarter in the trail. Where did this come from? Then, a little way down the trail, a dime. My weary body was forgotten—I was going to be rich! Why my father hiked with a pocket full of change that day I don't know, but his strategically tossed coins got me down the trail and back to the car.

A dozen years elapsed before I actually set foot on the summit of Katahdin. When I did I was in charge of a group of high school students. It was my second year leading backcountry trips, and the challenges and responsibilities I faced were very similar to those my parents had experienced with me as a child. Outdoor leadership demands many different skills, but at its heart—no matter whom you lead—is caring.

Caring and Leadership

What was my parents' role on Katahdin that day? It was the role of any parent anywhere—to reasonably protect their children from danger, to

Robert Kozlow

Participants place a lot of trust in their leader when they head off into unfamiliar and sometimes hazardous terrain.

nurture them, allow them to learn, allow them to enjoy. They were caring for my sister and me. Caring is feeling and exhibiting concern for others and accepting their well-being as a priority of your own. That day on Katahdin my parents were not only parents but also took on the unaccustomed role (for them) of outdoor leaders. While some of the skills involved are different, ultimately the aims of parents and outdoor leaders vary only in the time frame each has to accomplish their goals.

To the chagrin of some who expect outdoor leadership to be a "macho" undertaking, this is far from the case. Outdoor skills certainly play a huge role in effective leadership, and the caring leader must have these skills. But what makes great leaders is their ability to perceive participants' struggles and fears, to offer well-timed encouragement, to use consistently good judgment, to keep a sense of humor—and to know when to apply it.

Types of Caring

There are two types of caring that outdoor leaders may engage in: natural caring and contractual caring.

Natural Caring: In this type of caring, you as leader act not out of a sense of duty but rather because you want to. This is the type of caring that parents (ideally) exhibit with their children. It arises not out of obligation but out of a genuine desire to do the best thing for the other person. Natural caring, according to educational philosopher Nel Nodding, turns to action when you connect the desire to care with your own experience of being cared for. A positive memory of being cared for thus triggers action in order to reproduce this experience for others.

Outdoor leaders do not take on leadership roles for personal gain. They do so because they want to provide people—whoever they are—with a certain experience. Leaders *care* about their participants in an outdoor activity. As a leader gets to know a participant or group of participants, relationship caring comes into play. Adults may care for all children in a general sense, but parents most actively and intensely care for their own children—this is usually a very strong case of relationship caring. When you as a leader get to know participants and develop relationships with them, you may come to care for them not just as participants on the trip, but as individual people.

In her book *Caring*, Nel Nodding describes the result of natural caring: "To care is to act not by fixed rule but by affection and regard. It seems likely, then, that the actions . . . will be varied rather than rule-bound; that is . . . actions, while predictable in a global sense, will be unpredictable in detail." This quote, though unintentionally, beautifully captures the spirit of the best outdoor leadership. Outdoor leadership is too complicated to be governed by a simple set of rules. It is best accomplished through the judgment of skilled and informed individuals acting with the best intent and caring to carry their efforts through to completion.

Contractual Caring: This second type of caring occurs because it is obligatory for the leader. Even if you as a leader don't care for the participants in the sense of having a deep commitment to their experience or to them as individuals, you must still take care of them. Participants' experiences, and often their lives, are largely in your hands. They rightfully expect that a certain amount of care will be put into their experience and safety. This can be viewed as a sort of contract—participants agree to undertake the outdoor program, and you agree to provide an appropriate level of care.

An analogy can also be drawn between this type of leader caring and parenting. Even in the absence of a feeling of natural caring, parents still have a clear moral obligation to provide basic care for their children. Society has even constructed a contract between parent and child, with the state representing the interests of the child. Parents who fail to provide care for their child can face repercussions as severe as criminal charges. Similarly, leaders can face legal repercussions if they fail to provide an adequate level of care. More important than the legal issue, however, is the moral aspect of appropriate leadership. Participants in outdoor programs, particularly beginners, place a tremendous amount of trust in leaders. You as a leader have an obligation to live up to this trust.

Clearly, I have a preference for leaders who exhibit natural caring. Such caring, however, cannot be forced if you don't actually feel it for participants. The fallback position is the obligation of contractual caring that you agree to fulfill when taking on a leadership role.

Leaders can, however, develop relationships with participants, and through this develop a sense of natural caring. Slowing down to forge this relationship is a wonderful thing for leaders to do and will always be appreciated by participants. The pace of outdoor activities can be a fast one, so it's important to remember the critical one-on-one relationship that truly gives the work of leadership energy and meaning.

Challenges to Caring

Adventure is thought of as part of many outdoor activities. The presence of adventure implies uncertainty. There are, not unexpectedly, degrees of adventure. Advertisements for Sir Ernest Shackleton's famously unsuccessful 1914 Antarctic expedition read: "Men wanted for hazardous journey, small wages, bitter cold, long months of complete darkness, constant danger, safe return doubtful, honor and recognition in case of success." Now, that ad oozes adventure. Shackleton and his entire crew survived for more than a year, mostly living atop drifting sea ice, after their boat *Endurance* was trapped and crushed by the ice. In contrast, the level of adventure—and unpredictability—during the activities most leaders offer is far lower.

Nonetheless, as a child I was thrilled by the unpredictability of summer snowfall on Katahdin. The outcome of my outing with my parents became a little more uncertain as night began to fall, my legs began to falter, and I grew petulant. As a leader you will probably never lay down a trail of coins—instead you'll be called upon to create your own treasure in the form of solutions to the challenges that confront you. These solutions you generate will be essential to caring for your participants. The caring leader begins with good intention and follows through on that intention, but must also have the skills—creativity key among them—to make these intentions work. Little use my parents would have been as leaders if they had just yelled at me and told me to get my whiny butt down the mountain. I might have sat down right there for the night and refused to move; more likely, I would have sullenly descended the trail hating mountains every step of the way. Neither outcome was the one desired by a caring leader of a six-year-old.

The challenges may not all be external. As a leader you will, at times, be tired, hungry, dehydrated, annoyed, and even scared. In the face of such concerns, some of them deeply personal, you must maintain your caring. It is here, when the going is most difficult, that it really takes more than the obligation of contractual caring to be a great leader. When you're at your most miserable, your participants will probably be doing a lot worse. They will be best served by a leader who has a deep sense of personal investment in the finding the best possible outcome.

While outdoor adventures can and should have a degree of uncertainty, part of the role of outdoor leaders is to remove some of this. As a caring leader you understand that participants want an adventurous experience—but you also know that they want a reasonably safe experience. This is part of the unwritten contract between leaders and participants. The question sometimes is how far to go. When is an activity too risky to do at all? Should the leader always light the camp stove because of the danger of a flare-up, thereby depriving participants of the opportunity to learn and gain their own confidence? How direct should you be with a participant whose behavior is making the experience difficult for others? The caring answer to these and many other questions can be difficult to determine. Still, you'll be well served by looking to the best practices employed by other leaders, and observing how they find a caring balance. This book, and the training and experience it recommends, will also help provide perspective on these issues.

Fundamental Responsibilities of Outdoor Leaders

There are four fundamental responsibilities of outdoor leaders. The first two of these—to minimize risk and to minimize impact on the environment—are absolutely fundamental to caring leadership. The second set—to maximize learning and maximize enjoyment—are clearly important aspects of caring leadership, though they might, at times, take a backseat to the first two.

Minimize Risk: A leader's most fundamental responsibility is to manage participants' risk of injury, death, or psychological harm during a program. The risk of harm cannot be eliminated from any activity, of course, but it can be reduced with competent leadership.

Minimize Impact on the Environment: Individuals and groups have an obligation to leave areas in at least as good a condition as when they arrived. Without such continual care, our cumulative impact will diminish the very wilderness we love. Outdoor leaders have the opportunity to model and teach Leave No Trace principles, thus helping set the standard for all outdoor recreationists. This responsibility stretches the concept of caring used in this chapter. While people are the primary focus of outdoor leadership, it seems safe to assume that those who take others into the outdoors care equally for the wild lands they visit.

Maximize Learning: Within the context of a given activity, you as leader should seize upon opportunities to educate. While outdoor activities certainly aren't always educational in focus, all do present opportunities to educate participants. Even participating in mundane tasks can be a learning opportunity—let people learn just by getting them involved. When participants leave a program with improved outdoor skills or a greater appreciation and understanding of themselves, groups, or the natural environment, you've done a real service.

Maximize Enjoyment: Recreation, to most people, means fun. This is why most people sign up for outdoor programs. The participants' ability to enjoy their experience can influence whether outdoor activities become (or remain) a lifelong source of enjoyment. Even groups that put other goals ahead of enjoyment—successfully negotiating a particular river or building character in youth—can only benefit from a little fun along the way.

Implementing these responsibilities as an outdoor leader requires both a full understanding of the responsibilities and a variety of knowledge, skills, and experience. The rest of this book will help you along the path toward best living up to these responsibilities—something that even the most experienced and skilled leaders continue to work on.

Two Tales of Outdoor Leadership

In the Wind River Range

I first met Erin Lotz when we were both working as instructors for the Voyageur Outward Bound School. Erin, one of the most naturally gifted climbers I've ever met, is also a committed educator who has worked with a tremendous variety of different groups. Today she's a faculty member in the Adventure Education Program at Arizona's Prescott College. Her story of outdoor leadership involves a Prescott College Alpine Mountaineering course she co-instructed in Wyoming's Wind River Range.

The Winds, as they are often called, offer some of the finest wilderness hiking and climbing in the lower forty-eight states. Erin and her co-instructor had nine students in their course. During the first week, the group hiked in and camped at an unnamed lake marked only with its elevation—10,831 feet—on the topographic map.

Though unstable weather had thwarted much of their climbing for several days, on this day the group arose to find clear skies. Erin and four students set out for a rock climb a short distance from camp. The day before, on the same route, a group had reached the summit as a storm raced in. As they descended, alternating rain and snow made the descent treacherous and slippery. They watched as lightning struck the summit they had just left. On the day of this story, however, the sky remained relatively clear as they reached the base of the soaring granite, and everyone remained optimistic that the weather would hold at least through the morning. A few of the students accompanying Erin were strong climbers and had climbed the route the day before, so they took turns leading the rest of the group up the rock pitches.

The first clouds began to move in when they were still fairly close to the ground. As they climbed, the clouds become thicker, but their view of the incoming weather was partially blocked. The five climbers gathered on a small ledge to decide what to do. From their location on the cliff, the group could use existing anchors to make the rappels necessary to reach the ground. Those who had been on the climb before knew that if they progressed upward, there were no more existing anchors they could rappel from. Up or down? To Erin the answer seemed fairly obvious.

For two students it was an easy choice to rappel—and they did. While watching the two descend, Erin and the remaining two students discussed the decision and it became clear that the students wanted to continue climbing. They were both excited to be leading a long climb in the mountains. Because they had done the climb before, the students both felt that they could move quickly and be off the summit before conditions deteriorated. Erin felt that the clouds were moving in very quickly and they should descend to avoid being caught in a storm. The three discussed their points of view briefly. Unconvinced of the safety of continuing in the face of a potential storm, Erin unilaterally decided the group would rappel down.

Both of the students were very disappointed with Erin's choice—though they did respect it. They rigged the ropes for the rappels silently. By the time they reached the bottom rappel, the wind had picked up with intense gusts. Indeed, it was so intense that it whipped the rope into a crack, forcing Erin to climb back up to free it. As she did so, snow began to fall heavily, making the hike down across wet talus tricky. They headed back to the security of their camp, hoping that the weather would give them a break and they could get in some climbing in the days to come.

Analysis: In the Wind Rivers, Erin Lotz was a caring leader. She faced a decision and made the unpopular choice that was in the best long-term interest of the group. Her actions fulfilled the fundamental responsibilities of a leader: She minimized the risk to the group and also—though they may not have imagined so in the moment—probably maximized their learning and enjoyment. The actions of the good leader will not always please the participants, especially not in the short term. Of course Erin did consult with the students, listen to their opinions, and explain her decision. These, too, are caring actions, because they helped the students learn and probably made the experience more enjoyable. Erin was well trained for and experienced at her job, so she was able to successfully carry it out even as the situation become more difficult. In being proactive and making a conservative decision early on, Erin avoided a situation that might have had much more significant negative impacts for her participants.

Erin and her co-instructor had to make an appropriate plan for this trip with their participants—but their preparations began even earlier. The situation Erin contended with on the cliff was relatively routine for the program she was leading. Yet simply dealing with that particular incident required years of training and experience to effectively handle its complexities. She used climbing skills, weather-reading skills, decision-making and judgment skills, as well as interpersonal skills. If her abilities in these areas were not solid, she would not have been a caring leader. Caring begins long before the start of a program.

This particular trip was long, remote, and involved fairly complex outdoor skills. The demands on a caring leader on this type of trip are much higher than they might be if Erin had been leading a two-night backpack on the edge of the same range. But she also had students who started the course with a high skill level. If she and her partner had been taking out a group of complete novices, caring leadership would have involved even more attention to safety, developing positive group dynamics, and teaching climbing basics. This hypothetical trip with less experienced participants could almost be thought of as requiring a higher level of caring.

The Wild River

In mid-June 1998 a group from a high school outing club in Vermont set out for a backpacking trip in New Hampshire's White Mountains. The group consisted of six students and two adults, including the trip leader, who was also head of the school's outdoor program. On the first

A large part of leadership is caring for people, which involves taking the time to communicate with them.

night the group ascended to the South Baldface Shelter. Overnight the already poor weather deteriorated, with increasingly heavy rains.

The group's plan for the second day was to head to another shelter, a trip of about 8½ miles with 2,500 feet of elevation gain. In the morning the group leader decided that, due to the weather, rather than ascend nearby South Baldface Mountain over steep ledges, she would take the group over an alternative route. The new route—now involving more than 12½ miles of travel— added 1,000 feet of elevation gain. The route also traversed a ridge exposed to the weather and involved four crossings of the Wild River that can be difficult at normal water levels.

Torrential rains continued, and by one in the afternoon the group still had about 9 miles to go, including the traverse of the ridge and the river crossings. At this point the group leader gave a map to two girls in the group, ages fourteen and fifteen, and told them to go ahead to the shelter. Apparently, she felt the girls could move faster than the main group and would be better off if they made it to the shelter, so the two girls headed off on their own. Behind them, at a well-signed trail junction, the main group took a wrong turn and ascended Eastman Mountain.

After backtracking to the point at which they had made their wrong turn, the main group decided to camp there for the night. The group leader decided to set out alone toward the road to attempt to summon help. On her way out she slipped crossing what is typically a small brook. In the flood conditions, though, the leader was quickly swept 60 feet downstream and reported that she had nearly drowned.

Sergeant Bob Bryant works for the New Hampshire Department of Fish and Game, which has jurisdiction over search-and-rescue operations in the state. "The leader came out of the woods totally wet and confused," reports Bryant, who was involved in the rescue of this group, "and we headed in early the next morning." In continuing poor conditions, Fish and Game officers, along with volunteers from search-and-rescue organizations, headed in to assist the main group and find the missing girls. As Bryant tells it: "We were lucky that we had just practiced setting up tyroleans [rope traverses], because that was the only way we could get people across the streams."

The main group was found first, and rescuers set up ropes to assist them across swollen brooks. These ropes were also used by search teams as they fanned out on trails to find the two missing girls. "When we got to them they were just stranded by high water," says Sergeant Bryant. Rescuers set up more ropes to aid the girls to safety. Having lost a sleeping bag in a brook crossing on the first day, the two girls had then succeeded in making a risky crossing of the incredibly swollen Wild River. Realizing they would not make it to the shelter, they spent their night out sharing the one sleeping bag under the shelter of some dense conifers.

During the night, with water still rising, the girls had become trapped between steep, flooded brooks feeding the main river. That morning, fearing that they might have to remain where they were for several days, the girls improvised a shelter of hemlock boughs. They also rationed their supply of food. "Unlike the leader, it seemed like they did a great job given the circumstances," concludes Sergeant Bryant. With a little exasperation, he adds, "We spend most of our search-and-rescue time dealing with groups that have not kept together—usually because a slower hiker gets left behind. This situation was a little different, but like the rest, they probably would have been fine if they just stayed together."

Analysis: From all indications, I am sure that the outing club leader from Vermont cared about the participants on her trip. Unfortunately that care was not matched by her ability to fulfill even her most basic responsibilities to the group. The leader was not able to minimize risk; minimizing impact on the environment probably fell by the wayside under the circumstances. It is quite clear that participants' enjoyment was not maximized, though in an unfortunate way they may have been able to learn quite a lot from the experience. The best intentions can lead us in wrong directions. This leader needed to give much more thought to her leadership in advance of the trip. Once the trip began, the leader faced a difficult situation due to the intense rain. Unfortunately she made mistake after mistake after mistake. There is no simple formula for leadership—a caring leader must devote time and energy to learning to lead. It's very lucky that the outcome of this situation in the White Mountains was not a tragic one. As you continue reading this book, this is a good story to consider as an example of close to a worst-case scenario.

In Conclusion

Caring parents—to bring this discussion full circle—have the best of intentions. They educate themselves about parenting. They may read books, talk to their friends, and take classes on parenting. Most parents get hands-on practice almost every day for at least eighteen years. At times they serve as doctor, counselor, teacher, and friend. Sure, there may be some missteps along the way, but that's okay, as long as the damage isn't permanent. Parenting is the best analogy I can imagine for outdoor leadership. As an outdoor leader you must fill myriad roles, but in the end you must be driven by caring for the participants and 100 percent dedication to their safety.

This analogy with parenting may shatter a few people's conceptions of what it means to be an outdoor leader. A student in an outdoor education degree program told me as I was writing this book: "I thought I was coming here to climb and ski, but we have to learn about all this group stuff and working with people. I wish I had read something like your book before I started this." I hope that this book helps a few more people deepen their understanding of outdoor leadership.

The opportunities for outdoor leadership are almost unlimited. Whether you want to lead your friends on a nearby backpack or take a paying client sea kayaking off Greenland, if you have the right skills and experience, you can find the way. Some leadership roles require more of a focus on technical skills; some require almost none. The common element, however, is people. Four fundamental responsibilities of outdoor leaders—maximize safety, minimize impact on the environment, maximize learning, and maximize enjoyment—were outlined earlier in this chapter. The need to fulfill these responsibilities will be self-evident to the caring leader.

RECOMMENDED READING

♦ Noddings, Nel, *Caring: A Feminine Approach to Ethics and Moral Education,* Berkeley: University of California Press, 1984.

♦ = Advanced Recommendation

CHAPTER 2

Foundations

Leaders need, but unfortunately don't have always have, a solid foundation to support their outdoor leadership. One way to think of outdoor leadership is as a three-legged stool. The leader must perch atop this stool, the legs of which are hard skills, soft skills, and motivation. In the best of situations the legs are equal in length and the leader's stability is assured. As you can imagine, if one leg is a wee bit short, the stool becomes unbalanced. With two short legs, or one missing almost entirely, the stool becomes impossible to sit on. At this point the leader slides off—and the results can be bruising. In this chapter you will learn more about the legs of the stool and meet a leader whose stool was seriously off balance.

Observations on Orizaba

My friend Hampton and I had come to climb Pico de Orizaba, the third highest peak in North America, featuring relatively uncomplicated access to higher elevations. While both of us had extensive mountain experience in all seasons, we didn't have experience climbing at higher altitudes. Six dollars in bus fares transported us from a friend's home in Mexico City to the village of Tlachichuca at the base of the 18,700-foot volcanic peak. Viewed from the town square, the glacier-robed peak rises 12,000 feet in solitary reign above the unwatered plains.

The next stage of our endeavor was a rugged drive to base camp. We shared our sturdy four-wheel-drive "taxi" with Montana resident Bill and his children Cindy and Garrett. Neither Cindy, sixteen years old, nor Garrett, who was seventeen, had been outside the United States before. More important, neither had used—or seen—an ice ax or crampons before they arrived in town at the base of the mountain. Three years prior Bill had made a similar pilgrimage to climb the mountain with his brother. He had carried an ice ax that time, but altitude sickness had turned around their summit bid not far above base camp—well below the snow of the glacier.

The main hazard of the climb, besides the effects of rapid ascent to a relatively high elevation, is slipping on steep snow slopes. Our advance reading and a reconnaissance hike once we reached base camp indicated that the upper glacier reached an angle of about forty degrees. A fall there could result in a tumbling slide thousands of feet long. Hence the necessity of the ice ax, which reduces the risk of falls when used like a walking stick or can be used as a self-belay with the shaft plunged into the snow. Most important, the ice ax can be used to arrest a sliding fall on the glacier. Without an ice ax a climber would be helpless in a fall, and even with one a practiced technique is generally necessary to keep the tool from being wrenched from your grasp. Bill and family rented ice axes, at the insistence of the outfitter driving us up the mountain.

On the way down from our first day's reconnaissance hike, we encountered Bill and clan coming up the trail. After an exchange of greetings, Bill asked us if we could provide a lesson in the use of an ice ax. Hampton and I reviewed the basics, but we both emphasized that a practice session was invaluable. I was glad that we got in the review session, because we discovered that Bill misunderstood what part of the ax was used for self-arrest. We extracted a promise from all three of the Montanans that they would practice their new skills on the safe snowfield above us. Hampton and I headed back to base camp and set about trying to get some rest on the wooden bunks of the small shelter we were sharing with the other climbers.

The next we saw of Bill, Cindy, and Garrett, we were eating a hot meal cooked on our backpacking stove. The evening was rapidly cooling off, and Hampton and I bundled into our polypro underwear, fleece jackets, and warm hats. The Montanans were wearing jeans and T-shirts and donned what was their only warm layer—cotton sweatshirts. Then they climbed into their sleeping bags and ate candy for dinner. We soon learned that Bill and family didn't have a backpacking stove or any wool or synthetic clothes, which stay warm when wet. They also didn't have a way to purify water, wind pants, headlamps, or much of the other equipment that is today considered standard for a safe climb.

We gathered from Cindy and Garrett that their Orizaba climb was Dad's idea. They had done nothing more than casual summer day hikes in Montana to prepare for a mountain that unnecessarily claims multiple lives most years. Given the lack of appropriate judgment, technical skills, and equipment, Hampton and I were very concerned about the family's safety on the mountain. And while we were unsure how he would respond, we decided that we had an obligation to voice our concerns to Bill.

Not wanting to question his judgment in front of his children, I caught up with Bill outside camp. Carefully, I explained Hampton's and my concerns, to which Bill listened patiently. I said that we didn't doubt his or his children's ability to climb the mountain, but we felt that in doing so they would be taking unnecessary risks. I talked about technique, judgment, clothing, and equipment. I told Bill—who knew about my employment in outdoor risk management—that in my line of work I could never let a climb like his go forward. Bill, in his turn, was emphatic that he was going to climb the mountain. His one concession laid out a trap for Hampton and me: "If you think we need help, why don't you give us more guidance?" Our advice could be beneficial, but I was afraid that we'd only increase his confidence for a climb we thought he should abandon. Bill and I then spent half an hour discussing the dubious merits of his plan to tie the three members of his party closely together with a length of rope. This was even before I saw their "climbing rope"—though I probably should have guessed. It was little more substantial than a clothesline.

Three Foundations——————————————

Your leadership stool, we have learned, has the three legs of hard skills, soft skills, and motivation. To stay in balance you must understand these three components of effective outdoor leadership. You must also carry over from the first chapter the knowledge that it is the caring leader who can find success in developing these skills. Only as a caring leader will you have the focus and dedication to develop and use your hard and soft skills, or the motivation you need to be a good, well-balanced leader. The three foundations are described below.

Hard Skills

Bill and his family, but especially Bill as their leader, were all short on hard skills. These are the physical-activity- and knowledge-based skills necessary to engage in a given outdoor pursuit. Paddling a canoe, navigation, first aid, backpacking, and reading the weather are all examples of hard skills. There are two general categories of hard skills: (1) the core hard skills all leaders should have, and (2) activity-specific hard skills—such as those needed for alpine mountaineering—that are required only for leaders of that type of activity.

Core Hard Skills for Outdoor Leaders

► Trip planning

► First aid

► Crisis response

► Risk management

► Leave No Trace

► Nutrition and hydration

► Navigation

► Liability and legal isues

► Activity-specific skills

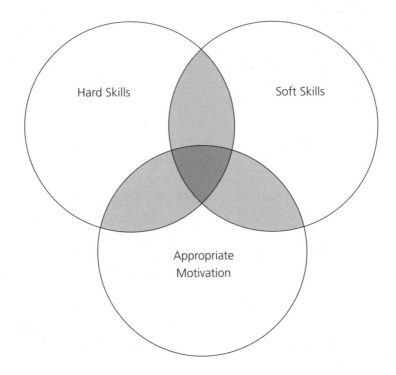

Effective leadership: hard skills, soft skills, and appropriate motivation converge to set the stage for effective leadership.

Those without solid hard skills for the activity they are undertaking cannot be counted upon to take care of themselves, let alone make decisions for a group. While leading a group in spring in the southern Rocky Mountains, for instance, I was surprised to run across another group from the same program in the field. Our routes were not supposed to cross, and as it turned out the other group was a bit off course. The other leader and his group were perplexed because the white areas on the map did not seem to match up with the remaining spring snowfields on the ground. (Of course these white areas actually represent spots free of dense tree growth.) While this leader had excellent skills in some areas, his deficient map-reading abilities meant he could not safely lead his group on a backpacking trip. He also should have been playing an instructional role, but couldn't because he hadn't mastered the skills he was called upon to teach others.

It's relatively easy for the experienced outdoor leader to assess an individual's hard skills through observation or an evaluation of experi-

ence, training, and recommendations. Evaluation is easiest with hard skills that can
be quantified. It's clear, for
instance, what a solid 5.7 rock
climber or a Class IV whitewater kayaker is capable of. The
emergence of relatively stan-
dardized training courses in
the United States—Wilder-
ness First Responder or Avalanche Level One, for example
—means that some skills that
people once developed piece-
meal are now essentially
quantifiable. Consulting with
others on skill development
is very helpful, because it's
often difficult to self-assess
your own skills. Guidance on
the development of both hard
and soft skills is provided in
chapter 3, Learning to Lead.

Robert Kozlow

Leading up this ice climb so group members can follow puts this leader's hard skills to the test.

Physical fitness is impor-
tant to mention. While not a hard skill per se, it's a critical component
of many hard skills. Leaders need to be in strong enough physical condition that they always have a reserve of strength even if their followers are exhausted. Most active outdoor pursuits require a leader to be
in decent to excellent physical shape.

Here's an example of some activity-specific hard skills:

Alpine Mountaineering Skills

▶ Mountain clothing

▶ Thermoregulation

▶ Mountain weather patterns

▶ Packing

► Backcountry camping

► Backcountry cooking

► Navigation

► Ice ax use

► Crampon use

► Roped travel

► Snow anchors

► Crevasse rescue

Not all of the core skills will be used on every outing, but they're all important to outdoor leaders. The list of skills for a specific activity—in this example, alpine mountaineering—varies because of the variable nature of such activities. Depending on the terrain, objective of the outing, and other factors, additional skills may be needed, and some of those listed in the chart may be unnecessary. On Orizaba, for example, knowledge of crevasse rescue does not appear to be necessary, but a basic grasp of Spanish became useful and made the experience more enjoyable.

Soft Skills

Soft skills is an apt term—the definition is vaguer than that of *hard skills*. Soft skills are also more difficult to teach and evaluate than hard skills. Teaching, awareness, judgment, and dealing with group dynamics are soft skills and require psychological and intellectual abilities that take experience and time to develop. In your brain hard skills camp in one location and soft skills somewhere else. Think about it: Many leaders have a big meadow for the hard skills and a little bivouac ledge for the soft skills (for a few leaders the opposite is true). Many leaders can develop a balance of skills, but for some this is a struggle.

On Orizaba, Hampton and I both realized what Bill did not—that Cindy was desperately unhappy about being on the climb. Group (especially family) dynamics are complicated, but it's critical for the leader to be aware of them. Time and again we witnessed Bill ignoring or dismissing his daughter's concerns. Cindy, as a result of the poor soft skills of her dominating leader, was unhappily engaged in a potentially dangerous climb. Clearly the caring leader would not push so hard for anyone to climb this peak. Along with a lack of hard skills necessary for mountaineering, then, Bill lacked the soft skills necessary for effective and caring leadership.

Core Soft Skills for Outdoor Leaders

- Communication
- Expedition behavior
- Leadership style
- Judgment
- Decision making
- Crisis management
- Facilitation
- Teaching
- Empathy
- Ethics
- Group dynamics
- Awareness of self
- Awareness of group
- Awareness of environment

When I began working for the AMC, I quickly realized that many of the volunteer leaders had strong soft skills. Prior to the AMC much of my own outdoor leadership experience had involved working with twenty-something-year-old professional outdoor leaders. Most volunteer leaders at the AMC are older and come with broader life experiences than the leaders I was accustomed to. These leaders have careers, are parents, and have been active in community organizations. Such experiences have allowed these leaders opportunities to develop soft skills that they carry over into their outdoor leadership roles.

Alex Kosseff

This leader needs hard skills to manage this rappel, but her soft skills are essential to teaching participants the necessary skills and making them feel comfortable.

Office careers, parenting, and community involvement all initially seem to have little to do with outdoor leadership, but a closer look reveals that success in these enterprises requires many of the same soft skills as outdoor leadership. Among the many relevant leadership skills that parenting may help leaders develop are those of teaching, communication, empathy, and even crisis management. A successful professional career often requires working in a group and skill in leadership, decision making, communication, empathy, and more. Many AMC leaders have also been participating in outdoor recreation for ten, thirty, or fifty years. They have seen what works for outdoor leaders and what doesn't. These soft skills, though hard to quantify, are a large part of what makes a successful leader.

Unfortunately, as we see in the account of Bill leading his family on Orizaba, age and life experience don't always add up to effective soft skills. For most people an intentional focus on the development of these skills and some constructive feedback from others are necessary. And yet people are generally more willing to provide critical feedback on hard skills than they are on soft skills. Many are willing to say, "Let me show you another way to tie the rope on the bear bag so it's easier to untie." Fewer people are comfortable telling you, "When you ignored my advice on where to put the bear bag, it made me feel like you didn't value what I had to say." Leaders of all ages need to do what's necessary to acquire soft skills; these sometimes neglected skills and approaches to developing them will be the focus of much of this book.

Motivation

The best leaders are excited about their role. They're enthusiastic about putting their hard and soft skills to work. They smile, they teach, and they make the experience enjoyable for others. Leaders who see their role as a chore (and there are more than a few) do not engage participants fully and often neglect important tasks related to safety and the quality of the experience. Outdoor leadership demands too much of you—physically, intellectually, and psychologically—for you to be really good without total commitment. The best leaders are able to maximize their potential because they are motivated.

> *"Technique and ability alone do not get you to the top—it is will-power that is most important. This willpower you cannot buy with money or be given by others—it rises from your heart."*
> —JUNKO TABEI, FIRST WOMAN TO CLIMB MOUNT EVEREST

Motivation, broadly defined, is everything that drives you to get going when the going gets tough and pushes you to be the best leader you can be. One source of motivation is the care you feel for your participants and the environment, as was discussed in chapter 1. Other positive sources of motivation for outdoor leaders include sharing your love of the outdoors, pride in doing a good job, satisfaction from shepherding your group through challenges, the respect you garner, or even a paycheck or free trip (ideally, these last two are not the primary factors).

Motivation must come from a variety of different sources. As a leader you will face human and environmental challenges; your motivation needs to be strong enough to keep you focused on addressing them. Leaders who remain consistently motivated are those who have many sources of motivation. If you're motivated to lead largely because you enjoy the teaching aspect, your motivation can be sapped by a group that's not interested in learning. Outdoor leadership, with its irregular schedule and unpredictable demands, can result in frustration and burnout. The motivated leader who proactively and enthusiastically tackles chores and challenges is more effective than one who shirks them. In this way and many others your motivation will impact your effectiveness as a leader.

In addition to being excited about leading, you must be excited for the right reasons. The peak you want to climb, the rapid you'd like to run, or the group member you'd like to get to know better are not where you should find your motivation to lead. Personal goals such as these should play, at the most, a tertiary role to primary and secondary goals of minimizing risk and attaining group goals. Likewise, ego boost—from running the show or strutting your skills—is not the reason to assume the leadership mantle.

With Bill on Orizaba we see an example of a personal goal—attaining the summit—comprising his primary motivation for leading his inexperienced children on the climb. Generally you should be able to have fun with your role, but any personal objective (even those common to the whole group) may have to take a backseat to the interests of one or more group members. Many disasters in outdoor leadership have their roots in the inappropriate motivation—often the personal objectives or ego—of the leaders.

Balancing Your Three-legged Stool ——

A leader should attempt to attain a reasonable balance of soft skills, hard skills, and motivation. Everyone is sitting on a stool that is a little bit off kilter. Awareness of your own abilities will help you focus your energy and learning on areas where you need improvement. Most outdoor leadership is done in pairs, and an awareness of your abilities may also help you pair up with co-leaders who complement your skills. While you might have excellent skills at working with groups, for instance, your partner might have strong safety skills. You'll learn from the others with whom you lead.

Simply advertising yourself as a leader or being hired to perform the role doesn't make you a one—a leader needs followers. Solid hard skills, soft skills, and appropriate motivation will help make those you lead most comfortable with your leadership role. It's true that a lopsided leadership style, weak in one or even two areas, may gain the buy-in of some participants in the short run. In the longer term, however, and in difficult situations, solid hard skills, soft skills, and motivation will best support your leadership.

To the Summit?

On summit day the five of us in the small refuge hut on Orizaba arose before two in the morning. Hampton and I had planned on another day to acclimatize, but we were unenthralled with life in base camp and I was eager to get on to climbing a technical ice climb on another peak. After wishing luck to Bill, Cindy, and Garrett, we headed up the rocky trail. In surprisingly cold temperatures under a partly clear sky, we ascended without conversation. A break would have necessitated quickly adding warm layers, maybe more than either of us carried. We kept a mountaineer's pace—slow and steady—through the early-morning hours.

By the time we were well onto the glacier, I was ill. I let Hampton know but felt that I could continue. There was no other appealing option—the steep couloir we'd ascended below the glacier would be a nightmare to descend until the sun softened the icy snow. Dawn was not yet a hint on the horizon, and given the unexpectedly cold temperatures hypothermia would quickly follow if we rested. Had we been readily able to descend, we might have done so, returning in a day or two. As it was, the idea of hiking around the glacier in circles until the warming sun rose was uninviting. We continued upward.

The slope angle gradually increased, which was paralleled by an increase in exertion and, for me, nausea. I was gasping for breath, though physically I still seemed to have sufficient energy. I stopped frequently, struggling for composure and oxygen. Hampton seemed unaffected. Up ahead of me, he'd wait patiently when I halted. Above us the featureless snow slope gave us little with which to gauge our meager progress.

The sun was rising, and its first rays hit the glacier, lending a fiery orange hue. Intellectually I acknowledged it as beautiful, but I didn't have much appreciation for the vista. I considered taking a picture of Hampton, but retrieving my camera seemed an insurmountable effort. I hiked on, halting, bent over, every dozen steps. Dawn became fully day, and with a miserable slowness features on the rim of the crater became recognizable. We trudged on until we were on the final pitch. At the rim I sat and stared without focusing anywhere. The crater rim we were on is the top of the long slope we had been climbing, but it's not the actual summit. One point of the rim, half a mile from where we sat, rises slightly above the rest. That half mile traverses above fatally long and steep slopes. To reach it, I'd have to go out and back, and then spend hours descending the steep glacier we'd only just ascended. While I was confident that I had enough energy to make it to the cluster of crosses marking the actual summit, I had some doubts about my balance. Following a brief discussion, Hampton concurred that from a safety perspective it made sense for me to go no farther.

We sat in the snow, resting. The hint of external warmth the sun provided was luxurious. I encouraged Hampton to continue on to the summit while I waited. After about ten minutes he headed off on the traverse trail, but five minutes later he was back at my side. I asked if everything was okay. "We're in this together—it isn't worth it," he replied. Moments later I was standing and the long trek down had begun.

With the force of gravity now on our side, the descent was relatively easy. We met Bill, Cindy, and Garrett about halfway down the glacier. They were tied closely together with the thin hardware-store rope around their waists.

Bill greeted us with an enthusiastic, if breathless, "How was the summit?"

"We only made it to the crater rim," Hampton replied.

"Gee, if anyone was going to make it I was sure you guys would," replied Bill, with genuine disappointment, not the condescension I'd half expected. Bill reported that they were keeping to their slow-and-steady plan, and were all feeling pretty good. Cindy—looking ragged and already sunburned, tied to the tail end of the clothesline—seemed a contradiction to the latter statement. Several times we urged them to be safe and turn around if they needed to. I suggested some sunscreen for Cindy, and we were back on our way down.

We had planned to leave the following day, but now we could catch a ride with the driver coming to pick up the Montanans. We packed up our gear and shortly the truck arrived. I sat reading in the sun, which slowly dipped toward a band of cliffs; the snowfields above began to hint of the alpenglow I had failed to appreciate in the morning. The cool of evening began to creep in and I climbed into the back of the truck to retrieve a jacket. The driver had spotted someone—only one person—descending below the glacier's terminus.

Garrett reached us first. They had summited, and he had gone ahead on the descent.

Excitedly he told us, "I slipped on the steep snow below the glacier. I started going pretty fast toward the rocks. But I used my ax to stop myself." They had never practiced their self-arrest technique. It was lucky he was able to stop his fall. Bill pulled in ninety minutes later, and a pathetic-looking Cindy finally reached base camp in the last of the day's light. She had the worst sunburn I've ever seen.

Final Analysis

Bill, Garrett, and Cindy reached the peak whereas Hampton and I—while close—did not. Humbling, perhaps, but we made a well-considered decision to turn back in the interest of safety. Between us, Hampton and I had thousands of days' experience playing and leading others in the mountains. Nevertheless we made a mistake: underestimating the effects of altitude. This is the clear reason we were not leading others on this trip. We were in a new environment with insufficient experience to take on the responsibility for others. Mistakes are more acceptable, and usually easier to rectify, when you do not have followers in tow. Leadership requires motivation, hard skills, and soft skills—all of which is very different from heading out with peers on an adventure.

Bill, responsible for his two children, made a less conservative decision than Hampton and I did on Orizaba. His goal—an apparent case of summit fever—was at the core of the problem. Had his motivation to lead his children on the climb come from a more thoughtful source, he might have been able to identify some of the shortcomings in his hard and soft skills.

The situation Bill, Cindy, and Garret were in is common to outdoor adventurers today. Given the recent explosion of participation in outdoor recreation and education, many leaders, like Bill, undertake or fall into leadership roles they are underprepared for. On the first trips I led I certainly did not have adequate hard or soft skills. Yes, Bill and clan made the summit and (like the participants in my early trips) suffered no lasting physical harm. Making a summit, however, is not the sole measure of a good leader. If you drive 30 miles an hour over the speed limit and fail to wear a seat belt you may still get to your destination safely, but this does not justify the risk. In both my early attempts at leadership and on Bill's family climb, participants were exposed to an unnecessary—and unacceptable—level of risk.

Imagine your reaction to this (fictitious) report from the annual compendium *Accidents in North American Mountaineering:*

> A father and his two teenage children, all from Montana, were reported overdue after their summit attempt on Orizaba. The following day a search effort was launched utilizing U.S. climbers on the mountain, local residents, and a helicopter from the Mexican military. All three climbers were found dead, separated at the base of the Jamapa glacier. All showed evidence of trauma resulting from a long, sliding fall from some point on the 4,000-foot glacier. A hardware-store rope, tied around their waists, had broken during the fall. Other mountaineers reported that the group had been unfamiliar with self-arrest techniques and had not used crampons prior to their summit attempt. Medical examination indicated that the two children survived the fall but succumbed to hypothermia during a night in which temperatures dipped close to zero degrees Fahrenheit. The group was equipped with only lightweight cotton clothing for their summit attempt. This peak is a modest climb but nonetheless requires preparation and respect. The report and others like it in recent years indicate an increasing number of climbers attempting this peak without proper equipment and experience.

In addition to the safety issues Bill's expedition posed, he also taught his children some negative lessons about working with others. It's unlikely that they will be enthusiastic about the outdoors as a result of this experience. If they do head out without their father, they're likely to repeat the same mistakes he made and fail to respect the hazards posed by this environment.

I picked this story about Bill and his children because he's an easy target. None of us has to look too hard to see the shaky foundations of his leadership. It's more difficult to turn the lens back on ourselves and realize that we all share some of Bill's weaknesses. As outdoor leaders we need to examine the foundations of our leadership for less obvious deficiencies. As this story from Orizaba should make clear, neither an abundance or a lack of experience always equates with success. Those who analyze the foundations of their leadership and rectify imbalances are, however, able to provide the best and safest possible experience for their participants.

The following quote from management guru Peter Drucker may seem a bit pessimistic, but it suggests a valuable point:

> Most people think they know what they are good at. They are usually wrong. People know what they are not good at more often—and even there people are more often wrong than right. And yet, one can only perform with one's strengths. One cannot build performance on weakness, let alone on something one cannot do at all.

As caring leaders each of us must make the effort to reflect on our strengths and weaknesses—but as Drucker makes clear, this may not be enough. We also need to obtain the input of others on our performance and analyze our past successes and failures. The following chapter, Learning to Lead, addresses different approaches to assessing and developing your skills. A true commitment to learning to lead is the only way any of us will fully develop the foundations of our outdoor leadership and thus get our stools in balance.

Questions Every Leader Should Ask

▶ What are my strong hard skills? Where do I need to improve?

▶ What are my strong soft skills? Where do I need to improve?

▶ What motivates me to be an outdoor leader?

RECOMMENDED READING

Ford, Phyllis, and Jim Blanchard, *Leadership and Administration of Outdoor Pursuits,* 2nd ed., State College: Pennsylvania: Venture Publishing, 1993.

Priest, Simon, and Michael Gass, *Effective Leadership in Adventure Programming,* Champaign, Illinois: Human Kinetics, 1997.

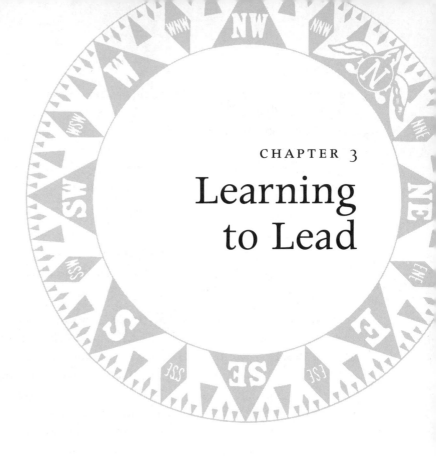

Learning to Lead

I had no formal training as a guide," relates Rick Wilcox. "I started out taking the AMC rock climbing course in Boston. Then, when I was a senior in high school, I became a winter hike leader." Today Wilcox has led twenty-five commercial expeditions as an owner of the International Mountain Climbing School, and in 1991 he summitted Mount Everest as leader of the New England Everest Expedition. On his home turf in New England he authored a regional ice climbing guidebook and pioneered many climbing routes. Since 1976 Rick has given back to the region's mountain travelers as president of New Hampshire's Mountain Rescue Service, a volunteer organization that takes responsibility for vertical rescues and winter rescues above timberline in the White Mountains. He has seen firsthand the tragic results of poor judgment in the mountains and has faced his own share of challenges.

Outdoor leadership has a long history in the United States of being undertaken informally. It was rarely pursued as a profession, and hardly any training was available outside the military. Today many leaders continue to become casually involved in outdoor leadership, but our expectations of leaders are much higher. Training programs for outdoor leaders are commonplace, and participation is almost universal, especially for professionals and those in formal leadership roles. A quick look at Rick Wilcox's experience will help explain the reasons behind this change.

"Today we have a system we use to train high-altitude guides," Wilcox says. "I never had anything like that, just experience at high altitude to teach me the bugaboos." Still, although Wilcox built his renown as a top climber and never had formal training, he knows the value of a well-educated guide: "Crummy people skills do not make a good guide. In the 1960s and '70s anyone who could do a pull-up was a guide." Wilcox believes this type of guide cannot provide what he calls "good customer service"—an experience both reasonably safe and high in quality. He has been active in developing training and certification programs for climbing guides and believes, as I do, that leaders need a combination of training and experience. He tells a compelling story of near tragedy on an expedition he led to the Himalaya—a situation he believes resulted from his lack of formal training and could have been avoided through the use of his current system for training guides.

On Langtang Peak in Nepal, Wilcox and his team were ascending via a rope that another guide had fixed on the infrequently climbed route. Above them one of the other guides stopped and was stomping a platform out of the snow for when the team arrived. Accidentally, the guide's attempts to construct a platform released a small avalanche. "All I saw was a wall of arms and legs," explains Wilcox. He, along with five of his team, went on a 2,500-foot sliding and tumbling fall down a snow-filled couloir. Given six people all falling together, there was no way they could arrest the fall. Amazingly, none of the six suffered serious injuries, but the incident did mean an end to the expedition.

When the uppermost guide knocked loose the snow, it hit the first person on the rope, a client. The rope broke where that client's ascending device was attached. Modern ropes are amazingly strong, but this one was only 6 millimeters in diameter—approximately the thickness of a pencil. The rope was anchored every 100 feet, but there were 6 people between the top of the rope and the next lower anchor. Once the rope broke, there was nothing to stop them. Today Wilcox—universally considered a model of safe high-altitude expedition leadership—

uses 8-millimeter ropes on expeditions, with 9-millimeter versions for the steep sections. Moreover, he learned more about the unpredictable nature of hazards in the mountains and the risks of trying to travel lightly. "It was an eye-opener," admits Wilcox, "and it made me a better big-mountain guide."

Learning

"To struggle and to understand. Never the last without the first. That is the law."

—GEORGE MALLORY, PIONEERING BRITISH MOUNTAINEER

The lessons that Rick Wilcox learned on Langtang Peak are indelibly etched in his memory. That learning benefited not only Wilcox and his future clients, but also the many guides-in-training he has worked with since then. Of course, as he well recognizes, such high-stakes approaches to learning are to be avoided. Nonetheless, on-the-ground experience is at the center of learning to be a leader. "You can't feel it, smell it, experience it in a video or book," believes Lieutenant Rick Estes, a friend of Wilcox's who, during a twenty-eight-year career with the New Hampshire Department of Fish and Game, oversaw search-and-rescue operations in a large area of the White Mountains.

"Mother Nature has no compunction taking life. It is not an easy life for a moose in the woods, or a black-capped chickadee bounced around and blown down by the winter winds." These animals live their entire lives in the outdoors, Estes points out, but are not immune to hazards. When humans venture out they may be faced with the same situation with less know-how and natural protections—things such as fur and layers of winter body fat—than animals. "Not that many people have been in a situation where your body is shutting down on you, like it does when you are hypothermic. Imagine how debilitated you feel being sick with the flu. Now imagine being on a mountain."

Learning to lead does not need to involve falling down mountains or slipping into serious hypothermia. It does need to involve being in real situations that allow you to learn from subtle cues about your environment and your group. It is this hands-on learning that enables you to make the judgment-based decisions that are at the center of effective outdoor leadership. The key to learning leadership is a slow progression. Training programs, participation in outdoor programs led by others, and personal adventures are the appropriate starting points. Over time the aspiring leader can progress to roles involving greater responsibility. It's vitally important that leaders not enter into positions of responsibility for others for which they are not ready.

Fundamentally, a leader must have ability. Ability has two components: knowledge and skill. *Knowledge* is understanding a task. *Skill* is proficiency at performing a task. The key to developing knowledge and skill is repeated exposure. Rick Wilcox's fast trip down the mountain in Nepal is stamped in his memory. However, Rick is unlikely to be in a situation that is exactly the same again. In order to generalize learning to a variety of complex situations, you as leader need to have a varied and extensive base of exposure to related situations. It is this experience that allows you to develop ability.

In *Mountaincraft and Leadership,* the official handbook of the Mountain Leader Training Boards of the United Kingdom, author Eric Langmuir is quite clear regarding the first order of business for aspiring leaders: "The chances of becoming an effective party leader are greatly reduced unless a considerable amount of time is spent on acquiring experience." His is an honest and accurate statement. In the United Kingdom the Mountain Leader Training Boards have historically imposed strict training and assessment standards on outdoor leaders, which we typically don't have at this time in the United States. Of course, training alone is insufficient if it's not driven by passion. As Langmuir describes it, "If going into the hills is done merely to gain sufficient experience to scrape through an assessment course rather than because of the inherent attractions of the hills, then it is necessary to think very deeply about whether or not to continue with it." Caring, motivated leaders are going to flourish and will, hopefully, enjoy the experience of gaining necessary skills.

Expectations of outdoor leaders in the United States have, historically, been much looser than those in the United Kingdom, and many aspiring leaders—myself included—developed experience while in leadership roles. My first paid outdoor leadership role involved, in part, instructing rock climbing—an activity in which I'd never even participated. To my knowledge none of my early participants suffered lasting harm; nonetheless, this is ill advised as an initial step toward becoming an outdoor leader. Those who dive into leadership roles too early often learn dramatic lessons at the expense of followers subjected to their trial-and-error approach.

As Eric Langmuir notes in (and referring to) *Mountaincraft and Leadership:*

> What such handbooks cannot easily convey, is the need for all these items of skill and knowledge to have been so well absorbed that they no longer exist in isolated compartments. It is necessary for them to have meshed . . . similar to the way in which tapestry threads interweave to form a pattern or picture. This mingling of threads underlines the fact that each of them has a relationship with all the others. The nature of these interdependent relationships must be understood by the leader so that when situations are faced requiring leadership skills, the interaction of all the factors will have occurred almost intuitively and spontaneously to the point where the key factors influencing the situation are identified. . . . It is these factors which influence judgements and subsequent decisions. The ability to scan them analytically and quickly select the appropriate skills . . . to deal with a situation should be an important aim for all aspirant leaders.

Weaving experiences together in the manner that Langmuir suggests requires extensive experience. Training, reading, sharing experiences, and mentoring all contribute to the development of outdoor leadership skills. The closer the learning experience is to the actual leadership experience, the more benefit it will bring to the leader. This realistic training helps familiarize leaders with the complex patterns that they must recognize and act upon as leaders.

As a tapestry will fade and even unravel over time, so too will a leader's skills. Leadership abilities are not permanent; they'll fade with lack of use. All leaders need practice to keep their skills current and new training to retain vitality and gain new ideas. Always remember that learning to be a great leader should be fun. Never shy away from sharing what you know and learning from others.

Skill Development

Experience of all kinds results in skill development. As I discussed in the previous chapter, two types of skills are required for outdoor leadership: hard skills, or physical-activity- and knowledge-based skills that are relatively easy to master; and soft skills, which involve more complex intellectual processes and social interactions. Hard or soft, skill development follows roughly the same process, with three major stages:

1. **Awareness of the Need for the Skill.** This may seem elementary, but looking back at my early forays into outdoor leadership I realize how ignorant I was about the things I didn't know. I also remember several poignant lessons in my early outdoor adventures. For example, when I was seventeen I traveled to Telluride, Colorado, with a good friend for my first skiing experience away from the East Coast. Both of us were passionate skiers, eager for fresh powder in a lean snow year. We transplanted our East Coast practice of violating trail closures at Telluride. Ducking into a bowl replete with knee-deep fresh powder, we could not imagine why the area was closed—until the slope started to move with us. Luckily the mini avalanche did not carry us far, but we immediately understood the reason for the Closed sign and our need to better understand avalanches. Just in case we hadn't learned our lesson, the ski patrol then began detonating explosives above us in a preemptive effort to set off avalanches and make the area safe for skiing. Subsequently we were arrested for violation of the Colorado Safe Skier Act (a misdemeanor with a penalty, as I recall, of up to a $500 fine and/or thirty days in jail—both of which we avoided as juveniles).

   Some lessons are less dramatic, of course; it may take repetition or guidance from another before you become aware of the need for a specific skill. As it was, I soon sought out avalanche awareness training and headed for the backcountry, while my friend has dutifully stuck to the open trails since then. Ignorance, we discovered, is not bliss.

2. **Understanding the Skill and Its Components.** Avalanche awareness—a hard skill—involves, among other things, understanding and recognizing different snow crystals, knowing the history of the

snowpack, understanding the effects of slope angle and exposure, building and evaluating test pits, and more. To understand a skill you need to have its components explained and preferably demonstrated to you. Depending on the complexity of the skill, this may need to happen one or many times.

3. **Practicing the Skill.** Avalanche awareness requires getting out into avalanche terrain and practicing your skills—perfecting your test pits, learning to assess slope angle, recognizing sliding layers in the snowpack. Any new skill—paddling a kayak, lighting a stove, recognizing hypothermia, or working to reach consensus in a group— will seem uncomfortable at first. Practice, especially with feedback on your performance, will allow you to overcome the discomfort and move into competence. Remember, however, that a developed skill is not with you forever—I have not spent much time in avalanche terrain in the past few years and don't enjoy anything close to the level of competence I once had. Mastery of skills is important not only for leadership, but also for teaching. As a teacher, knowing the ins and outs of a skill will enable you to individualize your teaching approaches to people with different learning styles.

Confidence

Along the way to developing hard and soft skills, most leaders also develop confidence. Confidence is the glue that holds your other leadership skills together. It allows you to put your hard and soft skills and your motivation to effective use. Experience brings you knowledge of similar situations that you can refer to in dealing with the one presently facing you. Confidence emerges because you know that you've successfully handled previous situations—and that you can apply your ability to a new situation, even one somewhat different from those you have previously encountered.

Take, for instance, a situation in which you and your group manage to misplace yourselves. While you may have never been in the particular area before, and you may never have lost the trail before, your experience tells you that in a situation like this you need to proceed calmly and methodically. You need to find the trail again because you need to get to the trailhead the next day for a resupply. Obviously you must employ a hard skill—navigation; when your group begins to become agitated, you also need a soft skill—communication—to explain the situation and reassure them. Confidence gives you faith in your own abilities in such a situation so you can choose a plan of action and proceed without constantly second-guessing yourself.

Again, Lieutenant Estes of the New Hampshire Department of Fish and Game emphasizes the importance of confidence. People who do not have confidence in their own abilities have a particularly hard time in a crisis situation—right about the time Estes and his staff get involved. "I once was able to reinstill confidence via a cell phone," relates Estes. "The leader was dealing with an ankle sprain. The leader didn't have confidence in himself—the call only got him answers he already knew." In this case a little boost to a leader's confidence and affirmation that he was doing the right thing saved the state from having to conduct a rescue. That confidence boost of an outside voice is not, of course, always available—or appropriate.

A lack of confidence can be stressful if you continually doubt your own decisions. Participants who detect a lack of confidence will also be more questioning of your leadership, further adding to your level of stress. On the positive side, a little confidence tends to generate more of the same—participants who sense your confidence will look to you for leadership. Having your participants believe in you goes a long way toward reaffirming your belief in your own capabilities.

Building Ability

So how do you develop your ability as an outdoor leader? The major approaches are training, mentoring, reading, and experience. These approaches are detailed in the following section, along with some of the many approaches that fall under these broad headings.

Training

Training is far and away the best bridge to becoming a leader. Well-designed training provides the aspiring leader with a well-rounded set of skills—other approaches to gaining experience may leave gaps and fail to expose you to all the skills you'll need. Training is particularly important for the development of outdoor-leadership-specific soft skills. Without it you'd be forced to move directly from a conceptual understanding of soft skills into an actual leadership role where the skills must be put to use. For example, a leader who has heard only about decision-making skills will be hard-pressed to use them in the field without prior practice in a controlled training environment. Certain types of training allow aspiring leaders to practice, serving as an intermediate step—a bridge—between understanding the basics of a skill and actually putting it to use. Training, of course, isn't just for new leaders—it's also critical for expanding and updating the skills of experienced leaders. The different types of training detailed in this section play a critical role in the development of both basic and advanced skills for the top-notch outdoor leader.

Soft Skills Training: Soft skills are difficult to develop though traditional classroom education, but they can be advanced through experiential education that puts you into situations similar to those you'll face as an actual leader. Unlike most traditional approaches, experiential education puts you in complex, often real-life, situations. These allow you to learn, in a safe environment, through your own and others' successes and mistakes. Experiential soft skills training includes everything from wilderness expeditions to role-playing scenarios that are feasible to work on in your living room.

The AMC Mountain Leadership School (MLS) is a five-day intensive backcountry training program designed for the individuals who have solid backpacking hard skills and want to move into a leadership role. Since its inception in 1959, the MLS has had experiential education at its foundation. Each group of eight MLS students is accompanied by two facilitators, drawn from the ranks of the AMC's best volunteer leaders, who gradually turn over the leadership of the group to the students. These students take turns in the role of leader and assistant leader. This structured setting allows students to venture into the mountains and practice leading with the security net provided by the two experienced facilitators. While the facilitators do teach some lessons, set up role-plays, and guide debriefing sessions to assist the learning process, their foremost role is ensuring the safest possible learning environment.

Mountain Leadership School and similar programs around the country certainly further hard skills—but MLS is particularly effective as a soft skills training program. The MLS program gives students experience dealing with a variety of simulated (and sometimes quite real) challenges—illness, interpersonal conflict, lost group members, slow hikers—and learning from their collective successes and mistakes. In the past forty-five years almost two thousand students have completed MLS, and every year their input and that of the facilitators has been used to further refine the program. The popularity and success of this program have made it the model for a variety of other leadership training programs operated by both the AMC and other organizations.

The AMC is also developing a new Leadership Training Institute (LTI) that incorporates MLS and several other existing leadership training programs. The LTI will model many of its training programs on the MLS style of experiential education. New offerings will allow participants to practice leadership skills in combination with different activities such as winter camping, paddling, or bicycling on programs ranging from a weekend to two weeks in length. Furthermore, the LTI will stretch beyond outdoor leadership to offer training programs in conservation leadership for those who wish to engage in advocacy around critical issues. In coming years, LTI programs will be offered from a base in Crawford Notch, New Hampshire, and in an increasing number of locations throughout the northeastern United States.

Other organizations around the country run outdoor leadership training programs with an experiential focus. Most notable among these is the National Outdoor Leadership School (NOLS)—a national leader in outdoor experiential education, and deservedly so. NOLS course curriculum tends at first to focus on the development of critical hard skills. Soft skills develop as the instructors allow students more and more autonomy in leading small groups. NOLS has the advantage of time—while the AMC's Mountain Leadership School is a five-day program, the standard NOLS course is a month long, and offerings range up to three months in length. This time frame allows the courses to successfully integrate the development of both hard and soft skills. For those with the time and money, NOLS courses are a wonderful learning opportunity.

More and more organizations are realizing the benefits of outdoor leadership training. Many of them see it as a necessity for their leaders in order to provide their participants with the type and quality of experience they expect. Individuals are also identifying outdoor leadership training as a way to hone skills they use indoors and out on a vocational or avocational basis. The response has been an increasing array of outdoor leadership programs—some open to the public, and some reserved for the staff or leaders of specific organizations.

Groups such as the Mountaineers and the Sierra Club offer training for their volunteer leaders. College outdoor programs and clubs such as those at Princeton or Georgia Tech offer training for student leaders. An increasing array of degree programs allow you to obtain a bachelor's or master's degree in outdoor leadership or a closely allied field, such as outdoor education. Such degree programs exist at the University of New Hampshire, Sterling College in Vermont, Prescott College in Arizona, and Minnesota State University at Mankato, among many others. Organizations such as Wilderness Inquiry in Minnesota and Outdoor Explorations in Massachusetts provide training specific to working with participants with disabilities. National organizations such as the American Mountain Guides Association and the American Canoe Association develop curricula and endorse courses around the country. Each program has its unique twists and often a specific focus, but all those listed here and many more offer valuable learning opportunities. A detailed list of training opportunities is included in appendix C.

This book cannot replicate the experience of an AMC course, a NOLS course, or any of the other programs mentioned. What it can do is provide information that can be referred to again and again. In some cases it may be useful as a text to accompany the courses.

Hard Skills Training: For every intrepid outdoor adventurer who wants to scale mountains or descend frothing rivers, there is someone who wants to show him or her the ropes. This has not always been the case, and it still isn't for some more esoteric activities. These instructors may be paid professionals or they may, if you're lucky, volunteer their services; one downside to this type of training is that good instructors can be quite costly. Still, a well-qualified instructor is generally the most expedient way to learn outdoor skills—and the best way to ensure a well-rounded understanding of the technical skills associated with an activity.

Good instructors follow an organized teaching progression, anticipate the mistakes beginners are likely to make, and have practiced

AMC file photo

A comprehensive course in wilderness first aid is an important learning step for every leader.

approaches to explaining and demonstrating skills. Working with an instructor is also a good opportunity for you to observe good teaching and leadership skills that you can ultimately put into practice yourself.

Even if you have a friend who offers to teach you to rock climb, it's likely that a skilled instructor will do a better job. As an instructor I have a different attitude than I do when I'm taking a friend out. Certainly I will teach the friend everything that he or she needs to know to be safe, but I'll also want to get in some climbing time myself. I may not cover every skill in the depth that I would strive for as an instructor.

The best approach to learning hard skills will vary depending on your learning style, time, financial resources, the danger involved in the activity, your tolerance for experimentation, and many other factors. Figure out what works for you.

First-Aid Training: This is really a subset of hard skills training—although good first-aid training programs certainly develop soft skills as well. I cover it as a separate section because of its importance and because leaders rarely have an opportunity to practice these skills (beyond blister care and handing out Band-Aids), rendering training critically important. First aid is the one aspect of leadership training that is almost universally accepted as mandatory. Every outdoor leader needs an appropriate level of first-aid training. Those who will be leading activities where emergency medical care is more than an hour away—which is most outdoor leaders—should have current training in wilderness as opposed to standard first aid. Wilderness first-aid courses address issues that are common in backcountry settings, teach you how to improvise equipment, and deal with care over an extended time period. Traditional first-aid courses only teach you what to do during the brief interval between calling 911 and the arrival of help.

In case you aren't convinced, here are a few additional reasons to take a wilderness first-aid course:

▶ You'll learn a great deal about avoiding a variety of problems.

▶ Role-playing scenarios help build both soft and hard skills.

▶ The courses are fun and interesting.

▶ The opportunity for hands-on skill practice cannot be replicated by reading a book.

▶ You'll develop a comprehensive set of first-aid skills.

▶ You'll learn the most up-to-date practices.

▶ On the street or in the backcountry your skills could save a life.

Four fairly well defined training levels in wilderness first aid have emerged with the increasing need and demand for such training. These courses are Wilderness First Aid, Wilderness First Responder, Wilderness Emergency Medical Technician, and, somewhat less commonly, Advanced Wilderness First Aid (full descriptions of these programs appear in the box on pages 47 and 48). These courses were developed by SOLO Wilderness Medicine of Conway, New Hampshire, Wilderness Medical Associates in Bryant Pond, Maine, and the Wilderness Medicine Institute, which has become part of the National Outdoor Leadership School in Lander, Wyoming. Contact information for these organizations is listed in appendix C. These three organizations remain the major providers of wilderness first-aid courses in the United States, although some new training organizations offering courses with the same names are emerging. Seek recommendations from past participants

WILDERNESS FIRST-AID COURSES

Wilderness First Aid (WFA): This two-day course is designed to emphasize prevention while teaching first-aid fundamentals and giving an introduction to the concept of improvising first-aid equipment in the backcountry. You'll learn how to conduct a basic patient examination and identify common problems. The course does not have time to go into particular depth on the extended-care issues faced in remote wilderness situations. The certification you receive is valid for two or three years, depending on which organization issues it. This course is most appropriate for recreational outdoorspeople who are not in leadership positions. It is also the minimum training level appropriate for leaders. WFA might be appropriate for leaders whose programs can be reached by emergency medical personnel within an hour, leaders of low-risk-level day trips, and assistant leaders working with a more highly trained leader.

Advanced Wilderness First Aid (AWFA): This four-day course is less commonly offered than the other three on this list. It's sometimes available as a two-day upgrade to the basic WFA training. The course builds on the basic WFA course, adding more training on extended care and more opportunity for practicing skills. This course is accepted as the minimum level of training for professional outdoor leaders by several of the top organizations in the outdoor industry. It's appropriate for leaders who will be leading activities of low risk in areas where emergency assistance remains relatively accessible.

Wilderness First Responder (WFR): This course is the industry standard for professional leaders and the level of training to which serious leaders aspire. It is usually taught over eight to ten days. Beyond WFA and AWFA this course provides much more information on care for both trauma and medical conditions. You'll learn to use standard rescue equipment, such as that found on an ambulance or used during a major rescue. The course may cover the administration of prescription medications such as epinephrine, used in cases of anaphylactic shock, or prescription painkillers for extended trauma evacuations. Substantial hands-on skills practice and role-playing scenarios add to the value of this course. It leads to a certification based on a

First Responder curriculum approved by the Department of Transportation (DOT). Recertification involves a two-day course taken every three years and generally retaking the entire course after some period of time. This level of certification is appropriate for leaders of everything but the most remote and dangerous activities.

Wilderness Emergency Medical Technician (WEMT): This is the gold standard for outdoor leaders. To be a WEMT you must be a certified "street" Emergency Medical Technician (EMT). The standard EMT course is 180 hours. To add the W to your EMT you take either an additional training module (usually four days) or a WEMT course that includes both the basic EMT curriculum and the wilderness component. Having taken the former route, I can recommend the latter—that is, taking the WEMT course as one package with wilderness skills infused throughout the course. Compared with a WFR, the WEMT will have more skills practice, much greater knowledge of basic physiology, and be able to utilize more sophisticated equipment—none of it typically available in the backcountry. The wilderness component of the training focuses on search and rescue, improvised equipment, extended care, and environmental injuries and illnesses. The standard EMT curriculum provides an excellent foundation, but the wilderness training component makes the training far more relevant for outdoor leaders. EMTs are certified for two years. Recertification as an EMT varies on a state-by-state basis but typically requires that you be affiliated with a rescue service, complete about seventy hours of refresher training and continuing education, and pass a practical exam administered by the state. Recertification of the wilderness component involves a day of training that can generally be counted toward continuing education hours. Among WEMTs who function purely as wilderness leaders and not rescue personnel, the percentage who recertify over time is fairly low. That said, this is valuable training, and I encourage anyone, even those lacking plans to maintain the certification, to undertake it. WEMT training is the best training a leader can realistically maintain and is appropriate for expeditions into remote areas, higher-risk activities, and activities in developing countries where trained rescuers are less likely and medical care of lower quality than in the United States.

and check the instructor credentials of other training providers—many of the newcomers in the field offer excellent training, but some are subpar. If you plan to apply for outdoor leadership roles, you may also want to find out if training by one of the newer organizations will fulfill the certification requirements. There are also outdoor clubs and colleges that offer nonstandardized courses in wilderness first aid and medicine. While the instruction in these programs may be excellent, the lack of a widely endorsed curriculum and acceptance of their certification make them less valuable for the leader.

Organization-Specific Training: Organization-specific training is provided by the organization for which you are leading. The AMC, for example, provides leader training for both professional staff and volunteers. These training programs are usually intended to train you in all aspects of leading, but they also cover any unique aspects of leading for the particular organization.

Different participant populations and different program philosophies demand different approaches from leaders. You would, for instance, run a far different sea kayaking program for troubled youth than you would for paying adults on vacation. The youth program might require each participant to share equally in the workload, with activities that focus on team building; the adults, on the other hand, might have all their meals cooked for them and expect to have the natural history of the area interpreted along the way. A variety of logistical operations and environmental factors will also dictate parts of the program. All these factors make the training provided by an organization very helpful—even if you are already an experienced leader.

Mentoring and Apprenticeship

My friend Brennan Brunner occupied the lofty position of outing club chairperson when I arrived at Macalester College. Though I participated only in one backpacking trip that he led, Brennan shared many of his insights into outdoor leadership with me over bowls of Cheerios in the dining hall. I went on to serve as chair of the outing club for two years and took several new assistant leaders along on spring break, fall break, and weekend trips. Although I realize in retrospect that these leaders could have learned more if I'd stepped back and let them do more of the work, they did gain a lot of experience without the pressure of serving as the primary leader on their initial leadership forays. After the trips these leaders continued to turn to me for guidance regarding their outdoor leadership activities.

A mentor serves as a guide who helps you to get the most out of the learning opportunities you have. A mentor is the person who gives you insight into your experiences, points you in the direction of additional learning opportunities, and provides helpful hints. You might have one mentor or—if you're lucky—you might have several people to whom you can look to guide your development as a leader. Many leaders and outdoor enthusiasts are glad to build a relationship that allows them to share their expertise.

An effective way for a leader to gain experience is as an assistant, intern, or apprentice leader. This is a popular way for both volunteer and professional leaders to expand their experience and polish their skills. These experiences as an assistant give you a chance to demonstrate your skills and gain a full leadership position. Many talented leaders in training move rapidly from apprentice to leader after demonstrating that they have what it takes.

To maximize your learning, be patient and take the time to appreciate your learning opportunity. As Scott Smalley, education coordinator for the Green Mountain Club, told me, "Being a good leader is being a thief and taking all the best practices from others." See if you can work with different leaders and try to adopt the best techniques you observe among them. In any apprentice situation, make sure that you'll have the chance to take on appropriate leadership tasks, and that you receive constructive feedback from experienced leaders. Some organizations view eager apprentices earning little or nothing as a source of cheap labor—be sure you maximize the value of the situation for yourself.

Reading

Because you're reading this book, you obviously believe that reading is one way to develop your leadership skills. Although this book is not a replacement for an extended outdoor leadership program, it does serve as a source of important information that can be referenced repeatedly. This book relates the experiences of many leaders, draws lessons from them, allows you to do the same, and supplements your own experience in the field. Remember the analogy of a good leader to a thief and take ideas for yourself as you read.

This book can make you aware of the need for certain skills as an outdoor leader. It can also help you understand some, but not all, skills relevant to outdoor leadership and their components. It cannot help you practice your skills. Many aspects of leadership addressed in this book can only be learned through doing. To maximize the usefulness of this book, follow these steps:

▶ Answer the questions that appear in some chapters.

▶ Use the structure of the book to identify specific areas where your skills need additional development.

▶ Reflect back periodically on various chapters as you gain experience and new perspectives.

▶ Develop a plan of action that will work for you.

▶ In addition to practicing skills in different settings, use all the learning approaches discussed in this chapter—training, reading, sharing experiences, and mentoring.

Reading materials other than this book are also very much a part of educating yourself as a leader. For recommendations look at the reference sections at the end of each chapter.

The following materials can be useful for developing your outdoor leadership skills:

▶ **Skills Instruction Books:** For most outdoor activities, selections of books and manuals explaining hard skills are now available. These books help beginner and expert alike master the appropriate techniques. Equipment and accepted techniques tend to change over time, so use the newest editions you can find. Also be aware that many books are written with the recreational outdoor enthusiast in mind—really the people you're leading. The technical skills that leaders employ are often more sophisticated. Attempt to find books or manuals that are targeted toward leaders, and never rely on a single book as the final authority.

▶ **Outdoor Education Books:** Books exploring various aspects of outdoor leadership such as ethics, risk management, and experiential education are available. These are useful for expanding hard and soft skills.

▶ **Periodicals and Websites:** These can provide more current or esoteric information than is often available in books.

▶ **Accident Reports:** While much can be learned from honest retellings of success stories in outdoor leadership, accident reports can be gripping and are remarkably popular. Accident reports for some activities are available in annual compendiums, as well as from many other sources. A selection of accident reports from the Northeast is published twice a year in the AMC's journal, *Appalachia*. Other sources of such reports are listed in the recommended readings at the end of the chapter. Every organization should also make appropriate internal accident and incident reports available to its leaders for educational purposes.

▶ **Leader Manuals:** Most organizations that offer outdoor programs have one. If done well, they give program-specific information and policies. Despite the importance of this information, reviews of programs often demonstrate that staffs are not familiar with their leader manual. Read yours!

Reading is the most convenient way to build your leadership experience—it can be done almost anywhere at any time. Recommended reading materials are listed on page 273.

Experience

"I was an Überguide," says Jane Imholte of her first summer as an outdoor leader. Eighteen years old, she solo-led trips for YMCA Camp Menogyn in Minnesota's Boundary Waters. "I was leading alone and doing all the work—for the thirteen days I was with my group I had cooked every meal and carried the canoes over every portage." Even years later, the astonishment that she would have ever done all of this is clear in her voice. Three days from the end of the

> *"I hear and I forget, I see and I remember, I do and I understand."*
>
> —CONFUCIUS

trip, the group of seven girls Jane was leading was portaging between two lakes. Jane was climbing over a downed tree when she heard a crunching and popping noise in her knee. Initially her injury did not seem particularly bad, and she continued on with her "Überguide" tasks, doing another 3-mile portage later in the day and then cooking dinner before she finally got to go to sleep.

During the night she woke up, and the pain in her knee was so intense that she had to take Tylenol with codeine to keep herself from crying out in pain. The next day "I couldn't do anything for myself— I needed assistance to go pee," relates the leader who'd been doing it all just hours before.

"For the next three days the group had to portage everything, including me," recalls Jane. "It was inspirational to see a small girl decide she was going to portage the seventy-pound cedar canoe I had been paddling." The group took over everything, even making chicken with dumplings for dinner one night—unfortunately using white cake mix instead of flour in the dumplings. Jane, who started the trip "getting a sense of self-esteem and -worth" from taking care of everything, was now just a passenger in the middle of her campers' canoe.

With the pain under control due to the medication, Jane cried with pride watching her group coalesce and learn to rely on one another. With a newfound cohesiveness and resolve the group made it back to camp. Jane, an attorney today, recovered from her knee injury to lead many more wilderness trips, working for Menogyn and the Voyageur Outward Bound School all over North America. For her the injury remains "one of the best things that happened to me" and her "biggest learning moment as a leader, because it forced me to relinquish so much control." Jane was able to give up some control of the group—allowing participants the opportunity to take on tasks she'd previously felt they were incapable of. The participants' success gave them confidence and a newfound sense of pride. While it was never again under such dramatic circumstances, Jane gave every group she led after that one the opportunity to develop some of that same confidence and pride.

Jane's story epitomizes the fact that the best way to learn to become an outdoor leader is experience in the field. What Jane learned in her first year of leading wilderness trips might have taken her years of training to understand so completely. Experience, of course, includes not only actual leadership of a group, but also participating in another leader's group, excursions with friends, or even outings by yourself that give you an opportunity to hone your hard skills.

Every time you engage in an outdoor activity you build your confidence, increase the volume of experience you have to refer back to, and improve your hard and soft skills. I am convinced that the experience gained from each outing helps you build valuable skills that will be useful as an outdoor leader.

Some skills are much easier to practice than others, and in general these are the hard skills. There are exceptions, of course; a hard skill such as first aid is difficult to find opportunities to practice outside simulations. Still, skills like navigation and paddling are simple to practice, hence leaders are generally more skilled in these areas.

It's a point that bears repeating: The easiest route to becoming an effective and inspiring outdoor leader is to gain a lot of outdoor experience. For *very* basic, nontechnical trips this might mean as little as twenty days' experience in an activity. For more complex trips and those involving technical skills, the leader will need hundreds of days of practice before assuming a leadership role. Becoming a leader does not end the need for practice. Leading is not a chance to push your limits, visit entirely new places, or build new technical skills. To remain vital and grow you must make time for personal outdoor adventures as well as for leading.

Even If You Ignore It, It Will Not Go Away: Unfortunately, people tend to practice what they're already good at. Everyone does it—we use our talents and avoid tasks that we find difficult. We more frequently enjoy recreational activities where we have some ability than those whose fundamentals we struggle to grasp. What has helped me understand this preferential engagement is my enthusiasm for rock climbing.

There are four basic types of rock climbing: slabs, faces, overhangs, and cracks. I'm a poor slab climber, decent at faces and overhangs, and I (to be immodest) can climb up and back down cracks that many of my climbing partners cannot get off the ground on. Unfortunately I abhor slab climbing and avoid it, while I love crack climbing and seek it out. The long climbs I like to do often encompass all four types of climbing. As much as I find slab climbing distasteful and downright scary, if I'm going to climb I need to practice that and all of the other skills. Some modest ability at climbing slabs will make me a better and safer climber.

The hard skills that leaders need for different activities are varied.

Marny Ashburne

Similarly, the outdoor leader needs to consciously develop a broad array of skills. The leader who finds facilitating a discussion distasteful is just as likely to need to facilitate as one who doesn't. The moment when the group really needs a facilitator is too late to start learning; the time for developing leader skills is before the trip (or in the case of my climbing skills, before I hit the cliffs).

Focus Your Experience: Focus your growth as a leader on two areas. First, decide what type of activity and program you would like to lead. Second, determine what areas of your leadership skills need the most attention. This focus will speed along your growth as an effective leader.

Determining what type of activity and program you're interested in leading allows you to focus your reading, training, practice, and mentoring in that area. While practicing rock climbing may in some ways be helpful to your role as a backpacking leader, you'd probably be better off backpacking. Also important is the type of population you'll be leading. You may want to lead adults, families, at-risk youth, or people with disabilities. Leading each of these groups requires somewhat different soft and hard skills. Given that there are so many ways to build your experience, you can tailor your experiences to fit your desired end result.

Determining which aspect of your leadership skills requires additional development can be difficult. As a leader you should always be open to feedback and give yourself time for reflection. People you lead with, mentors you can discuss your experiences with, and the participants in your trips can all give valuable feedback. Look for patterns in the feedback you receive. If you hear something once, give it a moment of reflection. If multiple people are giving you similar feedback about something you can improve upon, there's probably some validity to what they have to say. This feedback can help you focus your efforts to further develop your leadership skills.

Develop Solid Ability

If you're unsure of your leadership capabilities, experience and training will only help build them. Through experience and training you come to a better understanding of your motivations for leading. You will gain an important sense of your own limitations. Generally people can find an outdoor leadership role that suits them. For a few, training and other experience helps them determine that outdoor leadership just isn't right for them. Most people, however, find that gaining experience in outdoor leadership is an exciting and rewarding process of self-discovery.

Use this book as a framework for learning as you build your ability. Reflect back periodically on various chapters once you have gained more experience and perhaps a different perspective. Make a deliberate effort to use all the learning approaches discussed in this chapter. Find a peer group of leaders with whom you can discuss leading.

All this work to develop your outdoor leadership skills may seem like overkill. After all, people with no outdoor leadership experience have led successful trips. The difference is that you want to be a consistently good outdoor leader, and you recognize (or will, after reading this book) that expectations of leaders are rising with the increasing popularity of outdoor adventure. Finally, remember that gaining leadership experience should be fun—witness the popularity of various outdoor leadership training programs, even among people who have no intention of ever leading in the outdoors.

RECOMMENDED READING

Broze, Matt, and George Gronseth, *Sea Kayaker's Deep Trouble: True Stories and Their Lessons from* Sea Kayaker *Magazine,* edited by Christopher Cunningham, Camden, Maine: Ragged Mountain Press, 1997.

Daniel, Lucille, ed., *Appalachia,* Boston: Appalachian Mountain Club, biannual.

Ford, Phyllis, and Jim Blanchard, *Leadership and Administration of Outdoor Pursuits,* 2nd ed., State College, Pennsylvania: Venture Publishing, 1993.

Johnson, David W., *Reaching Out: Interpersonal Effectiveness and Self-Actualization,* 5th ed., Boston: Allyn and Bacon, 1993.

Langmuir, Eric, *Mountaincraft and Leadership,* 3rd ed., West Didsbury, England: The Mountain Leader Training Board, 1995.

Leemon, Drew, ed., *Adventure Program Risk Management Report,* vol. III, Boulder, Colorado: The Association for Experiential Education, 2002.

Leemon, Drew, Tod Schimelpfenig, Sky Gray, Shana Tarter, and Jed Williamson, eds., *Adventure Program Risk Management Report.* 1998 ed., Boulder, Colorado: The Association for Experiential Education, 1998.

Liddle, Jeff, and Steve Storck, eds., *Adventure Program Risk Management Report.* 1995 ed., Boulder, Colorado: The Association for Experiential Education, 1995.

Priest, Simon, and Michael Gass, *Effective Leadership in Adventure Programming,* Champaign, Illinois: Human Kinetics, 1997.

Williamson, John E., ed., *Accidents in North American Mountaineering,* Golden, Colorado: American Alpine Club, annual.

CHAPTER 4

Awareness

Without a steady flow of accurate information, effective leadership is impossible. As a leader you must rely on your own awareness—primarily direct observation—for all information. This awareness provides the foundation for every action you take. Keeping abreast of all you need to be aware of is a complex task. Most people are accustomed to gleaning much of the information they use from a computer screen, television, newspaper, or similarly explicit source. As a leader, it takes practice, knowledge, and skill to effectively cull the information you need from the sources available to you outdoors.

To provide a structure for everything the leader must be aware of, this chapter is broken into three broad areas of awareness: environment, group, and self. Environment is your surroundings; group is the people who are with you and the interactions that occur among them; self is your own abilities, opinions, and prejudices as well as your current mental and physical state.

In each of the three areas—environment, group, and self—it's possible to anticipate certain concerns you need to be aware of. A few specific concerns are mentioned in this book, including inclement weather (environment), dehydration (group), and assessment of your skills (self). There are many more specific concerns that go unmentioned, however, and vary with activity, region, population, season, and other factors. Experience or its substitutes, such as training, reading, and learning from other leaders, inform you of specifics to be aware of, as discussed in chapter 3, Learning to Lead.

More important than awareness of specific concerns is maintaining a broad awareness of environment, group, and self. The leader who focuses on a known set of concerns is more likely to be blindsided by unexpected occurrences. Experience or its substitutes are again critical here for developing your skills in filtering relevant information. Experience, combined with the framework provided by this chapter, will best enable you to evaluate and interpret information.

> *"Whether you are leading a group or going about your daily life, you need to be conscious. You need to be aware of what is happening and how things happen. If you are aware of what is happening and how things happen, you can act accordingly. You can steer clear of trouble, and be both vital and effective. . . .*
> *Consciousness or awareness . . . is the source of your ability."*
> —JOHN HEIDER,
> THE TAO OF LEADERSHIP

Before delving into the details, here's one more thought: Use your group to aid your awareness. Everyone who has hiked much in front of a group can recall stopping to look at the map and saying something like, "I think we missed our turn." Someone farther back in the line invariably pipes up with, "Oh, you mean the trail off to the right about a mile back?" The person in front asks why no one said anything, and the response is "Well, I was following you and I thought you knew where you were going." Nobody is omniscient, so set a tone of openness to observations. Developing your own awareness skills is the first order of business, but also consider how to instill these skills in others.

Awareness of Environment

Environment simply refers to your immediate physical surroundings. Your location and the weather figure prominently here, but the amount of daylight, the water level in a rapid you're about to run, the animal tracks crossing the trail, and myriad other details—some seemingly trivial—have relevance. While environmental awareness is important for all outdoorspeople, it's critical for leaders. The leader assumes responsibility for others' safety and experience—a high level of environmental awareness is requisite to meet this.

Environmental awareness is both conscious and subconscious. When I'm leading a group I firmly believe that my environmental awareness increases, even when I'm asleep. During the first extended wilderness trip on which I was a designated leader, my environmentally aware (or perhaps just lightly sleeping) co-leader woke me late on a dark and cloudy night. Annoyed, I mumbled, "Go back to sleep," and started to snuggle back into my sleeping bag. Moments later I heard the screaming call of the mountain lion investigating our camp. I froze. After two minutes of terrified inaction I got the door of the tent open. Tentatively, I peered outside to investigate. Fumbling for my headlamp, I froze as I heard house-cat-like footfalls approach. As the cat ran by, 5 feet from my face, I felt the air move. Nowadays I awaken at the slightest disturbance in camp, and I always sleep with my headlamp stashed by my side.

Experience in the outdoors, especially as a leader, is the best means of improving your environmental awareness. I don't think you can speed along the improvement in your level of alertness while you sleep; you can, however, consciously improve other areas of your environmental awareness. Many times I have been shocked by people who fail to notice an unusual odor, a stunning vista, or the moose crashing in the bushes nearby. A subtle change in vegetation may indicate a spring that is the only water source for miles. The indistinct rustle in the underbrush could be a clue to an exciting—or dangerous—wildlife sighting. Consciously endeavor to notice the diverse cues provided by all your senses.

In the environment, as with group and self, are also specific concerns that you must be aware of. Hazards vary by environment, region, and activity. These would include high-water stream crossings in the mountains, surf landings in a sea kayak, or more exotic ones such as the "assassin beetle" of South America (which transmits the fatal Chagas' disease). Special skills or knowledge are often required simply to recognize and understand hazards in the environment. Avalanche forecasting, reading whitewater, or assessing rockfall potential are examples of such skills.

Understanding where you are is fundamental to environmental awareness. Locating your position on a map is a start; however, you also need to know your route and the nature of what you'll encounter along the way. The locations of water sources, campsites, and other resources are important. Ideally, you'll be personally familiar with the route—but realistically this isn't always possible. At the least you should consult your map, any available written materials, and anyone available who has traveled the area. It can be tedious, but I follow my route closely on the map and pay more attention than I would on a personal outing. When the safety of others rests in your hands, be overprepared. Consistent attention to the map not only avoids route-finding dilemmas but can be invaluable in a crisis.

Any potentially dangerous location will prompt me to continuously reevaluate the best route to a safe location. I'm reminded of a body-width canyon in Arizona through which I led several groups a few years ago. Wading, swimming, and bouldering through this canyon with full expedition packs offered a once-in-a-lifetime experience for many participants. This, was, however, a committing undertaking: Once we were inside the canyon, there was only one potential escape route (in addition to the beginning and end of the narrows). We were careful to enter only under ideal weather conditions. Still, my co-leader and I carefully figured out the most expedient route to higher ground from each section of the canyon should there be any hint of rain or a change in water level. The canyon, once gave me a perspective on the potential danger—I was away for a few weeks and returned to find flood debris that included a smelly elk carcass lodged 20 feet above our heads. In this type of situation, advance planning is key to your environmental awareness.

Along with a route to safety, the leader should be conscious of where to turn in case of a situation the group cannot handle in the field. Two instructors I worked with were faced with a student on a course who severely sprained or fractured his ankle. One of the instructors, accompanied by a student, headed out to obtain assistance at a ranch house that was indicated on the map about a day's hike away. Unfortunately the ranch had been abandoned in the 1940s. As a result of their detour, it took another full day for them to reach a traveled road.

Robert Kozlow

Finding information like this in the backcountry is very rare; instead leaders must develop their own environmental awareness.

Thankfully the injury wasn't critical, because an evacuation team on horseback did not respond for three days. Consider potential evacuation routes, and know what phones, radios, or other communication points you can use to summon help.

All leaders need to be familiar with weather. It's surprising how many groups report being caught dangerously high on a mountain in a "sudden storm" that emerged from a "perfectly clear" day. Sometimes an approaching storm hides behind a ridge or trees, but more often people weren't paying attention. It has happened to me— more than once I've noticed what could be a distant storm front and forgotten about it for several hours until a nearby clap of thunder served as a wake-up call. Keep an eye on the sky, and if you haven't done so already, invest some time in learning simple weather forecasting.

Another, very different, piece of environmental awareness is knowledge of the equipment carried by your group. This equipment has the potential to modify the environment and thus is relevant to your environmental awareness. A headlamp turns night to day (or twilight, at least), a tent creates shelter in a storm, and a compact stove and a small packet enable you to turn snow into hot soup—imagine how different your experience of the environment would be without these or other material resources. In a crisis, thorough knowledge of the equipment your group carries can be a lifesaver.

Again, this is not an exhaustive list of what you need to be aware of.

Start with solid building-block skills such as map reading and weather forecasting. Spend as much time as possible in the outdoors, taking the time to observe your surroundings. Identify and acquire any specialized knowledge or skills required for environmental awareness in the locales where you aspire to lead. Take your time and make sure you're comfortable and familiar with any environment you aspire to lead others into.

Key Points

► *Environment* refers to everything around you.

► Environmental awareness is both conscious and subconscious.

► Experience is key to developing environmental awareness.

► Use all your senses in observation.

► Special skills and knowledge may be required.

Be Aware Of:

► Hazards.

► Location.

► Route.

► Weather.

► Equipment.

Awareness of Group

People are the reason for outdoor leaders. Without an awareness of the people in your group (this includes participants as well as other group leaders), making decisions will be difficult and contentious. Awareness of your group requires social interaction—you need to be friendly, or at least sociable. Some people naturally observe and interact; they sometimes

"You can learn more about an individual during an hour of play than in a year of conversation."

— PLATO

> **"***Potent leadership is a matter of being aware of what is happening in the group and acting accordingly. Specific actions are less important than the leader's clarity or consciousness.***"**
>
> —JOHN HEIDER, THE TAO OF LEADERSHIP

seem to intuitively pick up others' vibes. Others need to put more into it. Awareness of people is an art, but there are many different approaches, and with practice this awareness can be learned.

The intense physical nature of outdoor activities often pushes people to extremes of emotion. As you exercise your body produces chemical compounds that, combined with the experience of, say, reaching a beautiful and challenging mountaintop, can produce feelings of dizzying elation. On the flip side exhaustion, discomfort, dehydration, anxiety, and myriad other factors can push people to physical and emotional low points. It's also important to remember that the same interconnected mental and physical influences that act on your participants are acting on you. Awareness of your own physical and mental condition—self-awareness—is discussed in the next section and is critical to effective leadership.

Empathy, meaning understanding people well enough that their mood and motivations are apparent, is the hallmark of an effective leader. While many effective workplace managers employ empathy, the intense nature of outdoor activities makes this a particularly critical ability for the outdoor leader. Empathy allows you to better support group members and is particularly valuable on challenging excursions or when working with beginners. For example, I once saw a participant, Patrick, lash out at a fellow group member for setting up the tent the "wrong" way. Because of the empathy I had developed talking with him during the day, I realized that behind Patrick's anger was his frustration over how difficult he was finding the paddling on this trip. I also knew that he was exhausted after a long day on the water. I was able to pull Patrick aside and talk to him about what was going on. After a break and a snack, Patrick apologized to the person he had aimed his anger at earlier.

Be aware of physical fitness levels and any significant medical concerns or physical limitations among your group members. If possible, start learning this and other information about the people in your group before you meet, through initial phone calls or the written applications required on many trips. Obviously, a high level of awareness will be more difficult to achieve on a day trip than on an extended outing. For shorter outings, then, you may want to identify those you suspect will need more of your assistance. But be subtle; you don't want anyone to feel you're singling them out for special attention.

When I lead, I "float" around in the group, especially for the first few days of a trip. On the trail, the river, or while driving to the trailhead, I observe and talk to everyone in the group, if possible. I observe people's body language—are they smiling in a natural manner, are their shoulders slumped or held erect, do they appear attentive, or do they have a distant stare? This is the time to initiate a two-way relationship with members of the group. Talk to people and endeavor to be interested in what they say. Maintain eye contact and acknowledge comments with a verbal response. Steer conversations toward what is at hand and avoid topics such as popular culture or work that distract people from the moment. I ask people why they chose this trip or if they got a glimpse of the view we had a while back—try to be creative, although you can also have some standbys. Stay away from generic questions such as "how are you doing?"—you're likely to get a similarly canned response. Engaging in positive conversations with participants not only makes them feel important, but helps them feel positive as well. As the leader your attention can have extra meaning to participants.

While interaction with your group is important, a good time to step back and observe is when your group has tasks to perform together. Who is contributing and who isn't? How does the group make decisions? I learn and the group learns if they are allowed to make decisions early on. Have the group split up the equipment among their packs, or make decisions in some other predeparture task without the direct supervision of the leaders. This allows participants to experience group decision making and provides you with insight into how they will work together for the rest of the trip. These observations also provide a sense of the talents that individuals have to contribute to the group.

As you float, observe, and interact, use your experience to guide you to areas of concern. Try to pick up on subtle cues. A participant who challenges your authority as a leader may have a valid concern or may be nervous and looking for reassurance. Many cues aren't verbal. If the group hikes for hours without needing a pee break, for instance, they probably aren't drinking enough water. A hiker with an unusual posture may be struggling with an improperly adjusted pack. Look for changes in patterns and work on discerning the cause.

Passive observation and interaction are not enough to acquire the information about your group that you need. At times you need to be more direct. Early in a trip I'm often concerned that people are not drinking sufficient water to stay properly hydrated. I frequently "order" people to pull out their water bottles so I can see just how much has disappeared into their bellies—and if the amount missing isn't sufficient, we'll have a few group "toasts." Besides offering some a chance for bonding and humor, these "toasts" get everyone drinking and drive home the importance of proper hydration. Likewise, I usually stage communal foot checks with novice hikers on the first couple of days. These checks accustom people to caring for their feet and reveal "hot spots" when there's time to treat them—before they become blisters. I particularly like these and similar techniques, because they're nonconfrontational and don't single anyone out.

There are also times when you will need to ask direct questions of individuals or the group. As you float, there's nothing wrong with asking an individual how much water he or she has had to drink. The disadvantage to such direct questioning is that it may appear to the individual or others that you are singling someone out. Discretion in your questioning may be useful, so the whole group doesn't learn of your concerns about an individual—especially if you're asking about medical or other sensitive concerns. It's also important to approach individuals about whom you have a concern in a nonconfrontational manner. Participants who feel blamed for their problem—say, a blister—are less likely to accept help and more likely to suffer stoically until their breaking point.

Another way to initiate the sharing of information is convening a group debriefing session. This can be as simple as a group discussion after a meal, or it can be a more formally structured interaction. The practice of group debriefing has the advantage of building awareness and empathy among group members. For more information on these and other communication issues, see chapter 10. You need to experiment with techniques for checking in with participants that work for you.

On one particular trip, my co-leader and I were leading eight teenagers on a two-week backpack in New Hampshire's White

Mountains. We spent the rainy day hiking in our own private worlds, outside sounds excluded by the drumming of rain on our hoods. The temperature barely rose above fifty degrees. Upon reaching our campsite, group members pleaded for time in the small three-walled log shelter before setting up tents. My co-leader and I were feeling soggy, and with plenty of daylight remaining we agreed. Group members got out a stove for soup, and several of us started playing cards.

It was one of the participants who noticed that two members of the group weren't inside the shelter. We were missing two brothers—twins—who had not enjoyed interacting with others in the group. They were quickly located—sitting outside with rain pouring off the eave right onto them. First I noticed their bluish lips, and then their incoherent speech. After our miserable day of hiking through the storm—while we were enjoying our well-deserved ramen soup—we had failed our group by letting our level of awareness drop.

Never forget that many people are not comfortable in the outdoors and don't know how they should feel or behave given the newfound demands on their bodies and minds. Even the most experienced outdoorspeople can remain unaware while they become hypothermic, hyperthermic, or severely dehydrated. It's challenging to sort out routine discomfort and changes in behavior from those that may merit concern. Monitor your group as much as possible and look for patterns that may indicate problems. Observe, listen, interact, ask questions when necessary, and let your experience, intuition, co-leader, and the information in this book guide you.

Key Points

▶ Awareness of your group is critical to decision making.

▶ Group awareness requires social interaction.

▶ The physical nature of activities can produce emotional extremes in individuals.

▶ Building empathy with individuals is a key goal.

▶ As you lead, "float" in your group, interacting with everyone.

▶ Allow your group to make decisions together.

▶ Look for subtle cues regarding your group.

▶ Experience should guide your group awareness.

▶ Active techniques can be useful in obtaining information.

▶ Nobody is immune to problems.

▶ Prioritizing your observations is your key challenge.

Be Aware Of:

▶ Physical condition.

▶ Psychological condition.

▶ Mood.

▶ Motivation.

▶ Physical fitness.

▶ Medical concerns.

▶ Physical limitations.

▶ Group function.

▶ Change in an individual or the group.

Awareness of Self

Self-awareness is the foundation upon which you build your outdoor leadership. There are two components to self-awareness—one of which is fairly stable and the other in regular flux. The first, stable component, involves understanding your competencies, weak points, fears, motivations, and biases. Are you, for example, capable of leading three participants up a difficult climb? The second, dynamic component, is an awareness of your current mood and physical state. Is there reason to be annoyed at the participant who didn't put moleskin on his blisters, or are you frustrated because you're tired and hungry? Understanding these factors allows you to account for these influences during your decision making.

When it comes to awareness of your stable characteristics, remember that people do not inherently have perfectly objective views of them-

Alex Kosseff

Impending weather—sunny or stormy—can influence decisions and moods.

selves; nevertheless, increased self-awareness benefits leaders. Leaders who understand how they respond to stress, danger, exhaustion, difficult individuals, and other situations can compensate for any limitations these reactions impose. On a fundamental level, self-awareness allows you to understand which situations you can effectively handle and which require you to invest more effort or look for assistance. A balanced self-assessment also aids you in understanding which leadership roles are appropriate for you.

Mood is an ephemeral actor that influences all your interactions with your group. Unlike your more stable traits, you need to continually take stock of your mood, which can have a strong impact on your decision making and interactions with others. Any of these components of self-awareness that are relevant need to be factored in to a given decision-making process. This does not imply that outdoor leaders have to remain on a completely even emotional keel—in the real world, mental and physical challenges will always impact leaders' moods. Self-aware leaders are simply conscious of their mood and other factors that impact their thought process and behavior.

In addition to being conscious of their own mental state, self-aware leaders understand that their mood and attitude affects the entire group. A positive mood or a can-do attitude transfers to those around

Alex Kosseff

Lower down in this narrow canyon the author's lack of self-awareness resulted in a dangerous situation.

you. Enthusiasm is infectious—though, unfortunately, negativity can be even more so. While participants should understand that even leaders are human beings who experience mood shifts, it's your responsibility to prevent your mood from hampering the experience of the group.

Self-awareness is critically important for you as a leader because people may sign on to follow you through stormy seas, over desiccated deserts, or up to extremes of altitude. Especially on such rigorous adventures, you and everyone in your group will experience mental and physical stresses. You need to understand how interconnected the two are, not only for participants but also for you in the capacity of leader. Exhaustion, hypothermia, hyperthermia, low blood sugar, dehydration, and other factors—especially in combination—can have a profoundly deleterious effect on physical and mental capabilities as well as mood. The careless leader who becomes physically compromised will likely have a diminished mental capacity. This compromised leader may be unable to address his or her condition and can create a burden for the group.

Rating Your Own Abilities

Outdoor leaders make hundreds or thousands of decisions each day in the field. Most of these are made in a cautious manner, but leaders can sometimes overrate their own abilities and put themselves in risky situations they would never consider putting participants in. There have been a number of instances, for example, of climbing instructors falling off cliffs. These instructors were often at the top of the cliff, but in areas where participants would never be allowed to go unroped.

One dramatic instance in which I overestimated my own capacity occurred on a canyoneering trip I was excited to be leading in Arizona. Wearing running shoes and carrying our group first-aid kit, which I intended to keep above water, I lowered myself over a small waterfall and into a deep pool. Just after I dropped into the pool, though, my head went underwater. I struggled to the surface but rapidly went under again and gulped in some water. Survival became an issue—I could not easily climb back up, and the rest of the group was at the top of the pour-off. Luckily there was an easy solution—I dropped the first-aid kit and swam across the pool, pushing the kit ahead of me.

My mood—excitement at leading a group through the remote canyon—combined with a lack of awareness of my weakness—I thought myself capable of swimming the plunge pool wearing shoes and carrying five pounds above my head—both contributed to this close call (thankfully, the only casualty was the damp first-aid kit). While I probably could have made the swim successfully a few years earlier—I had performed a similar feat as part of a lifeguard training course—leading trips in the dry Southwest had not given me much opportunity to practice my swimming skills. There was also bias involved in this decision—I thought I could handle this task better than any of the participants. A couple of the participants were clearly better swimmers than I.

If they are open to being honest, other leaders whom you respect should be able to provide useful insights on your functioning as a leader. Discussing challenging events can be a productive way of improving self-awareness and preparing you for the future. You may want to join your co-leader in this discussion. Try this format:

1. Outline the incident that took place.

2. What are your feelings on how you (and your co-leader) handled the situation?

3. How might you handle a similar situation differently in the future?

Often you will find that you and your co-leader already know how you could have handled things differently. Another leader may have some different insights or be able to validate your existing feelings, but in reality you can also do this on a trip with just your co-leader.

Tracking your decisions and their outcomes is another effective way to improve self-awareness. This can be greatly aided by journaling and keeping an ongoing record of your observations as well as decisions you made and their outcomes. While much of your experience will remain clearly in your memory, a journal can help you recall your thoughts at the time of an incident and give you food for thought when reviewing the situation in the future. This technique can also provide you with some useful insights into your growth and development as a leader.

Self-Care

Your self-awareness and the resultant self-care are essential to effective leadership. Arlene Blum was expedition leader for the American Women's Himalayan Expedition that ascended Annapurna, the tenth highest mountain in the world. In her book *Annapurna: A Woman's Place,* Blum writes about the prospect of taking a respite from the demands of leading a major climbing expedition:

> It was a pleasure to imagine myself heading up to Camp I, lighthearted and relieved of all responsibility for the day. The problems at Base Camp could wait. I went to the supply tent and hurriedly threw a load into my pack, hoping to escape before one more problem came up. I didn't make it. As I was tightening the straps on my pack, Lopsang [their head Sherpa] came up with a worried look on his face.

Blum did manage to get away from camp that day, despite the new challenges that Lopsang informed her of. In the midst of several months of challenges, Blum had the self-awareness to recognize that a respite from her responsibilities would have many benefits. She was willing to relinquish control briefly and allow herself some downtime. Often a few minutes away from your group is precious—though as this example points out, escaping from a leadership role isn't always easy. Often it's important to accept that you cannot be present at all times and deal with every issue. If others are competent, let them take responsibility from time to time.

Amid all the responsibilities of leadership, awareness of your own needs and the resultant self-care often require extra attention to yourself that can seem selfish or overly time consuming. While there is clearly a limit, leaders who respect their own needs are generally able to function at a higher level than those who don't. This is particularly important to remember during a crisis, when it's easy to ignore your own needs. Self-awareness can help ensure that you consume enough water, or it can assist you in realizing that you aren't an especially strong swimmer. And don't forget that your self-awareness can inform your group awareness—their experiences will often be magnifications of what you are experiencing.

In summary, self-awareness involves knowing yourself and monitoring your mood, which is inextricably tied to your physical state. For the outdoor leader, self-awareness is critical to understanding your own perspective and using that knowledge to temper your actions. Perhaps even more crucially, self-awareness is fundamental to taking care of your mental and physical needs. Effective outdoor leadership is built on a foundation of self-awareness. Without knowledge of self, your other leadership skills will be undermined, sometimes to the point where you lose credibility.

Key Points

▶ Self-awareness provides a critical foundation for your outdoor leadership.

▶ Self-assessment assists you in determining which leadership roles to undertake.

▶ Your mood affects others.

▶ Mental and physical states are closely connected.

▶ Use your co-leader and debriefs to develop self-awareness.

▶ Self-care is critical to remaining an effective leader.

Be Aware of Your:

▶ Motivations.

▶ Fears.

▶ Competencies.

▶ Weaknesses.

▶ Mood.

▶ Physical state.

▶ Influence on the group.

▶ Self-care needs.

Focusing Awareness

A challenge can be focusing on what is relevant among all the information on environment, group, and self. You may be aware that the temperature is forty degrees and an osprey is flying overhead; that group members all have green backpacks and they all ate oatmeal for breakfast; that you also ate oatmeal for breakfast with a few raisins and that something small feels like it's crawling along your leg under your pants. This is just a start. There are many things that you are aware of. If you also consider that you're in an area where there are a lot of ticks and that you know from experience that the green packs your organization provides have a tendency to be uncomfortable, some of the other information becomes more relevant. Unfortunately, discerning patterns in the information you take in isn't always easy. Discerning patterns, however, is the key to awareness. This section will present two approaches to discerning what the useful information is—they can be used separately, but are very effective when used together.

Targeting the Most Relevant Information

This concept is best explained by the "bull's-eye approach" developed with regard to assessing avalanche hazard by Jill Fredston and Doug Fessler of the Alaska Mountain Safety Center. Their use of this approach with regard to avalanches is outlined in *Snow Sense,* their excellent book on evaluation of avalanche hazard. While this book addresses only avalanche hazard, the outdoor leader needs to be conscious of many different issues at once. This makes the task somewhat more difficult. Instead of an avalanche, consider this example of a river crossing.

Within the first circle lies all the information that you have available on the situation. For example, the river is higher than usual, the group has a total of nine people, there are pretty flowers on the far bank, and the water is fast flowing.

Within the second circle lies the relevant information. This still may not answer all your questions, but it's more finely tuned than the outer ring information. For example, the water is cold, one of the group members is less than 5 feet tall, the rocks on the last crossing were slippery, and the group is motivated to work together to get across the river.

Inside the bull's-eye lies the most useful information. This is the information that will allow you to make an assessment and decision—all the superfluous information is stripped away. Bull's-eye information might include: the crossing appears to be about 3 feet deep, the river remains relatively shallow downstream in case someone falls, the water and air are cold and hypothermia will be a concern if someone goes in, and the group has already done three equivalent river crossings after receiving careful instruction the day before.

This bull's-eye image can be a helpful way to think about all the information you have in front of you. It's more useful for approaching an issue you've already identified than for identifying issues of potential concern. This approach can be used to cull information for use in a decision-making process, as detailed in chapter 7. The following technique of pattern recognition is more helpful for looking at the bigger picture.

PRACTICING AWARENESS

One way to significantly advance your awareness is by making details something you consciously notice. Do this by choosing a set interval during your outing when you'll have a few moments for reflection. This could be a break on the trail, the top of each climbing pitch, or below each rapid set on a river. Reflect and make note of one detail each about your environment, group, and self of which you were not previously aware. Choose a regular interval that works for you and be creative—if you're too busy during hiking breaks, try picking out your three details just as you set off down the trail again.

The details you pick out don't have to be earth shattering; they can be things you're aware of on some level but were not part of your conscious awareness. For example, you might note that the temperature is dropping (environment), that several members of the group look tired (group), and that you're becoming annoyed with one member (self). Disciplined use of this technique will speed your development of a heightened state of awareness. If this becomes easy for you, try noticing more details at each interval. Do not, however, become too focused on this and ignore your more active leadership tasks.

Another helpful tactic is to compare your awareness of a day's events with that of your co-leader—this can often help reveal the strengths and weaknesses of your awareness. The more you can practice your awareness skills by making them a part of your conscious experience, the more awareness will become subconscious. As the basics become second nature, you'll notice further layers of detail. Noticing details as a leader can become an enjoyable, eye-opening experience and not just a job requirement!

Pattern Recognition

Jim Miller, a veteran outdoor educator and program administrator in the western United States and Canada, instructs the leaders he trains to look for patterns. He explains that leaders must group information, making quick assessments of it. An avid birder, he draws the analogy to the way he immediately categorizes a bird—especially one he's not familiar with—into a category such as seedeater, waterfowl, woodpecker, or bird of prey. Cues about environment, group, and self must be similarly grouped, or there's simply too much information to deal with.

Cues about impending weather are grouped together, as are behaviors observed in the group and physical strain you might experience from an activity. Beyond just grouping these observations, Miller feels that leaders need to make a quick judgment based on patterns they have observed before. A bunch of weather cues are useless unless you're able to make some basic assessment using them. Instead of thinking, *Gee, there are some clouds moving in, and the temperature has dropped,* Miller's ideal leader uses these observations to deduce that a cold front is moving in. Regarding group awareness, Miller is timid about using the obvious word—*stereotype.* While he's the first to advocate that leaders must get to know participants, Miller also argues that at the beginning of an activity the leader must often work off some quick judgments. There can be a lot going on right from the start— leaders need to tailor their leadership to the group. The only way to do this is to get some impression of the group members. Are they confident with taking charge? Are some members quiet and perhaps need a little personal attention? Perhaps you, the leader, are getting tired and feeling a little headache—right away you know that this is an obvious pattern indicating dehydration.

One way to think about pattern recognition harks back to the days when you learned how to drive (if you don't drive, think about learning to ride a bike or paddle a canoe). At first there are too many cues. You push on the accelerator and you sense motion, you hear the engine noise increase, and you see the landscape move by more rapidly. Soon you connect all those cues and learn to push the accelerator the right amount to get the proper response. Then there's merging onto the highway. You learn to observe your speed, the speed of cars already on the highway, how far you have until you have to merge into traffic, and other factors. Soon you can make a quick assessment of any merging situation. Developing your pattern-recognition abilities as a leader functions in the same way—it comes with practice. This ability to recognize and categorize patterns feeds directly into the primary way leaders make decisions, which is detailed in chapter 7.

RECOMMENDED READING

Blum, Arlene, *Annapurna: A Woman's Place,* San Francisco: Sierra Club Books, 1980.

◆ Fredson, Jill A., and Doug Fesler, *Snow Sense: A Guide to Evaluating Snow Avalanche Hazard,* Anchorage: Alaska Mountain Safety Center, 1994.

Heider, John, *The Tao of Leadership,* Atlanta: Humanics Limited, 1985.

◆ Johnson, David W., *Reaching Out: Interpersonal Effectiveness and Self-Actualization,* 5th ed., Boston: Allyn and Bacon, 1993.

◆ Klein, Gary, *Sources of Power: How People Make Decisions,* Cambridge, Massachusetts: MIT Press, 1998.

◆ Luckner, John L., and Reldan S. Nadler, *Processing the Experience: Strategies to Enhance and Generalize Learning,* 2nd ed., Dubuque, Iowa: Kendall/Hunt Publishing, 1997.

◆ = Advanced Recommendation

CHAPTER 5

Planning

Prior planning prevents poor performance. It's that simple. The more organization that goes into the trip, the less likely something will go wrong, and the more likely you can recover gracefully when faced with potential disaster. This chapter provides an outline for trip planning that can be adapted to any imaginable scenario.

It's important to remember, though, that while good trips can be planned using the outline in this chapter, trip planning is ultimately more art than science. The best leaders do not work with a formula but have a feel for what will work in a given situation, what pace will work for people, and what a group will most enjoy. They also know not to sculpt their plan in stone, but to mold it out of clay so it can be shaped and then reshaped again (and again) during the trip if need be.

When it came time to consult a master trip planner for this chapter, I didn't have to think long. As a volunteer, Joe Kuzneski has planned (and led) uncountable AMC trips in both the Northeast and the western United States. I have seen college students in awe after spending five days with Joe on a backcountry leadership training program. Joe does not rely on trail skills and brawn alone on these wilderness outings. He's backed by a trip plan with a level of detail that would make any engineer (an occupation from which Joe is retired) proud. One of his frequent co-leaders has accused Joe of planning out the thickness of the toilet paper his groups carried. It was, of course, an exaggeration, but it reflects Joe's dedication to thinking through the details of his trips in advance (his cost-benefit analysis on the toilet paper issue was inconclusive). While some accuse him of going a bit overboard, Joe's planning standard is the golden one to which leaders should aspire.

Joe's own experience is testimony to the value of good trip planning: "When I first started leading outings, the trips would conclude, we would smile, hug, and say good-bye. After a while, participants started asking as the trip neared conclusion, 'When is your next trip; what are you planning?' Eventually I realized this was a compliment. The participants enjoyed the outing sufficiently to want to go with me again. I tried to identify the factor that made my trips seem better to the participants. My style and personality hadn't changed—I was still me. The outings were going to the same or similar places. Finally, I realized that the factor here was that my trip-planning skills had improved, and as a result my trips were better. I was becoming more meticulous, paying more attention to detail, overlooking fewer things, and including more things in the plan that I knew would have a positive impact on the participants. And I was having fun doing it. So that's what I try to achieve with each trip, to hear: 'When is your next trip?' as we smile, hug, and say good-bye. To me, that is the ultimate compliment for a leader."

Organization

Trip planning is by nature focused on details. As a leader, particularly one who is inexperienced, it'll be easiest for you to proceed in a systematic fashion. On one of my first trips my co-leader forgot to pack tent flies for our two largest tents—rendering them useless in wet weather. Improvisation with a tarp and the fly from our two-person tent did not keep everyone terribly dry through several nights of rain. In this situation the results were merely unpleasant; had the weather been more inclement, we might have faced hypothermia or been forced to end the trip early.

Checklists are useful for guiding you through the stages of planning a trip. They are critical for equipment. It's usually difficult to remedy lapses in your planning process once you're in the field. As you run through the planning steps listed in this chapter, be sure that whoever is responsible for the different planning aspects is keeping a written record of the plan. Checklists, as Joe Kuzneski points out, are not an additional burden, but a tool for making sure everything goes smoothly.

Elements of a Trip Plan

The trip-planning system included here is based on six simple prompting questions:

▶ Why?

▶ Who?

▶ Where?

▶ When?

▶ What?

▶ What if?

The answers to these questions will form your trip plan. Each question helps answer the one that follows. You will not, however, be able to run through the list and answer every question in the order it appears. You may determine under "Who?" that you want to take people who've never backcountry skied before. When you look at "Where," you may be unable to find a location that's close enough but also has good terrain for never-evers. You would have to go back and change "Who?" to "more experienced skiers." It helps if you think of trip planning as sort of a puzzle. The answers to some questions will be obvious to you— start by filling these in. Use the answers you do have as cues to guide your efforts as you fill in the rest of the blanks.

Why?

Why are you leading your outing? Is it to teach skiing, improve people's self-esteem, climb a specific peak, or just have an enjoyable time? Some objectives are common to most trips—others may be unique to yours. Joe Kuzneski, not unexpectedly, sets a high standard: "I plan my trips with the goal that everyone enhances the quality of their lives as a result of going on this adventure. This can be in the form of learning new things, experiencing new environments, accepting new challenges, and making friends with great people. I may not always be 100 percent successful, but I try."

Whatever objectives you establish will guide the planning and development of the rest of the trip. Trip objectives are very flexible—as long as participants understand and agree with what they're getting into. I encourage you to use your imagination. The following are some common objectives, beginning with the most important. Use these objectives as a starting point, reprioritize them as you see fit (except the first one, safety), and add details specific to your trip.

Minimize Risk: As Kuzneski tells it, "The primary objective on all my trips is to have pizza and beer at the end of the trip. That means," Joe continues, "that we all have to make it safely back to our cars." Joe's point is that to be successful a trip needs to come back with all the participants it started with, in good health and spirits. This is not exactly why you lead a trip, but it is critical to allow the rest of your objectives to occur. Thus safety is the first, nonnegotiable, objective for every trip.

Fun: Most people participate in outdoor programs to enjoy themselves. Without some level of enjoyment few people would come back. While there are a few programs that are so goal focused that fun may be lower down on the list, I hope to never go on any trip where fun is not an objective at all. If all this serious leadership stuff leaves you in need of relearning how to have fun, see chapter 15, Don't Forget to Have Fun!

Learning: What an opportunity! The learning can involve outdoor skills, group dynamics, conservation, cultural history, natural history, or legions of other topics. Many people participate in outdoor activities in part to gain new knowledge and skills. Be sure participants have at least one structured opportunity to learn something new each day— even on a recreational trip of a few hours. Then take advantage of informal learning opportunities that present themselves along the way.

Specific Objectives: What specific things are you setting out to do? Climb a certain peak, run a certain river, bike a certain trail, learn about the natural history of an area, develop better self-esteem among group members, expose children who have never been out of the city to the outdoors? The possibilities are almost endless. While you and your group may be willing to sacrifice a lot to obtain your goal, always remember the first objective, safety. Those who put any goal above safety place themselves and their group in grave peril. If you would like this lesson reinforced, read Jon Krakauer's *Into Thin Air,* on the fatal 1996 season on Mount Everest.

Once you've decided upon your objectives—why you're leading the trip—you can move ahead planning the rest of the trip around meeting them. If something you do on the trip doesn't fit with these objectives, you should question it—either drop it or decide that it's important enough to become part of your objectives. On a longer trip you don't need to plan every objective. Participants' understanding of and commitment to these objectives are what allows the best objectives to be met. This means participants must buy in to your objectives and adopt them as their own. It helps if the participants can have some role in sculpting at least some day-to-day objectives, so they feel ownership. Participants' connection to your objectives is covered in more detail in chapter 11, Expedition Behavior.

Who?

Who is the trip for? You may have an exact group of individuals in mind, or you may be looking to have people sign up. As a professional leader you will often have little or no control over who a trip is for, although it's always your ultimate responsibility to ensure that those going are appropriate for the trip and can complete it safely. You must also know how the trip has been presented to them to help you understand their expectations. Some questions to ask as you plan the trip include:

▶ Population—retirees, scouts, college students, at-risk youth, amateur geologists?

▶ Special skills required—kayaking, rock climbing, backpacking?

LEADER'S INTERESTS

Participants, not your own personal interests as leader, must come first when planning objectives. Imagine that you've led sea kayaking groups on a paddle around Scenic Bay a dozen times over the course of a summer. You know the route and the currents well, and you know just where to find the sea lions, otters, seals, and seabirds—the reason most people sign up for the trip. You've heard that Majestic Island has similar terrain and wildlife to that of the bay but has some unique cliffs you would love to see. Unfortunately, you aren't familiar with Majestic Island and will not have time off to visit before your summer of guiding comes to an end. You've heard that a combination of large ocean swells and unexpected winds make paddling in the area treacherous at times. Because Scenic Cove is getting a bit boring, it might seem that you would take the chance to visit Majestic, but this is not the decision of a caring (and ethical) leader. Objectives must be determined with the interests of the participants coming first. Paddling to Majestic Island would be less safe than going to Scenic Bay, and because you don't know it as well, you'd be less likely to be able to find the wildlife that people come to see. Especially in light of the safety issue, there is no justification for going to Majestic Island—participants will not benefit. While this example may seem dramatic and clear-cut, this issue plays itself out frequently—in big and small ways—in the actions of every leader. This does not mean that leaders can't enjoy themselves, just that they should set and follow objectives that benefit participants first. The caring leader finds satisfaction in leading and not just in new challenges and new surroundings.

▶ Fitness level—anywhere from none to Ironman level?

▶ Specific focus—birding, mountain biking, leadership development?

▶ Special needs—what types of disabilities or medical conditions are you prepared to accommodate?

▶ How many—numbers of people who will go on the trip? (See below for more detail.)

Of these questions, the issue of how many people to take is one that needs more discussion. In many areas regulations now limit the maximum group size, especially for commercial groups. When regulations do not determine a group size, there are three issues to consider: safety, group management, and impact. Safety and management are intertwined. The largest group you can effectively monitor, teach, and communicate with will also be the largest group for safety purposes. If you have two leaders and a group of twenty people strung out along a trail, it gets hard to be a caring leader and aware of what's going on for everyone. On the other hand, from a management perspective there's really no such thing as a group that's too small. Certain activities, such as long rock climbs, work only with small groups. In other cases a group size of four or more people has safety advantages. With four people, if one is injured, one person can stay with the victim and two can go for assistance. The group's impact on the environment and fellow outdoor users is a key consideration. On land a group size of ten or less seems to be emerging as the consensus ideal. Issues related to impact are fully addressed in chapter 14, Conservation.

Come back to the answers to these six questions regarding "Who?" once your trip plan is nearly complete and see if the people you've identified at this stage still fit with the trip you have planned. The only consistently wrong answer to the question, "Who is this trip for?" is "Me." As a leader, your own interests need to be, at most, secondary to the interests of participants.

"Who?" is also about the leaders. Leaders should each be capable of independently leading the trip if circumstances demand it. When working together, the leaders will ideally complement each other's skills. On a paddling trip, if one person is strong on paddling skills and weaker on issues of group dynamics, the other should be better at dealing with people.

Where?

Where will you go on your trip? Answering this begins by identifying the general area you'll be traveling in, and narrows down to include the specific route you'll be traveling. It may be that your client or organization dictates where you go. Or one of your objectives—say, "Climb the West Peak of Mount Bond"—might make it clear where you're going. In other cases the activity you wish to lead may determine where you go. The resources listed later in this chapter will be of assistance to you.

As much as possible, you want to plan your entire trip and travel route in advance. On shorter trips this will likely include the exact route, location of campsites, water sources, resupply points, points of interest, hazards along the way, bail-out routes, and turnaround times. On a longer trip your planning may need to be less specific—it would be hard to plan your exact camping spots for a monthlong wilderness trip. Focus not just on the backcountry but also on how participants will arrive and depart and any issues specific to the region you will be in.

Prior Knowledge: Ideally you will have traveled the route of the trip before, but this is not mandatory if the difficulty of the trip is well within your abilities and you have experience in similar areas. If your experience is leading backpacking trips in the forests of the Northeast, you'll need to gain some experience in the terrain of the Rockies before leading a trip there. "I used to feel safe coming off the summit of Colorado peaks by noon," relates trip planner Joe Kuzneski. "I had read and heard that storms would not build until midafternoon, but then I encountered storms well before noon." Experience on the ground gives relevance to any research you have done in the past. Of course, Joe would be fine leading trips to a new area of the Colorado Rockies, but he would need some hands-on experience before he led a backpacking trip in, say, Alaska.

If you haven't been in the exact area you're headed, the onus is on you to do the additional research to make up for your lack of firsthand knowledge. Prior knowledge of an area gives practical information that makes a trip run as safely and smoothly as possible. It also helps enable you to educate participants on the natural and human history of an area. Again, good research can give you some, but not all of this. The best leaders are usually those who have an intimate knowledge of and affection for an area.

Transportation and Support: In the enthusiasm of mentally walking the trip in your mind, it's almost possible to forget how you'll get where you're going. Will you have cars or will you be dropped off and picked up? Do more elaborate travel plans including plane, trains, or boats factor into the planning? Also consider what support, such as food or equipment resupplies, you'll need. Transportation and support are

Good trip planning usually involves a lot of work with maps.

mostly straightforward, but the key is in the detail. I will relate two quick anecdotes about pitfalls. The first involved a daylong canoe trip I was on. Because we had only one van, we left my bike securely locked at the takeout point. The idea was that one person would bike back and get our vehicle after the trip was over. As I locked up the van, I decided I needed only the van key, so I left my key chain in the van. When we got to the takeout point the bike was still securely locked—and I had no key. An upstream paddle was not feasible, so I enjoyed a long hike back to where we had parked.

In another, more serious situation, some friends of mine were on a six-week wilderness trip in coastal Alaska conducted by an out-of-state organization. The bush pilot they hired failed to show up with a planned drop of two weeks' worth of food. Because the group was far from any road, they hiked down to the coast and after a week were able to hail a passing boat that carried them back to civilization.

Be certain that all your plans are well constructed. Recheck any arrangements, especially if safety depends upon them. If support is required, make sure that more than one person is responsible. The organization offering the Alaska trip, for instance, could have had someone follow up with the pilot to make sure the food drop had been successful. If that group had not been able to contact the boat, they might have faced a life-threatening situation trying to get back to civilization with almost no food.

Rules and Regulations: As much as it seems contradictory to some people's concept of "wilderness," more and more wild areas are closely regulated. On all federal lands in the United States, commercial groups need a special permit to operate. Many other areas require backcountry permits for everyone. Generally the regulations are easy to find out, but if you're planning a trip to a new area be sure to ask a long time in advance. The permitting process for some areas can be very time consuming. Also find out about any rules or guidelines pertaining to the type of activity you'll be conducting. Remember that most of the rules and regulations were developed with the goal of preserving the type of backcountry experience we all seek in the face of growing pressure from users. While rules and regulations may pose a challenge to the trip plan you first envisioned, the land managers who develop and implement them have good intentions in doing so.

Simulation: The Joe Kuzneski standard is to "walk the trip in your mind." What does the map tell you? No two 6-mile stretches of trail are the same. What is the elevation lost and gained? Picture yourself hiking through the narrow canyon you see on the map and then climbing the steep headwall. Would it be better to do the headwall at the end of the day or perhaps camp at the base and tackle it in the morning? If there is a guidebook, does it say the route is "very exposed" or "slippery when wet"? According to Kuzneski, those slippery-when-wet sections are always wet when he gets there—assume they will be for your trip as well. If you're on a river, what will the effects of high or low water be? For sea kayakers, consider waves, currents, tides, and wind. Develop alternative routes in case your planned route is too long, too short, or impassable. Consider bail-out routes that might be used in a crisis situation.

When

The "When" is very dependent upon the "Where" but addresses the exact dates of the trip and also the impacts those dates have. Different locations will have different seasons that are best for visitations. Snow levels, water levels, bloodsucking insect populations, storm patterns, and many other factors vary with the time of year. In some areas there can be dramatic changes within a week's time.

What

What equipment and supplies do you need for this trip? Two types of equipment need to be addressed: personal gear and group gear. Personal gear includes a participant's sleeping bag, clothes, toothbrush, water bottle, and so forth. Group gear is those items of equipment that are used by the entire group or at least several people, such as cookstoves, tents, climbing ropes, and the like. Supplies are consumable items, such as food, that are used during an activity.

Personal Gear: As leader, it's your responsibility to ensure that trip participants have the appropriate personal gear. Unless they're true experts themselves or the trip requires no equipment (not even a water bottle), participants must be provided with a clear list of *everything* they need to bring. Most people will really appreciate having a checklist. Be specific and try to educate people about the reasons behind the gear they need. If you say "rain jacket," you may wind up with someone with a full-length dress raincoat, another with a plastic poncho, and a third with a nylon windbreaker that is not waterproof. I've seen all of these on trips—and under some circumstances they may be okay, but often they are not appropriate. Tell people they need a "waterproof rain jacket made of a waterproof material like coated nylon or a waterproof-breathable fabric like Gore-Tex; the jacket must have a hood and be snug fitting so it will not catch gusts of wind above treeline." If this sounds like overkill, wait until you're backpacking on a windy day in cold rain and sleet and your most inexperienced participant has inadequate rain gear.

Beyond providing a list of gear, you must check participants' critical gear before going out into the field. Despite the description of the rain jacket, people may still bring something less than ideal. It's very helpful at this point if you have some alternative equipment that can be loaned out. Besides bringing inappropriate gear, people sometimes forget things—you'll be a hero if you can supply a substitute.

Some participants will bring critical medications that they may not

Katherine E. Jones

Planning also involves getting all the gear ready.

be able to live without. On a multiday trip it may be worthwhile to have participants bring two sets of these medications, one to be carried by the leader in case anything happens to the first. This is a good practice for people who know they are vulnerable to anaphylactic shock and need to carry injectable epinephrine (although this item may be in some well-stocked first-aid kits). The same goes for people who are totally dependent on eyeglasses—a backup pair can be a blessing if the first pair are lost or destroyed.

You may also choose to provide a list of things *not* to bring. This is especially important with youth programs. Depending on circumstances, this might include alcoholic beverages, cell phones, portable video games, radios and CD players, cosmetics, firearms (you might be surprised), or other items incompatible with the activity you're leading. It's helpful to have a clearly stated policy on tobacco products, especially if they are not permitted. For certain individuals, heading into the woods is viewed as a good chance to use recreational drugs—while it should be obvious, a statement that illegal drug use will not be tolerated may also be necessary.

Group Gear: Leaders are often responsible for bringing group gear, but depending upon the exact activity, participants may also need to bring some to share. As with personal gear, it's important to have an exact list of what's needed so items can be checked off. Make sure everything is in working order. Backpacking stoves and any other finicky equipment should always be tested before heading out on a trip, and it's often important to set up tents and check for holes or missing poles. Also essential is a repair kit that includes spare parts for gear such as stoves and water filters, as well as multipurpose repair supplies such as duct tape and light wire.

Supplies: Though primarily food, this category also includes other consumables such as stove fuel, water purification chemicals, and first-aid supplies. When it comes to food, the quality (and quantity) of meals, especially dinner, has a significant effect on your group. A tasty, nutritious, and hearty dinner brings closure to a satisfying day, while a poorly planned meal of modest appeal only adds to the burdens of a long, hard day. As such, time spent planning dinners will have a big payoff for the leaders. Play the "What if?" game (see the following section) with your dinners. Get it perfect before you head out—using backcountry gear, experiment with cooking any meals you haven't made before. If you have to carry it, plan to keep the weight of the food as light as possible. Your backpacking participants will love you for this.

There should always be one or two group first-aid kits on a trip. These must be methodically restocked before any trip. If you carry any communications equipment, make sure the batteries are fully charged. For cell phones or satellite phones it may be worthwhile to obtain disposable alkaline batteries; these are more reliable than rechargeable ones, especially at low temperatures. Even if you use a water filter or plan to carry enough water on a day trip, a backup supply of water purification chemicals is a good idea. When relying primarily on chemical purification, make sure to have supplies in several places. Stove fuel must be carefully planned out to ensure an appropriate amount. The amount of stove fuel you need to carry varies greatly with the type of stove you're using, the type of food you're cooking, the season, and especially if you'll have to melt snow for water. In general, under summer conditions, a group of eight to ten people will use a quart of fuel a day.

The "What" question requires significant planning effort, especially if you're undertaking a trip different from those you've completed before. Your energy will be well spent carefully planning out what needs to go on the trip and making sure that it actually comes along. This is a situation where checklists are most certainly your friends—don't be shy about making and using them.

What If?

This is what you should be asking yourself as you develop your plan. It's possible to plan for some of the more likely problems, though obviously it's impossible to cover every contingency. What you can do is build in some redundancy so that one relatively minor problem does not escalate into something more serious. Really good leaders play the "What if?" game extensively, and as a result anticipate the unexpected and are prepared for it. As you walk the trip in your mind, picture your group trekking across the 2-mile-long above-treeline knife edge. Picture it on a nice clear day with great views. Now what if the picture changes and you and your group are caught on the middle of the knife edge with lightning flashing all around you? Your "What if?" should allow you to plan to keep this last picture from becoming reality.

Trip-Planning Resources———————

Your most valuable resource is often a guidebook specific to the area and activity you wish to undertake. This guide will usually describe trails, rivers, and climbs, along with interesting attractions of the area. Referencing a guidebook is rarely sufficient to develop a trip plan, however. Guidebooks are inaccurate or provide incomplete information; trails, trailheads, and permit requirements change. For some locations (often the best ones) and activities, there will be no guidebook.

Other Sources of Information

Maps: The standard maps for many backcountry activities in the United States are the topographic quadrangles produced by the United States Geological Survey (USGS). These are available either from the USGS itself or through a wide variety of outdoor outfitters and bookstores. Similar government-produced maps are available in many other countries. Maps produced specifically for hikers and paddlers or other

Alex Kcsseff

Foreign destinations may require significantly more planning work—pictured here is Lake Titicaca in Bolivia.

recreationists, such as those the AMC publishes, are also available in some areas. These maps have the advantage that they are often updated more frequently and may contain more relevant information than USGS maps.

Topographic ("topo") maps show elevation through the use of contour lines and are the only kind of map useful for most outdoor activities. When trip planning, you always want to look at elevation change and distance. A very general rule of thumb for foot travel allows for half an hour to travel a mile and an additional half an hour for each 1,000 feet of elevation gain. Maps can tell you where water sources, river crossings, and trails are. Maps also give you a clue as to how exposed your route will be to the weather, what the terrain may look like, and where potential campsites lie.

Internet: Obviously, an increasing amount of information is available on the Internet. Most areas of public land have a website, and these often provide a significant amount of useful information. Area-specific or activity-specific private websites often feature bulletin boards that allow you to connect with other people who've been in an area. User beware: There's a lot of inaccurate information available on the Web do not trust everything you read. Among the best Web resources are the several online outdoor bookstores. A search of one of these will inform you about books and often maps that are available covering the area you're interested in.

Government Agencies: When planning a trip, one of your initial steps should be to call, write, or visit the Internet site of the agency that manages the area you plan to visit. These agencies generally have a lot of useful information. In particular the management agencies can inform you of any restrictions, regulations, or guidelines they have for use of the area. With increasing use many areas have instituted regulations, particularly with regard to camping. Permits are required for camping or even day use in many areas.

People: Often the best resources for trip planning are others who've been there. Things that you may not have thought of and helpful tidbits of information will often reveal themselves in a conversation with someone who has visited the area. This firsthand knowledge is particularly helpful if your source also happens to be a trip leader.

Summary

Value of the Trip Plan

The plan for a day trip may exist largely in your head, but for more complex trips much needs to be written down. For a sample trip plan prepared by Joe Kuzneski, see appendix A. Even on a short outing some responsible person should have a clear idea, in writing, of where you're going and when you'll return. A written trip plan serves at least seven purposes:

1. Ensuring that the leaders have a shared vision for the trip

2. Giving structure to the trip, including objectives to work toward

3. Providing information to share with participants or potential participants

4. Recording information necessary to locate you in an emergency

5. Cataloging information you need in an emergency

6. Documenting any logistical support needs, such as transportation or food drops

7. Giving you a checklist for tasks, equipment, supplies, and so forth

The trip plan continues to be valuable after the trip, making it easier for you or others to skip much of the research and repeat the trip. While overkill is possible, the more detailed the trip plan, the more useful it generally is before, during, and after the trip. Just be willing to modify a plan—no matter how much work went into it—if the situation calls for it.

Expectations for Trip Plans

Organizations, if you are leading for one, have varying expectations for trip plans. At a minimum you should always have a detailed itinerary including the "Where" and "When." Some of the other factors, such as the "Why," may remain fixed if the trips you lead have standard destinations and objectives. Even then it can be helpful to develop new objectives for a trip, perhaps based on avoiding the less successful aspects of previous trips. If you usually raft the Salmon River and your objectives are safety, fun, and ensuring client comfort, challenge yourself. Because a couple of evaluations mentioned this on previous trips, make it an objective to give a talk on the flora and fauna of the area.

Hundred Mile Wilderness

A final lesson on trip planning from Joe Kuzneski originated with a situation in which he put his trip planning to use to modify his trip plan. He was co-leading a trip along the Hundred Mile Wilderness section of the Appalachian Trail from Monson, Maine, to just south of Mount Katahdin. As Joe tells it, "This section of the trail does not cross any public roads for a stretch of about 100 miles." Unfortunately he developed a knee problem early in the trip. "On the third day of the trip, about 30 miles into the hike, it became clear that the problem was getting worse and it would be unwise for me to continue hiking." Luckily Joe had done the trip planning and was aware of all the possible bail-out points from this remote area. "There was a side trail just ahead, which led to a logging road after an easy 2-mile hike," he explains. "As soon as my co-leader and I discussed the issue with the group and decided I had to go out, we were able to able to implement a plan to make it happen." Luckily there was another experienced leader on the trip who was able to take over Joe's role. "The strategy worked as planned," Joe reports. "I was able to hitch a ride, and I was back in Monson within four hours after we decided I needed to go out."

Joe's evacuation from an area he had never traveled before is a testament to the value of careful planning. By taking the time to get to know the area he was going to, Joe was able to identify the easiest option right away. Without Joe's prior research the group might not even have been aware of the possibility of finding a ride from the remote logging road. While they probably would not have wound up making the 30-mile hike back to the trailhead, the group might have been more inconvenienced as they tried to determine the best course of action. This is just another reminder that the value of a trip plan continues throughout the trip. Never discount the value of asking "What if?" at all the junctures of trip planning and even once you're under way. It's good practice, and someday you'll likely get to use one of those alternative plans.

RECOMMENDED READING

Curtis, Rick, *The Backpacker's Field Manual: A Comprehensive Guide to Mastering Backcountry Skills,* New York: Three Rivers Press, 1998.

◆ Ford, Phyllis, and Jim Blanchard, *Leadership and Administration of Outdoor Pursuits,* 2nd ed., State College, Pennsylvania: Venture Publishing, 1993.

Gorman, Stephen, *Winter Camping,* 2nd ed., Boston: Appalachian Mountain Club, 1999.

Harvey, Mark, *The National Outdoor Leadership School's Wilderness Guide: The Classic Handbook,* New York: Simon & Schuster, 1999.

Krakauer, Jon, *Into Thin Air,* New York: Villard Books, 1997.

Lanza, Michael, *The Ultimate Guide to Backcountry Travel,* Boston: Appalachian Mountain Club Books, 1999.

Petzoldt, Paul, *The New Wilderness Handbook,* New York: W. W. Norton, 1984.

♦ = Advanced Recommendation

CHAPTER 6

Participants

Participants follow a leader because they perceive a benefit in doing so. Becoming a follower is not a willy-nilly decision or an unchangeable decision if the participants see no continued benefit. Minus the participants, there is no need for the outdoor leader (this may seem obvious, but the behavior of a few outdoor leaders indicates a lack of understanding). Leaders need to have some influence over participants' behavior, which necessitates an understanding of the motivations and needs of the participants. Through understanding of the participants, the leader will be best able to meet their needs. A skilled leader can also use this understanding to influence participant behavior in a manner favorable to the goals of the group.

As a leader, your awareness of each participant's needs will help you make the experience as safe and enjoyable as possible. These individuals, of course, are members of the larger group. Individuals with unmet needs usually focus on these needs and hinder the accomplishment of group goals. A participant who feels unsafe, for example, may not engage fully in activities and will continue to return to questions on safety topics. On the other hand, individuals whose needs are met will be contributors to the meeting of group goals. Understanding the group, and its successes and failures, begins with understanding the individuals who comprise it.

Participants in outdoor activities, like leaders, come in all shapes, sizes, ages, genders, and colors. The same is true of participants' motivations and needs. Your awareness depends on interactions with and observation of each participant. Even a general impression—often all you'll have time to develop on a shorter trip—can be very valuable in helping you ensure that an individual's needs are met.

Needs

Participant needs are many and varied, so it may be helpful to have a framework within which to understand them. The metaphor presented here requires a bit of background on expedition climbing.

The history—and much of the present—of Himalayan climbing is based on what's referred to as the siege-style expedition. Team members travel to the mountain—usually accompanied by several tons of supplies and equipment carried by pack animals or porters—and establish Base Camp. In addition to transporting all of this equipment, establishing Base Camp involves setting up kitchens, tents, and—on many modern expeditions—satellite communications and laptop computers. While this setup is taking place, the climbing team may venture a short way up the mountain to acclimatize to the altitude, but they always come back to Base Camp for the night.

Edmund Hillary and Tenzing Norgay first ascended the South Col route on Everest, and that remains the most popular route up the mountain today. Once a South Col expedition establishes Base Camp, the team begins to set up a chain of camps up the mountain. Climbers first make a day's journey up the treacherous Khumbu Ice Fall to establish Camp One. That done, climbers often return to Base Camp to rest before returning to climb even higher on the mountain. Later, once Camp One is fully stocked and climbers are acclimatized to the altitude, they will move upward and set up Camp Two.

This siege-style climbing provides a neat analogy to the needs of your participants. Much the way an expedition establishes a Base Camp and then a series of higher camps up the mountain, the needs of your participants must also be fulfilled in a certain succession. You cannot establish Camp Three on the mountain without the camps below, just as you cannot satisfy higher-level needs for personal growth if people's bellies are empty. Establishment of a higher camp—or fulfillment of the next tier of human needs—is dependent on the ongoing support of the level below.

In 1954, a year after the first ascent of Everest, psychologist Abraham Maslow's *Hierarchy of Needs* was first published. This work delineates distinct tiers of human needs. The most fundamental needs —Base Camp level—are the *physiological needs*. The need for food, water, shelter, and other elements essential to survival will be a primary motivation for an individual's behavior until these needs are largely satisfied. The next level in Maslow's Hierarchy are the *safety needs*—related to an absence of threats to one's physical well-being. As their physiological needs are met, individuals will become motivated to address their safety needs. These safety needs will gradually become the primary focus of the participants' attention—just as establishing Camp One becomes the focus of the climbing expedition.

Moving up the mountain, the needs become more sophisticated but remain dependent on the continuation of the support structure below. Above the safety needs are the desire for *belonging or social needs* (Camp Two) and, one step higher, the *esteem needs* (Camp Three). Finally, at the rarely attained summit, is what Maslow termed *self-actualization*. These highest needs still remain dependent on the fulfillment of the more fundamental needs below. If the participants' security is threatened, they regress to prioritizing safety ahead of belonging needs. Likewise, if the climbing team at Camp Two realizes that Camp One has been destroyed in an avalanche, they will ensure it is reestablished so it can continue to play a supporting role.

In describing both participants' needs and the manner in which these needs motivate behavior, Maslow's Hierarchy is particularly useful to outdoor leaders. During an outdoor program individuals are likely to focus, at least initially, on meeting lower-level needs that are not customary worries. Participants may find that their needs are being met; but if they don't, their progress up the hierarchy may be blocked by that deficiency. According to Maslow, ". . . gratification becomes as important a concept as deprivation in motivation theory, for it releases the organism from the domination of a relatively more physiological need, thereby permitting the emergence of other more social goals."

Despite the emphasis on the defined tiers, it's important to understand that individuals do not need to have a set of needs satisfied 100 percent before needs in a higher tier can begin to be addressed. Expedition climbers may venture up and establish Camp One and part of Camp Two, perhaps even climb up toward Camp Three and then return to Base Camp. The camps are partially established and climbers are partially acclimated to that altitude. Participants, likewise, will be addressing needs at different levels of the Maslow's Hierarchy simultaneously. A participant in a climbing program may have a safety need that has not been filled—she is untrusting of her climbing partner and believes that he will drop her if she falls onto the rope. This participant may simultaneously be addressing belonging needs and building relationships with those around her. This need for belonging may even assist her in working out the safety need by building trust with her partner. This participant is also motivated to climb because it helps fulfill her esteem needs. Thus this particular climber might have 90 percent of her physiological needs met, 80 percent of her safety needs, 60 percent of her belonging needs, 30 percent of her esteem needs, and 10 percent of her self-actualization needs met at this point in the program. The shifts between different tiers on the hierarchy—like the shifts between camps on the mountain—will be ongoing.

Physiological Needs (Base Camp): Maslow wrote: "It is quite true that humans live by bread alone—when there is no bread." For most members of our society, meeting basic physiological needs is not a major concern. Thus people focus on higher-level needs. Because people are so accustomed to having their physiological needs met, the prospect of any deprivation may be disconcerting to participants.

To maintain optimal performance—and ultimately to survive—humans need adequate air, water, food, sleep, and shelter. Although it's detrimental to our physical and mental performance, it is possible to go for periods of time without food or sleep. Deprivation of the other physiological needs can have serious effects in a short amount of time. Adequate fulfillment of the physiological needs—like the establishment of Base Camp—is in most cases a prerequisite for significant fulfillment of higher-level needs. It's easy to imagine that the participant

Summit
SELF-ACTUALIZATION
doing what one is fitted for

Camp Three
ESTEEM NEEDS
respect of self and others

Camp Two
BELONGING NEEDS
relationships with others

Camp One
SAFETY NEEDS
freedom from dangers

Base Camp
PHYSIOLOGICAL NEEDS
food, sleep, water, shelter, etc.

According to Maslow's Hierarchy, each level or camp is dependent on
the support and refuge provided by the level below.

with inadequate air, water, food, sleep, or shelter would not be well
motivated to address even basic safety needs. This is why the Base
Camp level need is the strongest of Maslow's Hierarchy—these needs
cannot, in any more than the short term, be denied.

Safety Needs (Camp One): Part of most Outward Bound courses is a solo
experience in which participants spend time alone in a designated spot
for one, two, or even three days. Ideally this is an opportunity to peace-
fully reflect—for many participants, it's the high point of the course.
Unfortunately this opportunity can be lost for participants if their
safety needs have not been addressed—spending time alone in the

backcountry is a daunting prospect for many people. They worry about wild animals, shelter from storms, providing treated drinking water, unknown people coming into camp, and many other issues. These concerns are not unwarranted—participants on courses I've led have faced hazards ranging from a curious bear that visited several solo sites, to two days of torrential rain, wind, and hail that tested the shelter of the best-rigged tarp, to—memorably—a UFO that participants reported hovering nearby. Unless they're adequately prepared to address their safety needs, participants will be distracted from fulfilling the higher-level needs that likely brought them to the program.

The fundamental safety need of participants is to be reasonably free of fear. While participants may perceive some increased risk on outdoor programs—and this is not always a bad thing—people need to be able to be free enough of fear that other needs can receive proper attention. Outward Bound students who spend the entire solo in terror will miss out on many of the opportunities that the experience is intended to provide. They won't get to appreciate nature and their own company or have the opportunity to reflect on their other course experiences. Participants' fears vary but include physical or psychological dangers; the threat that physiological needs will no longer be met; and, broadly, the unknown.

Unfortunately—this is addressed more in chapter 12, Risk—participants are not always good at understanding the level of risk they face. The leader's task in addressing participants' safety needs is not only to provide a reasonable level of safety on the program, but also to explain the risks and safety precautions to participants. Addressing safety needs begins in the very first moments of a program, when you greet participants in an open and friendly manner. First impressions go a long way toward making people comfortable. Throughout the course you address these needs by letting participants know what is going on in advance, greatly reducing anxiety. Finally, the leader always keeps participants informed of safety concerns and creates a partnership with them to help reduce them. This involvement not only reassures people but also makes for a safer experience, because the leaders are not the only ones looking out for the group.

For many participants, addressing safety needs—establishing this first camp on the mountain—is tricky. In part this is because safety needs vary greatly. While one participant may want to jump into a kayak and paddle difficult rapids on the first day, another may still be

PHYSIOLOGICAL NEEDS

Water: We require a steady replenishment of water to keep our blood volume at a constant level and maintain vital body functions. For most people with relatively sedentary lives and plenty of water and other beverages close at hand, hydration does not seem like a major concern. For the participant on an outdoor program, constant exertion will greatly increase the need for water. High elevation, high temperature, low humidity, and wind also contribute to increased loss of liquid, as does the food people eat in the outdoors, which is often lower in water than what people eat at home.

Thirst, surprisingly, is not a very good indicator of the need for water—it only kicks in once you are mildly dehydrated, and even then only intermittently. Thus it's important to consciously consume water—especially when it's cold out and the thirst mechanism is further depressed. Two liters a day is a bare minimum—I have led groups where the five liters a day (at almost two pounds per liter) we carried was insufficient in the hot and dry desert.

Dehydration leads to decreased energy, impaired judgment and reasoning, and increased susceptibility to hypothermia or hyperthermia. As dehydration increases in severity, it increasingly can cause serious health problems. Of course, preventing this is not as simple as sitting down and dipping your water bottle into the nearest stream. Water for your participants must be purified by boiling, filtering, or chemical means before it's consumed. Science and the personal experience of many backcountry travelers tell us that even the purest-looking spring may be contaminated by nasty micro-critters.

Food: In addition to providing the nutrition necessary to keep our bodies functioning, food also has important psychological impacts. A tasty meal will leave a group in higher spirits than a bland one. The caloric requirements of participants in outdoor activities may be almost double their needs at home and must be consumed throughout the day to keep up energy levels. The

uncomfortable with that level of difficulty after days of practice. As a leader your job is to encourage a realistic perspective on safety and bring the two ends of the spectrum together.

Belonging Needs (Camp Two): As safety needs are addressed, the participant begins to focus more on companionship. The need for relationships

food provided also must contain sufficient quantities of carbohydrates, protein, and fat. Carbohydrates—starches and sugars—provide quick energy. Protein provides the building blocks for muscle and other tissues—or can be converted to energy, providing about the same amount as carbohydrates. Fats provide the most energy per pound, but take longer than carbohydrates to convert into energy, making them useful for dinner, when participants will need energy to stay warm all night.

Air: Most people are completely unfamiliar with having an inadequate air supply, but this is exactly what happens at higher elevations. At decreased atmospheric pressure, our bodies are able to take up less oxygen. Above 8,000 feet (and rarely down to 6,000 feet), individuals can experience altitude sickness—itself potentially a serious problem—or the life-threatening conditions of pulmonary or cerebral edema. Given time at altitude, our bodies, thankfully, can add more oxygen-carrying capacity in our blood, allowing for a degree of acclimatization.

Sleep: Sufficient sleep keeps a person's mental and physical skills in top condition. Well-rested participants will be better able to assist with making their own experience a good one and will, in general, have a more enjoyable time—beginning to sound somewhat familiar? Eight or more hours of sleep may be appropriate during a trip—and in the days leading up to it.

Shelter and Clothing: Shelter and clothing are what we use to maintain a body temperature that is neither too hot nor too cold. Shelter and clothing protect us from the chilling effects of wind and precipitation as well as from the damaging effects of the sun's rays. Conduction, convection, radiation, and evaporation are the ways heat can be lost from the body—each can be a good or a bad thing, depending on circumstances. When it is a bad thing, inappropriate shelter and clothing may lead to hypothermia or hyperthermia—being too cold or too hot. A wilderness first-aid course will address all these environmental safety concerns and is invaluable for prevention as well as treatment.

with others and to feel a part of a group is indeed what motivates many people to participate in outdoor programs. According to Maslow, "We still underplay the deep importance of the neighborhood, of one's territory, of one's clan, of one's own 'kind,' one's class, one's gang, one's familiar working colleagues. And we have largely forgotten our deep animal tendencies to herd, to flock, to join, to belong." The small group outdoor activity can be a way for people to experience this sense of community and to feel like they are making a contribution to it. Some participants have a very strong need not just to participate but to actively contribute to the group—washing dishes, carrying extra weight for someone who's not as strong, reading the map, making dinner, and so forth. Such activity contributes to these individuals' sense of belonging.

Unfortunately, individuals sometimes have difficulty finding acceptance within some groups. A group that successfully engages its members and is not exclusionary is said to have good expedition behavior—a subject fully addressed in chapter 11. By helping cultivate good expedition behavior in their groups, leaders enable the fulfillment of this stage of Maslow's Hierarchy of Needs.

Esteem Needs (Camp Three): As belonging needs are met, participants will transition to a focus on esteem needs. Esteem involves valuing and liking yourself and is based on both self-respect and the respect you're accorded by others. For many individuals the two are difficult to separate, as self-esteem is dependent on respect from others. Self-esteem comes across as confidence and self-assurance—often leading to increased respect from others—and is based upon mastery of skills, achievements, confidence, and independence. In a universal sense, respect from others, according to Maslow, involves prestige, reputation, fame, and glory. In an outdoor program respect from others is likely to come in the form of recognition or attention.

When Mary compliments Steve on his navigational skills, which led the group through a stretch of off-trail travel, her compliment helps address this second aspect of his esteem needs. If the group is attentive when Carmen speaks, that attention will influence her sense of the esteem in which the group holds her. A supportive group that uses good expedition behavior will help its members meet their esteem needs. The group filled with disagreement and infighting will lower people's self-esteem and make them feel bad about themselves.

Self-Actualization (Summit): When other needs are reasonably satisfied, Maslow believed that "we may still often (if not always) expect that a new discontent and restlessness will soon develop, unless the individual is doing what *he* or *she* individually is fitted for." According to Maslow, individuals must do what is most appropriate for them—

Participants must feel comfortable that their physiological and safety needs will be met when venturing into new territory.

"Musicians must make music, artists must paint, poets must write if they are to be ultimately at peace with themselves." Only as other needs are reasonably met are individuals able to focus on making the greatest possible use of their inherent talents. This is an ongoing process. Unlike the physical summit of a peak few, if any, ever make the greatest possible use of their talents and become fully self-actualized.

Unlike the needs of the lower-level camps, there is little that you as an outdoor leader can do to help your participants attain the summit of self-actualization. For some people, participation in an outdoor program may be an important step toward self-actualization. For some a day of sea kayaking or a hike up a local peak will fulfill this need, while others will feel the need to paddle unexplored whitewater gorges or ascend storm-swept Patagonian peaks. Still others may want the experience of working closely with a group. The best a leader can do is to forge a group setting where the lower-level needs are addressed, freeing participants to focus more fully on their self-actualization goals.

In a later work, *Toward a Psychology of Being,* Maslow actually developed a concept of the "peak experience" that is much like the experiences many people seek in the outdoors. More recently Mihaly and Isabella Csikszentmihalyi at the University of Chicago have continued in this vein with the development of their concept of "flow," which describes the best and most memorable experiences in our lives. They use the term *flow* to encapsulate the idea that human beings have evolved an inherent excitement in confronting the unknown limits of their world: "Flow describes a state of experience that is engrossing, intrinsically rewarding, and 'outside the parameters of worry and boredom.'" The Csikszentmihalyis' work has resonated with the outdoor world because it fits so well with the experience of many outdoor leaders and the experience that those who come on outdoor programs are often seeking.

Activities that produce a state of flow are, to the person involved, totally engrossing and present constant challenges to be met with appropriate skills. The result is immediate and gratifying internal experiences. These flow experiences are characterized by a clear goal, with clear steps toward that goal, and immediate feedback regarding the steps taken toward that goal. Because goals and feedback are so clear, there is a merging of action and awareness, and all other stimuli are screened out. As an outgrowth of this process, people lose themselves in the task and begin to feel as if they transcend themselves; they are greater than they were as they become one with the activity in which they engage. They feel in control without fear of loss of control—sometimes even when faced with danger. According to the Csikszentmihalyis the flow experience is strongly self-reinforcing: "The components of the flow state are usually so enjoyable and psychically rewarding, and so unlike the drudgery of most of life, that there is a desire to repeat activities that produce the flow experience."

While flow experience may be only a brief stop on the road to full self-actualization, it does represent the pinnacle of many participants' outdoor adventure experience. As Mihaly Csikszentmihalyi writes, "It is what the sailor holding a tight course feels when the wind whips through her hair, when the boat lunges through the waves like a colt—sails, hull, wind, and sea humming a harmony that vibrates in the sailor's veins." With luck your participants will experience flow, and you can know that the experience is likely to be one they treasure for years.

Exceptions: After departing in 1995, Goran Kropp bicycled from his home in Sweden across Europe and Asia and arrived at Mount Everest, approximately seven thousand miles away on the border of Tibet and Nepal, in spring 1996. Then—climbing by himself and using only equipment he had towed behind his bike—he ascended the world's highest peak. Shortly after he got down off the mountain, Kropp got back on his bike and pedaled home. Needless to say, Kropp did not establish the usual system of well-stocked camps up the mountain. While most climbers still rely on the siege-style expedition to get them to the summit of Everest, there are exceptions, and Kropp's ascent is a remarkable example of one. There are similar exceptions to the way people progress through Maslow's Hierarchy of Needs.

Maslow noted one particular exception to his hierarchy that is of interest to outdoor leaders and directly relevant to the story of Goran Kropp's adventure. Individuals who have long had their basic needs amply fulfilled are able to endure remarkable deprivation of needs—all the way down to the physiological level—in order to accomplish objectives they strongly believe in. We see this fairly frequently in outdoor activities: people will push their bodies to the limits, going without adequate food, water, or shelter, in order to achieve their strongly held objectives.

Summary

In a single outdoor program participants may experience the depths of physical deprivation and the heights of personal enlightenment. Though it was never specifically intended to explain the needs and motivations of participants in outdoor programs, Maslow's Hierarchy makes sense of the full range. Of course there will always be exceptions. Not all behavior is motivated by the Hierarchy of Needs, and not all behavior motivated by the hierarchy will be immediately recognizable as such. Like any tools that leaders use to understand and categorize what is going on around them, this one is useful but should not be applied exclusively in every situation.

The importance of the hierarchy to leaders will vary with the length and rigor of the activity you're leading. While physiological and safety needs will be important during every activity, awareness of self-actualization needs is likely to be more relevant on something longer than a weekend trip.

It's also critically important that we separate what motivates people to participate in a program from what motivates them once they are participating. An individual may embark on a group backpacking program with the self-actualization goals of improving fitness, better understanding the natural environment, and developing enhanced interpersonal skills. On day one of the trip—when he realizes that his physiological needs are not automatically provided for—this same participant may tumble from the metaphorical summit back down to Base Camp. With time and good leadership, though, he should be able to work back through the hierarchy, have his needs addressed, and return to functioning at the summit level.

Helping participants keep track of their original goals for participating can help motivate them to work though any issues they have and function at a higher level. This can be as simple as having people share with others or the leader why they came on the program and what they want to get out of it. Reflecting their original goals back to people—or better yet, having participants help each other keep focused on these objectives—can be a powerful force keeping individuals and the group focused on higher-level needs. More information about helping participants stay focused on their goals is found in chapter 11, Expedition Behavior. Not only is this important to the individual, but ultimately, if the needs of individuals in the group are largely met, the group has a much greater chance of reaching its collective goals.

RECOMMENDED READING

♦ Csikszentmihalyi, Mihaly, *Flow: The Psychology of Optimal Experience,* New York: Harper & Row, 1990.

Csikszentmihalyi, Mihaly, and Isabella Csikszentmihalyi, "Adventure and the Flow Experience," in *Adventure Programming,* edited by John C. Miles and Simon Priest, State College, Pennsylvania: Venture Publishing, 1999.

Johnson, David W., and Frank P. Johnson, *Joining Together: Group Theory and Group Skills,* 7th ed., Boston: Allyn and Bacon, 2000.

Maslow, Abraham, *Motivation and Personality,* 3rd ed., New York: Addison Welsey Longman, 1987.

♦ Maslow, Abraham, *Toward a Psychology of Being,* 3rd ed., New York: John Wiley and Sons, 1999.

♦ = Advanced Recommendation

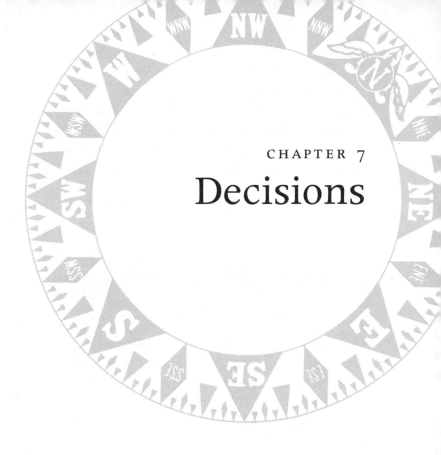

CHAPTER 7

Decisions

As a leader, your usefulness to the group is dependent upon your ability to make and implement effective decisions. These decisions are based largely upon judgment, which is the capacity to assess a situation and draw conclusions. But how is it that some leaders have good judgment and can make rapid and effective decisions? This chapter explores the mysteries of judgment and decision making that are central to outdoor leadership—and indeed all aspects of our lives.

Your decision-making ability is based on your awareness of group, environment, and self as outlined in chapter 4. The more information you have and the better you're able to home in on what is relevant, the better your decisions will be.

Key lessons are identified throughout this chapter that will help you in making decisions and in learning better decision-making skills. These are lessons and not rules because there is no one correct way to go about making decisions. While the lessons can be helpful, there will always be exceptions; you must expect this.

Only superficially does this chapter delve into how groups make decisions. This subject is largely left to chapter 8, Leadership. Regardless of the nature or involvement of the group, the leader must be comfortable making and implementing decisions. The ultimate responsibility for a decision lies with the leader or leaders in a group. Thus even when the whole group is involved in a decision, it's still the leaders' judgment that prevails, especially with regard to safety. The leader or leaders in a group must be comfortable making decisions—thus this chapter is focused on their decision-making process.

Basics of Decision Making————

A Bear's Tale

Our wilderness campsite was a half-mile bushwhack from the trail in New Hampshire's White Mountain National Forest. Two of our participants were cooking dinner while the rest finished setting up their tents and getting camp established. It was the final night of a two-week backpacking trip with eight teenagers. My co-leader, Steve, and I were enjoying the reduced workload that came with the increased experience of our participants.

I was a short distance away from camp when I heard someone yell, "Bear!" Oddly, I didn't take it seriously at first, but as the cacophony of yells increased I headed rapidly back to camp. Sure enough, the largest black bear I have ever seen was in the midst of our cooking area and was looking thoroughly in control of the situation. Our group had been routed, and members were distributed in the woods well away from the cooking area. We had actually talked about this type of situation, with Steve and I advising that if we encountered an aggressive bear we would stay in a group and make as much noise as possible. That advice had not been heeded as this bear lumbered into camp.

Steve and I got everyone to regroup well away from the cooking area. He and I discussed the situation and decided that our problem was the bear and that we should get it to go away, ideally before it ate all of our remaining food. We instructed our group to find the best noise-makers they could. With sticks banging on pots, whistles blowing, and much yelling, we approached. To its credit, the bear was looking quite relaxed, sitting and licking the last remnants of peanut butter off the pieces of what used to be a plastic jar.

As we approached, the bear looked up and then went back to its peanut butter licking. I was in the front of the group, beating a stick on a pot. Suddenly the bear rose up faster than I had previously given bears credit for being able to move and charged toward us with its teeth bared. We retreated rapidly, and the bear casually returned to its peanut butter jar.

Lesson: *Make small, frequent decisions whenever possible.* You will have many opportunities to make small decisions that move you toward an overall solution—use them as best you can. Your reaction time will be too slow if you always try to come up with a comprehensive plan, and the situation may change, rendering your plan irrelevant. Constant re-assessment is possible if you work in small steps. Once a group comes up with a master plan, people can become overly committed to this route. This rigidity can be an encumbrance in situations where the circumstances are changing rapidly and hence demand decision-making agility.

Dusk turned to night and we still had the pleasure of our uninvited dinner guest, so we decided to light a fire. We hoped that this would shed some light on our surroundings, help keep group spirits up, and perhaps serve as a deterrent that would keep the bear away from the group.

Steve and I reassessed our situation and adjusted our definition of the problem. Getting the bear to go away was no longer a priority; our problem was simply ensuring the safety of the group. We saw two options, the first being to stay put, assuming the bear would finish the food and leave. The second option was to pack up what we could and move camp.

We had little information on which to base our decision. The fact that, statistically, black bears in the eastern United States very rarely harm people was an argument for staying. We assumed that the bear was after our food supply, which it already had. We were fairly certain that once it finished eating our food, the bear would lose interest and leave, but neither of us had previous experience with a bear acting this aggressively. Waiting made sense in that if the bear did not leave eventually, we could always leave later. However, we were also clear that this large bear was potentially very dangerous if it did choose to attack.

On the other hand, if we left we'd have to leave behind some of our gear. We then faced a half-mile bushwhack to the trail with no prospects of a camping spot nearby. After a long day of hiking, we were concerned that making our students pack up and then bushwhack in the dark could lead to falls or sprained ankles.

Steve and I agreed that the bear was fairly likely to leave us alone if we kept our distance. We felt that the risk of an attack was almost non-existent if we left the bear to eat in peace. The risks of packing up and moving seemed more serious. After carefully and rationally identifying the problem, the possible solutions, and the possible consequences of those solutions, we stayed put.

Lesson: *Do not wait until you have every piece of information to make a decision.* Often, especially in crisis situations, you will have insufficient time to gather all the necessary information. Many decision-making models presume all the necessary information is available. Outdoor leaders must have a high tolerance for ambiguity and be comfortable making decisions based on less-than-complete knowledge.

We told the group our plan: They would go to bed with their clothes on, and Steve and I would stay up to watch the bear. In discussing the plan, the group was justifiably nervous, but soon they headed off to bed. It wasn't long before the bear abandoned the food and wandered off into the woods. We tried to monitor its progress but assumed that it had finished its meal and was departing. We were wrong. As we headed over to our tent, the bear emerged from the woods. It had avoided us by circling around through the woods and was now right next to one of the occupied tents, which it proceeded to sniff and paw at. This time our noisemaking took on a new fervor.

We yelled our hearts out. I picked up a tent and waved it in the air. Steve armed himself with a large stick. The bear moved on to investigate a nearby—and now empty—tent. We did not have to have a discussion this time. Steve and I—and the whole group—knew we needed to leave. The only question was how much of our equipment we would bring with us. The bear had not yet come near the fire, and we all worked to pull as much gear as we could toward it. Each had one eye on the bear as we packed. The bear did not rip any tents, apparently interested only in sniffing and pawing. As it moved away from a tent, we moved in and took it down. We were ready to leave—without our equipment if need be—if the bear showed any interest in us, but it did not.

Lesson: *Aim for the 70 percent solution.* In other words, take action once you conclude that your chosen plan is the best one and more likely than not to succeed. However, you must also ask yourself "What if" and weigh the likely consequences of your plan failing. The more serious the repercussions of failure, the more confident you must be in your plan. If serious injury will result from the failure of your plan, you must be as close as possible to 100 percent certain it will work—unless the risks associated with alternative plans or doing nothing are even worse. (The opposite, of course, is also true—if the consequences of failure aren't so bad, you can act with less than 70 percent certainty.)

With most of our equipment packed, we put out the fire with several potfuls of water and departed—implementing our contingency plan. The group, Steve and I very much included, was worried that the bear would follow us. Some members wanted to run, but Steve and I vetoed that plan quickly, as we were off the trail with full packs. We did instruct our group that if the bear approached us, we'd abandon our packs and proceed quickly.

The energy in the group, considering that by now it was approaching midnight, was quite high. In what seemed like no time we had made it back onto the trail with no evidence that we were being followed. The sky had cleared and the moon had risen, leaving the trail dappled with light. The walking was easy, and Steve and I hung back while the group hiked energetically and actually broke into song.

Steve and I knew there were limited camping opportunities nearby. Without saying so we also knew that we were both eager to put some distance between our group and the bear. The idea of camping in the open without room to set up our tents didn't have much appeal psychologically. We hiked on, reaching the road and our van in the early-morning hours.

After a short night of sleep we went out to a big breakfast.

Then the final step. I was actually able to get volunteers to accompany me on a hike and jog back into the previous night's campsite. Once there we cleaned up what the bear had left of our food packaging and gathered up the cooking equipment we had left behind less than twelve hours before. As it turned out, we could have shared—the one thing the bear did not eat was the lentils and rice that had been on the stove for dinner.

The peanut-butter-loving bear provides us with a story rife with decision-making lessons. First of all, knowing that we were hiking in bear country, Steve and I had instructed the hikers about what to do if we ran into a bear. Although they did not heed our instructions at first, having previous awareness of the bear presence in the area and the sense that the leaders knew how to address the situation may have prevented some panic. At each juncture, we clearly identified the problem, considered our options and their possible outcomes, and made well-thought-out decisions that we attempted to carefully explain to the group. With each decision we made, we also developed an alternative plan—if the bear had followed us out of the camp, for instance, we would have dropped our packs and run. Neither Steve nor I had had an experience just like this one, but we were able to safely evacuate our campers and gear because we used good decision-making practices.

Leverage Points

Leverage points are critical junctures at which decisions are made and judgment must be employed. Each leverage point presents opportunities for new directions; however, the path each option leads to is rarely obvious. In his fascinating book *Sources of Power: How People Make Decisions,* Gary Klein draws a useful analogy between leverage points and selecting moves while rock climbing. As a climber I can relate to the situation of choosing moves. As you are perched on a precarious ledge, you might notice a series of thin edges ahead of you, a short, diagonal crack off to this side, and a series of larger-looking holds traversing in still another direction. This is a leverage point. Each route you take may eventually lead you to the same place, or it may lead you into a totally different direction and preclude reconnecting with the other options.

It's possible that waiting at the camp while the bear pawed our tents would have eventually allowed us the opportunity to reclaim all our gear and exit safely. Our decision to hike to safety at night and return the next day for the equipment offered the same conclusion. However, different endings could have occurred with these different paths if, for example, we had waited at the camp and the bear had attacked a camper. Return to the original leverage point would have been rendered impossible at that point.

The decisions you make at any given leverage point inevitably lead to another leverage point, which offers its own, somewhat unpredictable options. Any of the routes taken from the precarious perch on the ledge could lead to a smooth section of face that precludes further passage—or to easy climbing on nice ledges. The character of each handhold is often impossible to determine from a lower vantage point. What looks like a ledge may be sloping, a crack may be too shallow to jam a hand into, or a little edge that was undetectable from below may appear and be just enough to make passage possible. Experienced climbers will look for recognizable patterns in the rock both close at hand and far away. Even on a face that has never been climbed before, it's often possible to chart a safe passage.

Leverage points provide options to solving the problem at hand, but each option leads to further leverage points. Even the best leader cannot guarantee success. Nevertheless, the experienced leader's pattern-recognition ability allows the best odds for success.

Simple and Complex Decisions

The first consideration in looking at decision making is to realize that there are many different types of decisions a leader makes. If you look closely, the outdoor leader is making many decisions on essentially a constant basis. These decisions range from when to stop for a snack to whether to remove the tiny rock in your own shoe to what route to take through avalanche terrain. There are a tremendous range of types of decisions, but for now let's consider them as two types: simple and complex. Simple decisions have limited consequences and outcomes that are relatively predictable—say, deciding where to stop for lunch. Complex decisions are characterized by uncertainty in terms of at least one of the following: information, options, or outcomes. Unfortunately many of the decisions that outdoor leaders must make are of the complex variety.

Simple decisions need not be time consuming to make. Typical simple decisions do not significantly alter the nature of the experience for the group, and group members usually don't have much investment in the outcome. Because of these two factors—time and low group investment—simple decisions are often made by the leader or other designated group member. In most groups it's not an efficient use of time or the group's emotional energy to involve the full group in a decision such as where to hang the bear bag or how to treat a participant's small blister.

While the concepts discussed in the rest of the chapter can be applied to simple decisions, our focus will be on complex decisions (these terms are somewhat subjective, but as a leader you'll know whether a decision is a complex one for you). Within the category of complex decisions there is still wide variation in the type of decision and the level of seriousness of the issue. A complex decision might involve deciding where to camp, how to run a rapid, or how to search for a lost group member.

Natural Decision Making————————

Lessons from Chess

To begin to understand what natural decision making looks like, let's turn to two revealing studies not of outdoor leaders, but of chess players. The first study was conducted by Roberta Calderwood, Beth Crandall, and Gary Klein and is detailed in *Sources of Power: How People Make Decisions*. In this study the researchers demonstrated that top-ranked chess players were able to maintain their high quality of play even under extreme time pressure.

To investigate the effects of time pressure, two study groups were used. Chess players were useful as subjects because of a rigid classification system that made it easy to identify players at distinctly different skill levels. The first group was composed of chess players rated as masters—one step below the best players, the international grand masters. The second group was composed of class B players, three ranking tiers below the masters in the first group.

Two tournaments were held, one for the masters and one for the class B players. The games counted toward players' official rankings, and cash prizes were offered to the winners. The first set of games each group played was done under regulation conditions, in which each player has about two minutes and fifteen seconds for each move. The second set of games was played under blitz conditions, where players averaged six seconds per move.

After the tournament the international grand masters consulting with the project rated the quality of each player's moves. The result that makes this interesting to outdoor leaders is that the quality of moves made by the master players under time pressure remained similar to the quality found in normal play. Among lesser players, the quality of moves declined. Some of the most salient results are reflected in the grand masters' judging of how many blunders each player made. For the master players, the rate of blunders remained steady in the 7 to 8 percent range. For the lesser players, the percentage of blunders increased from 11 percent during regulation play to 25 percent under blitz conditions.

Developing Natural Decision Making

So how does this decision making by expert chess players connect with outdoor leadership? The outdoor leader, like the chess player in blitz mode, will often be called upon to make rapid-fire decisions. Even in the unlikely event that all the information you need to make a decision is available, there may not be enough time to gather it. Many of us have been taught to analyze our decisions in a step-by-step manner. Not only does this rarely happen in the field, but it may not even be desirable. So how do we make decisions? Some more clues emerge from a second study with Gary Klein's involvement.

The second study demonstrated that skilled chess players were able to pick remarkably good moves under time pressure—meaning that they recognized the moves almost immediately. How is this possible? There were an average of thirty-one moves available to the players. Did they generate all the possible moves subconsciously and without realizing it home in on one that offered a reasonable solution? This seems unlikely. More likely is that expert decision making develops over time and is based in an ability to recognize and respond to patterns.

In the case of the bear that charged into our camp, Steve and I had no personal experience dealing with an animal that aggressive. We did have anecdotal information, gleaned in the form of oral and written stories from others. As experienced group leaders we also had the experience of having led many groups and dealt with other crisis situations. We had the ability to quickly connect experience in a somewhat similar situation to the one at hand. We knew how to manage the group and address their fears. We knew not to let the situation create more problems—by running off the trail away from the bear, for example. While we did not have all the information we needed, we did have some experience we could apply to the situation. The ability to quickly connect an experience to a similar situation is an extremely valuable asset for an outdoor leader.

This expertise-based model of decision making presents a problem for someone who is writing about decision making. What I have suggested is that there is no step-by-step process to achieving the best decisions. Instead of presenting a formula for decision making, this chapter will focus on investigating how leaders do make effective decisions and how that process can be reinforced.

Analytic Decision Making————————

I have been fairly critical of decision-making approaches that present a formulaic plan for success. Typically these models are based on several stages, which is what many people have been taught to think of as the logical approach to problem solving. Under the analytic model, a series of decision-making steps leads from defining the problem to identifying a solution. Instead of totally tossing this model out I will present it here and give some situations in which it is helpful for leaders.

Analytic Model

This analytic model presents seven stages of decision making. This is not the simplest model (which has as few as four stages and is easier to implement but less accurate), nor is it the most complex (more accurate, impossible to implement in the field). This analytic model presents a good balance.

1. **Define the problem:** What is the end result or results you are looking for?

2. **Gather relevant information:** Collect information that may assist in the development or evaluation of solutions.

3. **Generate solutions (problem solving):** This is a brainstorming step. Anything is possible. Encourage and do not critique unconventional options.

4. **Evaluate solutions:** Weigh the benefits and risks of the different options.

5. **Choose a solution:** Select an option that best resolves the problem at hand, balancing benefit of the solution versus its risks.

6. **Implement the solution:** Decide who needs to do what and make your solution a reality.

7. **Reevaluate:** As implementation proceeds, continue to assess the solution. If it isn't working, restart the decision-making process.

Like most decision making, the analytic model does not always manifest in a linear process. In other words, you may not start out with step one, move on to step two, and so forth—while this is ideal, the reality is that you may need to jump around to answer different questions as more information becomes available. Some questions may not be answerable with the information you have. In this case you will need to find more information or make a judgment without it.

Applications for Analytic Decision Making

Analytic decision making can be very useful when involving the entire group in a decision. The steps involved allow for the dissemination of relevant information and ideas to the entire group. The defined stages provide a ready framework for facilitating group discussion. Working through a decision in this manner can be a valuable experience for the less experienced group members as the various aspects of the decision are vocalized and discussed. In fact, the more complex a situation is and the more people involved, the more valuable an analytic approach becomes. This useful application of the analytic process

Alex Kosseff

Leaders decide how to accomplish a tricky river crossing.

will be covered in more detail in chapter 8.

The analytic model can also be useful for inexperienced leaders who are attempting to make the best of an insufficient experience base. The analytic model can impose structure on their thinking and, in particular, can help these leaders to identify what they *don't* know. Unfortunately this framework cannot compensate for a lack of experience-based judgment, so inexperienced leaders will have difficulty making the decisions needed at the different stages. One of the greatest difficulties will remain a lack of full information necessary for decision making, especially for time-pressed decisions.

In situations where time is plentiful, there is also use for the analytic model. If information in plentiful and more can be gathered, it's possible to conduct a real analysis. Leaders, however, should be careful of the tendency to waste time validating decisions that have already been made via natural processes.

Limitations of Analytic Decision Making

It would seem that analytic decision making is a logical process and should result in a reliable decision. An advantage is that a full analysis can keep leaders from leaving things out. Ultimately, however, the many small decisions that are necessary to apply an analytic model require the same judgment-based recognition to resolve as the overall decision does. The analytic model has the disadvantage of being cumbersome, time consuming, and less adaptable to limited information than are a leader's natural decision-making abilities.

Those trained in analytic decision making typically do not make use of the technique. Especially in natural settings (as opposed to closely controlled situations with few variables), where information is incomplete and the situation in flux, skilled decision makers turn to the natural decision making with which they are most comfortable. If applied at all, analytic models are used to seek confirmation of decisions that have already been reached.

One of the early lessons of this chapter was that leaders should make small, frequent decisions. Analytic decision making is more conducive to developing a master plan and less practical for prompt decisions at each of the many leverage points that arise in a dynamic environment. Investment of too much energy in an overall plan can result in a situation where leaders resist adjusting to new circumstances. Unless care is used, analytic models can result in the belief that decision making is a linear process leading directly from identification of the problem to its resolution. The reality is that decision making is not nearly as neat and simple as this would imply.

When Steve and I faced the situation of the bear's takeover of our camp, we employed a variety of decision-making techniques. At all times we maintained a flexible attitude. The plan we invested the most time in developing and most closely analyzed was the plan to monitor the bear while our group went to sleep. It didn't work. Many of our other decisions were made based on quick applications of judgment— some in very urgent situations. Analytic decision making was too cumbersome for most of our decisions.

Real-Life Decision Making

Recall that master chess players were able to make effective decisions even under time pressure. Each turn on the chess board is analogous to a leverage point for an outdoor leader. The decisions you make at each leverage point open up certain options and eliminate others. Sometimes you'll be able to foresee the consequences of your actions, but sometimes there will be unintended results. Although there is some utility to analytic decision making, natural decision making is still the process by which leaders make the vast majority of their decisions. Natural decision-making ability is derived from experience. Knowing more

> *"Managers are continually taking calculated risks. Indeed, one sign of . . . promise is his or her ability to calculate those risks better than others. . . . Moments arise, however, when strict analysis does not serve well. Sometimes what is required is simply instinct."*
>
> —MICHAEL USEEM, *THE LEADERSHIP MOMENT*

about how this works allows leaders to optimize their decision making and benefit more from learning opportunities.

Referring back to another analogy, chapter 4, Awareness, drew a parallel between the awareness a leader develops and the awareness you develop learning to drive a car. When you first get behind the wheel, you don't know what to make of the feel of the steering wheel or the feel of the brake pedal. Things get even more complicated if you learn on a stick shift. Slowly you develop an awareness of all the cues that are present under normal driving conditions. Later you may develop a broader awareness encompassing how the vehicle handles under different conditions—on wet roads, in the snow, perhaps on dirt roads or ice.

As a driver or a leader you become aware not only of cues, but also of the appropriate responses to these cues. While the novice driver knows that there is a rule that one must stop when confronted with an octagonal red sign with the word Stop written in it, the experienced driver has little use for the rule. The experienced driver stops almost without thought. These cues are triggered by recognition; when asked to explain a quick decision these drivers—or leaders—will often say that they "just knew what to do." What's actually taking place is pattern recognition, perhaps the most powerful of decision-making tools leaders use. This is the first of three real-world decision-making techniques detailed below in order of increasing complexity.

Recognition: What people often call intuition or even a "sixth sense" is actually more humble recognition. This is what makes you (assuming you're an experienced driver) stop at a stop sign even when you are distracted talking on your cell phone and turning down the radio. Over time we learn to identify patterns. Remember that experienced chess players are able to select good moves even under extreme time pressure. These chess players were not analyzing all the potential moves and their consequences; what they were able to do was recognize patterns on the board and make a decision with remarkable acuity.

Outdoor leaders also come to recognize patterns. Some of this recognition comes from learned rules that become deeply ingrained with experience. A simple example is that leaders learn the signs and symptoms of dehydration, but over time come to recognize a dehydrated person with little more than a glance. Recognition can also be based on accrued experience that provides a "sense" of when things are not going well for an individual or the group. Leaders may have a bad feeling about a potential avalanche slope or river-crossing site. Although even the most experienced leaders may not be able to identify the source of these feelings, they are worthy of attention. This pattern-recognition ability is obviously not unique to outdoor leaders. Recognition has been studied and shown to be critical not only for chess players but also for firefighters, military commanders, medical personnel, and other experts.

Satisficing: When initial recognition does not produce a viable response, leaders will use the first viable option they develop. Nobel Prize winner Herbert Simon called this decision-making strategy "satisficing." When satisficing, leaders will consider the risks and benefits of a single option at a time and accept or reject that option based only on its own merits. This process continues until a workable option is found. Obviously this does not always result in the optimal solution; it can, however, be efficient, and it usually results in a solution that works. Satisficing is utilized by not only those under time pressure, but also by those in less urgent decision-making situations.

If I'm with a group in the morning and notice that a participant is cold, I might employ satisficing to find a solution. I might think that we'll get moving soon, and he'll probably warm up, then reject this because I see breakfast is still cooking on the stove. Then I might consider asking him to put on some more clothes, but I realize that he let the rest of his clothes get wet in a rainstorm the night before. Finally I decide to lead the group in some jumping jacks and a little running around to get everyone warmed up. The decision reached by satisficing may not have been optimal—I never even considered loaning him some dry clothes—but it would work.

Simulation: When faced with more difficult situations, leaders often employ simulation, attempting to run though a plan in advance. This is not easy, taking more time and expertise than it may initially seem for a difficult decision.

In a crisis you might simulate different options for a carry-out rescue considering different plans in terms of weather, route, and available assistance. In *Sources of Power,* Gary Klein concludes that mental simulations rarely consider more than three variables or more than nine steps into the future. Beyond that, the ability to perform the simulation overwhelms our brains' impressive, but still limited, processing power. Every aspect of the simulation requires expertise to forecast what the most likely outcome will be. While the more detailed simulation will theoretically be more accurate, it becomes mentally unwieldy and introduces more sources of potential error due to the many projections the leader must make.

Simulation can be a valuable technique, time permitting, for two or more leaders who talk each other through it. A larger group can also employ simulation in this manner. These approaches will often result in individuals pointing out potentially important variables that have not been included in the simulation.

Across the Bay

My first paid outdoor leadership position involved leading middle school students in southern New England. We offered some interesting programs and had plenty of opportunity to use our decision-making skills. My favorite program was a five-day canoe trip following a watershed from near its source all the way to its outlet in the Atlantic. We paddled undeveloped sections of the river as well as past abandoned mills and through bits of suburbia. Along the way my co-leader, Carolyn, and I taught our participants about the ecology of the river and the lands surrounding it.

In the early reaches of the drainage we sometimes had to step out and drag our canoes through short sections of shallow water. Soon the channel grew deeper and the water—a deep tannic brown color—was uninviting to wading. Later the growing river passed through a couple of sections of Class II rapids. After four days of paddling we emerged into a wide tidal river. Our fourteen participants seemed to be enjoying themselves—especially the water fights, but perhaps even the paddling and ecology lessons.

On the final day of the trip we let the group slack off in getting out of camp because our planned pull-out site was a relatively short paddle. We paddled out into the small bay where the river met the sea and pulled off on a sandbar for lunch and to study some of the marine life in the estuary. As we ate, the wind began to pick up. By the time our canoes were repacked, the route to our pull-out site across the bay lay directly in the path of a very stiff breeze. Worse still, the shift in the wind brought with it surf that angled through the mouth of the bay and rose to large rollers and breakers in the relatively shallow bay.

Lesson: *Anticipate.* Leverage points are often most useful before they even become apparent. Advance recognition gives you more time to plan an alternative plan of action.

Stuck on the wrong side of the bay, my co-leader and I—who barely had the skills to teach the students how to paddle the river—were faced with a difficult decision. We had little experience paddling canoes in open water, and none under these sorts of conditions. It was obvious that paddling into the wind and waves would be difficult, especially for some of the weaker paddlers. What concerned us the most was the prospect of canoes capsizing if our paddlers could not keep their bows pointed into the wind and waves.

Overdue groups were not something we had discussed at our program, and we didn't know what the response would be. We spent some time trying to simulate what would happen if we didn't make our preplanned pickup. Ultimately we were unable to reach a conclusion. Lacking resolution in that area, we began to discuss whether the wind would die down and if the outgoing tide might make the waves larger or smaller. Again we had no answers.

Our students relaxed on the beach, ignorant of our dilemma, as we tried to figure out how to proceed. Using a form of the analytic model, we tried to compare the two options of going for it or not, but again had a difficult time reaching any conclusions. On the one hand, the waves and wind looked and felt daunting. The counterpoint was that we could probably make it across the bay. As Carolyn pointed out, there didn't seem to be a strong current and the wind and waves would push any capsized boats and their participants back toward the beach. Life-jacketed participants who were all swimmers, combined with warm water temperatures, meant that participants in the water would not be in immediate risk.

We saw the question as one of yes or no. The option of staying put meant being overdue for our pickup and potentially spending the night where we were on the spit of land. The option of going meant a difficult paddle, the risk of capsize, but the opportunity to be at our pickup location close to on time. We decided to go for it. Perhaps we could have towed the canoes close to shore, back toward the mouth of the river, and then paddled across and back along in the shelter of the far shore. I don't think the two of us ever considered this option.

Lesson: *In a difficult situation, consider all the options.* When your experience isn't up to the task of rapidly identifying a viable option, generate all reasonable options. Don't limit yourself to the conventional options that are right in front of you. Once you have all the options—time permitting—weigh the pros and cons of each.

By the time Carolyn and I were ready to talk to the group, they had gathered that something was up because of the delayed departure. We explained to them where we needed to paddle to, and they immediately understood our concerns about the waves. Of course they, for the most part, seemed to think that canoeing through the surf looked like fun. After a short safety briefing, focused on keeping the bow into the waves and sticking together as a group, we were ready to go.

Having picked out the best route through the surf, we began to launch one canoe at a time. The first five canoes, including Carolyn's, went well. The sixth canoe had almost made it through the worst of the swell near shore when the bow paddler turned to speak with the stern paddler, who stopped paddling as well. I yelled as the canoe turned sideways, but it was too late: The next big wave was already dumping out the occupants and their gear. Seeing the two participants tossed in the surf and clinging to a partially swamped canoe made the danger in our plan very real. Thankfully, the canoe wasn't very far out and I was able to swim out to help the two canoeists, their canoe, and their gear back into shore.

Lesson: *Consider how your plan will fail.* Hindsight is 20/20, or so the saying goes. Review your decision as if you have already implemented it and it has failed. What was the cause of the failure? This new perspective may cause you to look at alternative plans, or it may help you to implement your chosen plan more effectively.

◆

By the time we got the now very attentive paddlers launched, Carolyn and the others were well across the bay. They were struggling to make headway, and I wasn't certain they were aware we were having any difficulty. I decided that the best thing to do was to catch up, so we redoubled our efforts to get the canoes out. My canoe—the last—finally launched. Once we cleared the shore area, the paddling remained very demanding and the wind made verbal communication with other boats nearly impossible. I felt I had to hang back with the slowest in our pack while others struggled to catch up with Carolyn's group. Soon our seven boats were spread out over more than half a mile. Worse still, some of the boats were trending too far toward the mouth of the bay. If these boats got in trouble, they faced the potential of being pushed out into open water.

I paddled hard forward, leaving some canoes behind me, and got the outermost boat to come farther into the bay. Then I dropped back again. Carolyn also recognized the issue and slowed her group to allow us to regroup. Thus we all made it into a safe landing. Our program director, who was waiting with the van, had been able to see part of our crossing. While he could not see some of the more dramatic moments, he was not impressed with what he saw and was quite direct about this in our program debrief. The discussion that emerged made it clear to me that we would have been better off looking at different options or even spending the night on the beach instead of taking the risky route of making the crossing under the conditions we faced.

Lesson: *Ask yourself, "What would my mentor do?"* Often we gain a good sense of how other leaders we work with respond to situations. If a situation is difficult for you, consider how a leader you know well and respect might respond. It's not the same as having the person there, but it may bring a new perspective to the situation.

♦

While everything wound up all right with our decision (it usually does), the process was far from perfect. As leaders we simply did not have the relevant experience to make this decision. We also didn't have experience making leadership decisions like this with insufficient information. The simpler, natural decision-making strategies were out. In this case we would have benefited from a careful analytic decision-making process. I also do not believe we would have gone ahead with the plan if we had fully considered "How will it fail?" and "What would my mentor do?" These are vital questions in more difficult and drawn out decision-making processes for leaders with limited experience.

Conclusion ——————————————————

Crossing the River

This is not a paddling story, like Crossing the Bay was, but a backpacking one. This took place while I was observing a backpacking group as part of a safety review I was conducting. It is included to demonstrate how decision making ideally works.

The group I was with was part of an outdoor leadership training program conducted in spring. On their second to last day I awoke to a tarp pressing down on my face under 4 inches of new snow. The day before it had been raining, so in my mind this was a turn for the better. I figured the snow would stop, but it didn't.

The first task of the group was a long descent into a valley. As we descended the snow began to turn to sleet at times, and there was much less accumulation on the ground. Some of the students were not prepared with ideal boots for the snowy and wet conditions and had allowed all their socks to become wet. Breaks became longer than usual as students helped each other warm their feet on each other's stomachs (a remarkably effective way to warm cold feet). When the group finally reached a stream crossing the trail near the base of the mountain, they were well behind schedule. The leaders knew that they had to make it to a campsite on the far side of the valley that night to reach their pickup point the following day.

Their tardiness in reaching the stream wouldn't have been significant except that the bridge across the stream had been washed out over
the winter. At the same time, what was usually a modest stream was
now more of a raging river due to the spring snowmelt combined with
new rain and snow.

As the group took a brief snack and foot-warming break, the two
leaders dropped their packs and scouted a short way up and down the
stream. Both immediately recognized two potential river-crossing locations. One leader suggested that the lower crossing would be safer
because the water below it wasn't moving as fast. Having employed
recognition and then satisficing, the leaders were comfortable with
their decision, but because they were involved in a leadership training
program they wanted to let the participants have a crack at it.

The group members came into the program with a variety of experience levels, and everyone had gained some river-crossing experience
on the trip. To make their decision they sent out scouts for a long distance along the river. They used an analytic approach to consider three
potential crossing points, including the one the leaders had selected.
The group was clearly nervous about the crossing. They verbally simulated what the crossing would be like using different techniques they
had been taught.

Eventually, one participant who was looking at the map suggested
that they could hike a quarter mile on the same side of the river and
reach the trail in the valley, which actually had another bridge. The
group decided that the risks of the crossing site in front of them were
greater than the risk of the off-trail hike to the other bridge. They presented their decision to the instructors, who accepted it, impressed.

Both the experienced instructors and the full group made good decisions. The instructors' decision took less than five minutes. The students took seventy-five. Both processes worked, even under mild time
pressure, but one was obviously more efficient—though it didn't arrive
at the more creative option. The leaders were more comfortable selecting the best among those options right in front of them, while the participants were less confident in their judgment and looked for a more
conservative option.

So Where Do I Go from Here?

Natural (or recognition-based) decision making is the ideal in many situations, but the leader's fallback is in the direction of the analytic process. When you're working with a co-leader, you may have different approaches to making decisions. You're usually well advised to go with the more conservative approach (generally the more time-consuming one) to make decisions, unless there is severe time pressure.

You now have a better awareness of the different ways in which leaders make decisions. When you get out, pay attention to what decision-making tools you use, and remember the lessons that will help to make all the approaches easier. The approaches to developing decision-making ability are the same as those for learning to lead, as outlined in chapter 3. It all comes down to gaining experience. Chapter 8, Leadership, will discuss in more detail approaches to making decisions in groups.

RECOMMENDED READING

Freedman, David H., *Corps Business: The 30 Management Principles of the U.S. Marines,* New York: HarperBusiness, 2000.

◆ Klein, Gary, *Sources of Power: How People Make Decisions,* Cambridge, Massachusetts: MIT Press, 1998.

Langmuir, Eric, *Mountaincraft and Leadership,* 3rd ed., West Didsbury, England: The Mountain Leader Training Board, 1995.

McCammon, Ian, "Decision Making for Wilderness Leaders: Strategies, Traps, and Teaching Methods," in *2001 Wilderness Risk Management Conference Proceedings,* Lander, Wyoming: National Outdoor Leadership School, 2001, pp. 16–29.

Petzoldt, Paul, *The New Wilderness Handbook,* New York: W. W. Norton, 1984.

◆ Plous, Scott, *The Psychology of Judgment and Decision Making,* New York: McGraw-Hill, 1993.

Priest, Simon, and Michael Gass, *Effective Leadership in Adventure Programming,* Champaign, Illinois: Human Kinetics, 1997.

Useem, Michael, *The Leadership Moment,* New York: Times Books/Random House, 1998.

◆ = Advanced Recommendation

CHAPTER 8

Leadership

L eadership, the focus of this book, is difficult to define. At its simplest it can be thought of as the activity of influencing others in order to achieve group objectives. The leadership ideal is to influence others in the most unobtrusive manner possible. The unobtrusive leader allows group members to take ownership of group objectives and successes. Although the best leaders strive to minimize their presence in the group, they also understand that a more assertive role is sometimes needed. There exists a leadership continuum with a laissez-faire attitude on one end and a dictatorial approach at the other. This chapter will address how effective leaders, depending on the situation, make use of all of the leadership styles in this continuum.

Vision and Implementation

Leadership begins with a vision of what the group will accomplish. This vision can be the leader's or it can be developed collectively.

> "*A leader is best when people barely know he exists. . . . When his work is done, his aim fulfilled, the people will say, 'We did this ourselves.'*"
>
> —LAO-TZU,
> TAO TE CHING

Whatever the origin of the vision, it is the leader's responsibility to ensure that group members understand it so they know what to expect from the trip and, in turn, what the expectations of each participant are. Should participants expect to scale a peak, run a river, or just have a fun time in the outdoors? Are they expected to carry a heavy pack, know how to travel on a crevassed glacier, or sit back and enjoy gourmet meals cooked by a professional chef? An overview of the trip at its outset provides participants reassurance that they are capable of its challenges—better yet is this initial briefing combined with advance information provided before participants arrive. The issue of clear expectations is also discussed in the text and a sidebar in chapter 9; the point here is that this initial communication is absolutely fundamental to effective leadership. Whenever possible, participants should understand the leader's plans for the group—starting with the initial goals and continuing with every step along the way.

Once there is a vision and it is communicated to the group, the leader's role is the implementation of the plan. No plan covers every detail or goes off without some unanticipated events. As the trip unfolds, the leader's job is to adapt to each situation. Each task that the group must accomplish needs a plan of action. Decisions must be made on an almost constant basis. If someone needs to get water from the river, will it be the leader, a participant, or every member of the group? How is the decision about obtaining water made, who makes it, and how much time is devoted to this decision making? The leadership style you choose to employ forms the framework for putting all your other skills to use for the group. The constant communication and decision making you do as a leader draw upon the skills discussed in all of the other chapters in this book.

Selflessness

It is the guidance of the leader that allows the group to implement its vision, yet the leader must be as unobtrusive as possible. As Lao-tzu wrote in ancient China, the group must be able to say in the end: "We did this ourselves." Effective leaders shun the spotlight and attempt to reflect praise for group accomplishments onto their participants, while at the same time putting participants ahead of themselves in many respects. Paul Petzoldt puts it well in *The New Wilderness Handbook:*

> No matter how skilled or experienced a leader may be, he cannot be effective if he is selfish. . . . Just as a good cowboy will feed his horse before preparing his own meal, one in authority must think of the welfare and enjoyment of his party before satisfying his own wishes.

This statement harks back to the first chapters in this book and the concepts of caring leadership and having a positive source of motivation for your leadership role. The effective leader—the selfless leader—finds satisfaction in the success and enjoyment of each participant and the group.

Power

Leadership is the activity of influencing others. Power is the capacity for influence that enables leadership. To some outdoor leaders *power* may seem a heavy-handed term for the influence they wield through personable interactions. However benign it is, though, the ability of leaders to influence participants is always based in some form of power. While you may never need to wield your power in a manner that negatively effects others, it's important to understand why you're able to influence others.

Outdoor leaders make use of expert, position, personal, reward, and occasionally coercive power. Following are simple explanations of these different sources of power.

Expert Power is based upon knowledge and skill applicable to a given situation. You might have significant expert power as a leader of mountain bike trips but find yourself without this power if you attempt to lead an unfamiliar activity. Participants who feel that your expertise has value for them and their outdoor experience will be more willing to follow you.

Position Power is the formal authority given to you when you are put in the position of leader. In outdoor leadership situations most people

PARTNERING FOR LEADERSHIP

While much of this book refers to the singular leader, many outdoor activities have two or even more leaders. "A co-leader is a gift—a person who will look out for you," says Katherine Byers, the AMC's Outdoor Leadership Coordinator. Byers, who develops outdoor leadership training programs for the AMC, continues, "Leaders are often people who put the needs of the group before their own. Participants won't be able to take care of you, but your co-leader can."

The ideal partnership involves communicating on decisions and supporting each other. Again, Katherine Byers: "A good co-leader dynamic is the same as a good relationship. The better you connect and understand your co-leader, the better the partnership will be." In addition, Byers points out that "this can be the number one route to improving your leadership." A trusting and caring co-leader relationship allows for effective feedback in the partnership.

Most co-leader relationships require effort to succeed. The foundation of a successful partnership is setting expectations. Simple objectives enable you and your partner to focus on achieving the same results. Partners should establish expectations for communication, feedback, and conducting the trip.

will follow the leadership of a designated leader—unless they perceive some reason to doubt that person's competence.

Personal Power is based on the relationship of participants with the leader and the desirability participants find in interacting with him or her. Leaders with significant personal power typically have friendly personalities or are admired for their accomplishments. Personal power is also reinforced if participants see following the leader as a way to achieve shared goals. Personal power must be cultivated over time and will be much less effective if the leader waits until the influence is needed in order to develop the necessary relationship. This can also be a dangerous source of power. Charismatic leaders must be careful that they are facilitating the achievement of the participants' goals, not their own. Participants may follow a leader and adopt the leader's goals as

"We were wary at the start of having three leaders," Katherine Byers says of a trip she led with Princeton University's Outdoor Action Program. Because they were unaccustomed to working as a triumvirate, Byers and her co-leaders put extra time into planning. They discussed decision making and what lessons they would each teach. The trip was a success and the leaders each learned a lot—including a lesson on the importance of planning to successful leader partnerships.

Learn your partner's strengths and the areas where they are least confident. This is useful in selecting a co-leader and valuable for partners to discuss prior to a trip. Regardless of differing strengths or experience levels, Byers teaches that partnerships work best if the leaders are viewed as equal partners in the eyes of the participants. Equality means an "assistant" leader won't feel superfluous and sets the stage for leaders to tackle major issues jointly. "Maybe one leader will learn more in the process, but not everyone in the group needs to know that," Byers concludes.

Your co-leader relationship, Byers says, "is intensive, and even if you come to dislike that person you can't and shouldn't avoid your co-leader." Caring leaders, focused on group goals, will resolve conflicts that arise in their partnerships. Setting expectations is critical prep for success, as is the use of the communication and expedition behavior skills addressed in chapters 10 and 11. Your co-leader is a gift, but one that comes with the responsibility to create a partnership and realize the many potential benefits for your group.

their own simply out of a desire to be with the leader and enjoy the relationship. Leaders must always keep participants and their own goals first and foremost.

Reward Power influences participant behavior if the rewards are seen as worth pursuing. This power may be derived from a reward as simple as praise or recognition of an individual in front of the group, or it may be based on something more concrete. Concrete rewards might be a special meal cooked by the leader, an opportunity to engage in a fun activity, or being relieved of dishwashing duty.

Coercive Power is based on perceptions of a leader's ability to punish. Coercive power should be employed with more care than any of the other forms of power; it has very few appropriate uses for the outdoor leader. More commonly practiced with youth but also with adults, it may be used to deal with clear violations of established standards of behavior. In rare instances, a participant's behavior may threaten his or her own safety or the safety (emotional or physical) of others. Coercive power—the threat of removal from a program, in particular—may be used in these situations but must never be used to pressure a person to engage in an activity or in other routine circumstances.

Power is not a permanent attribute. It ebbs and flows depending on the situation and participant perceptions of the leader. Imagine how fast your expert power would evaporate if the group found out that you led them 10 miles out of the way in grueling heat because you confused north and south on your compass. Effective leaders use different types of power to influence participants, and they use all of them as gently as possible.

Leadership is a response to the needs of the participants. A leader who is perceived as moving the group toward achieving shared goals will be influential. The opposite is also true, and the leader who is perceived as incapable of assisting the participants in realizing goals will lose some power. The gain or loss of power occurs regardless of other traits. As a leader you may be incredibly charismatic, but if your group travels to Nepal to climb a mountain and you insist instead on searching for snow leopards, you are unlikely to have much influence with the group. The leader who can move participants toward their goals while keeping everyone happy and not stepping on any toes has achieved true success.

Personality

No single personality type makes the ideal outdoor leader. Most types of people have traits that allow them to play this role, although some may find it less enjoyable or rewarding. Leadership seems to come naturally to some, while others must work harder to achieve success. Usually, people with different personality traits bring different positive attributes to their leadership role. This, in part, makes working with another leader who complements your strengths ideal.

As discussed in chapter 3, confidence is an essential personality trait for leaders—it's the glue that holds your other leadership skills together. Confidence allows you to put your hard and soft skills and your motivation to effective use. It emerges because you know that you have successfully handled previous situations and you know that you can apply your ability to a new one, even if it's somewhat different from those you've previously encountered. Thus confidence is key to allowing your personality and skills to be put to the best use.

Beyond confidence, other traits of the effective outdoor leader are touched upon throughout this book. Outdoor leaders are adaptable, energetic, personable, dependable, decisive when needed, and work well in groups. Caring outdoor leaders do not try to micromanage the group in all situations, and they are not self-centered. Few outdoor leaders excel in every trait; fewer still manage to be adaptable, energetic, and so forth all the time. Leaders work with what they have and use these skills and a positive outlook to make up for what they lack.

Situational Leadership

Outdoor leadership constantly demands that leaders deal with ever-changing circumstances. Leaders know to employ a variety of tools to cope with different situations. An ice ax is very useful when ascending a steep snow slope. You could also use the ice ax to chop down a tree, but there are better tools for the job. Leading groups is similar—there are many tools you can use to do the same job. As a leader you need to understand how to use the different leadership tools (or styles) and when to employ them.

Situational leadership has two components—leadership style and situation. Through understanding different leadership styles and different types of field situations, leaders can identify the optimal approach to working with their group in any situation.

Leadership Style

Task behavior and relationship behavior are the defining behaviors of every leadership style. The participant's view of what leader behavior is being utilized defines the type of leadership style being used.

Task Behavior (or directive behavior) is focused on one-way communication telling participants what task to perform and when, where, and

Leadership Style Continuum

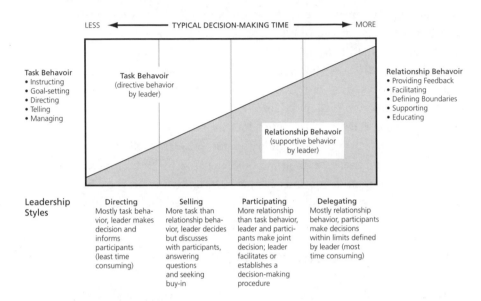

LESS ◄─────── TYPICAL DECISION-MAKING TIME ───────► MORE

Task Behavior
• Instructing
• Goal-setting
• Directing
• Telling
• Managing

Task Behavoir
(directive behavior
by leader)

Relationship Behavior
• Providing Feedback
• Facilitating
• Defining Boundaries
• Supporting
• Educating

Relationship Behavoir
(supportive behavior
by leader)

Leadership Styles	Directing	Selling	Participating	Delegating
	Mostly task behavior, leader makes decision and informs participants (least time consuming)	More task than relationship behavior, leader decides but discusses with participants, answering questions and seeking buy-in	More relationship than task behavior, leader and participants make joint decision; leader facilitates or establishes a decision-making procedure	Mostly relationship behavior, participants make decisions within limits defined by leader (most time consuming)

how to perform it. Leaders establish standard approaches to organization, communication, and accomplishing tasks.

Relationship Behavior (or supportive behavior) involves two-way communication and is centered on the establishment of personal relationships between leaders and participants. Leaders open broad channels of communication, provide emotional support, and facilitate effective group process.

The ratio of task to relationship behavior defines the leadership style as illustrated by the Leadership Style Continuum. While the continuum represents an infinite variety of leadership styles, four broad styles—directing, selling, participating, and delegating—are identified to aid in the discussion of situational leadership.

Situation

Like the cardinal compass points—north, south, east, and west—there are many degrees of variation between the four defined leadership styles on the Leadership Style Continuum. While the continuum explains the styles on your leadership compass, the "needle" pointing you in the direction of the best style is provided by the situation. The Situational Application of Leadership Styles diagram employs four situational variables—participant ability, participant willingness, available time, and situational risk—to point toward the optimal leadership style for a given situation. The first three situational factors—ability, willingness, and time—are together considered the Situational Resources.

Ability is the level of knowledge and skill that a participant or group of participants possesses in relation to a specific task. Knowledge is an understanding of a task and the information needed to successfully complete it. Skill is the demonstrated ability to execute this type of task. Group members might have the ability to paddle through a rapid, but not to serve as the sweep boat, which requires knowledge and skill in performing rescues.

Willingness is the confidence and motivation of a participant or group of participants in undertaking a given task. Confidence is the level of assurance a group or individual has in accomplishing a task, and it is typically the most important component of willingness in outdoor activities. Motivation is the desire to perform a task. Group members may have the confidence necessary to set up a tent, but lack the motivation, and thus this participant would not be willing. (The same applies to the reverse situation of a participant who is motivated but not confident.) The willingness of individual participants will change depending on how their needs, as identified in chapter 6, are being met. Similarly the dynamics and skills of a small group change over time, often increasing the ability and willingness of the whole group. This process is addressed fully in chapter 9.

Time available must be considered in all situations, and can limit the amount of relationship behavior employed by the leader. As a rule relationship behavior is more time consuming than task behavior—consider the time it would take for one or two leaders to make a decision versus the time it takes an entire group to be involved in the same decision. Many groups or individuals will have the ability and willingness to be involved in making a decision, but there will be insufficient time for the leader to engage them. This is particularly true in crisis situations.

While time is frequently a limiting factor to the amount of relationship behavior employed, it's important to note that any of the three situational resources (ability, willingness, time) can be the limiting factor. The group might have all the necessary ability and time to take on a task, but if members have limited willingness their leader may need to put the selling or even directing style to use. A group that is ready for a participating approach from the perspective of ability and willingness may require a telling approach if tasks need to be accomplished very quickly.

The final situational factor, risk, is represented on the Situational Application of Leadership Styles diagram as the axis opposing the situational resources (ability, willingness, and time).

Risk is the potential for suffering some harm or loss. From a situational perspective we look at each task and the potential for harm or loss, but also factor in the severity of that harm or loss. The risk of a participant cooking dinner is that the meal will be burned (a highly likely occurrence, in my experience). While the likelihood that a participant may incorrectly tie a climbing knot may be lower, the severity of the outcome—falling—could be far worse than burning a meal. Thus we think of the level of risk in tying a climbing knot to be greater. In another example, the likelihood that a beginner will incorrectly pack a canoe might be high, however the severity of this might be low if the packing could be adjusted after input from the leader. Attempting to quantify risk is always somewhat subjective; however, detailed approaches are addressed fully in chapter 12.

Of course, the Situational Application of Leadership Styles that employs these four variables is not scientific in that the variables aren't quantified in any way. It's simply a graphical representation of a useful concept. The implementation of the different leadership styles is dependent upon your personal approach and subjective assessment of situational resources and risk. Even though no two leaders will use this model in exactly the same way, it will point you in the right direction.

The Situational Application of Leadership Styles illustrates that an increased level of risk indicates an optimal leadership style higher in task behavior. In other words, you as a leader generally exert greater control of higher-risk situations, unless your participants have a high

Situational Application of Leadership Styles

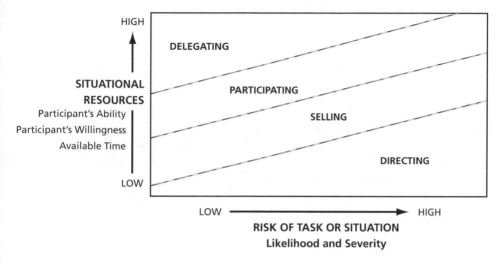

level of ability and willingness and there is plenty of time in which to make decisions. Take for example a rock climbing trip for beginners. The risk level is clearly high. On the situational resources side you have low participant ability, moderate participant willingness (due to limited confidence), and plenty of available time—thus the low ability is the limiting factor and the situational resources are considered low. According to the Situational Application of Leadership Styles the leader would thus employ a directive style at the start of the trip.

On that same first day of the climbing trip the risk of preparing lunch is probably low—that task could be delegated from the start. But by day five of the climbing course, situational resources would likely increase (due to increased participant ability and willingness) and the risk would actually decrease (the likelihood risk may decrease with increased participant skill). In this situation, on day five of the climbing course, you might employ the participating or even a delegating leadership style with regard to some climbing tasks.

There are, of course, exceptions to this model. In particular, it may not be appropriate to significantly involve participants in decisions on some types of trips. These might be short outings where it is difficult to get people to work together or guided outings where participants expect the leader to do much of the work and make the decisions. Even in these situations, however, it is often effective to use a selling style so participants have a thorough background on what to expect and have the opportunity to ask necessary questions.

Integration

What's discussed here and included in the charts is only a framework within which to think about leadership style. You shouldn't need to memorize the details and think back to the chart when faced with a leadership challenge—it's the general concepts that are most helpful. It is useful simply to identify the leadership styles you do frequently employ. This awareness will then assist you in considering if there are other styles you could be using under some circumstances. The stories of successful leadership included below help explain how the different leadership styles are used under varying situations.

A "Classic Example" on Tronador ———

"On a mountaineering expedition, the leadership style on the approach hike might be totally different from on the mountain," Brady Robinson observes. "It's a classic example of how leaders must employ different leadership styles." Robinson is the Chile Program director for the North Carolina Outward Bound School (NCOBS). He spends seven months a year as director, logistics coordinator, resupply driver, and sometimes leader for backpacking and mountaineering programs in the Andes and sea kayaking programs on the Pacific coast. Even when not working, he's often found among the peaks, and he has established difficult new climbs in far-flung locales such as Pakistan and Patagonia.

Robinson recalls an ascent of Tronador, an 11,414-foot peak in the southern Chilean Andes, during an NCOBS mountaineering course: "The approach was mellow through the forest, and students were using skills they knew well. We just let them go and trailed along behind." Here the risks were low and the group had the necessary willingness and ability, so the leaders delegated leadership to the group.

When they reached their base camp location at the base of Tronador, the group set up camp and received a resupply that was brought in on horseback. The instructors became somewhat more

A leader uses the telling style in working with his group.

involved with the group, stepping in to teach new skills such as snow camping and mountaineering. "The students also got their crash course on being stormbound in their tents," Robinson laughs. "It's mandatory." The Tronador region is notorious for unstable weather and extended stormy spells. The instructors used the selling and participating leadership styles as they first explained and demonstrated skills and then encouraged the group to put their new skills to use.

Once the storm clouds cleared it was time for the ascent. On summit day the instructors took over in a new way; "the students essentially become guided clients." "They understood," says Robinson, "because they knew they don't have the skills they needed in that environment. We tried to teach more skills along the way and involved the students as much as possible, but they had their hands full just taking care of themselves." A higher level of risk on the peak combined with decreased student ability and confidence meant that the instructors needed to employ a selling style. Time constraints often mean instructors do not have time to explain themselves, so they're forced to adopt the directing style.

The climb began with several miles of post-holing through deep snow. Instructors led the whole way—breaking trail proved too laborious for the students, who were not used to the task. Hours later, nearing the summit, the group completed a traverse that placed them above

Leadership has been delegated to these two student-leaders who discuss their route before beginning a technical canyon descent.

Alex Kosseff

a sheer 600 feet of vertical ice—the students, Robinson mentions, "were really wowed by the location and exposure." One final rope length of climbing was the only barrier between the group and the summit, but this pitch included the most difficult rock and ice climbing of the whole route.

"I was belaying students up the final pitch, but we had to bag it," Robinson recalls. "It was getting too late and there were lenticular clouds approaching." Lenticular (or lens-shaped) clouds are often a sign of incoming winds and poor weather. The student Robinson was lowering down the final pitch was going very slowly, not trusting the rope with 600 feet of exposure below his feet. "I was very directive. I told him to 'lean back and lower,'" Robinson explains. "At that point how the students felt about me and even about themselves wasn't that important. The key was to get back down." The safety imperative took precedence over any other leadership concerns at that moment. The student was not fully aware of the safety issues Robinson was concerned with; he also had low confidence and limited ability, and time was in short supply. Robinson was forced to take the most directive possible leadership style.

The key to taking charge in a difficult situation is being "calmly directive, no shouting or panic, just a firm edge on the voice and a direct command that makes the student know you mean business, *now*," explains Robinson. It's important not to give the impression of being nervous or panicked—that will only backfire and result in panicked participants. Employed correctly, a very directive leadership style can be highly effective. Robinson explains how he puts it to use: "This is a leadership style I keep in my back pocket only to be used once or twice, if at all, during a course. It has so much more power if it is fresh and catches the students a little off guard—sometimes you can use anger or even being really silly in a similar way." The shift in style on Tronador worked—after the student was successfully lowered down the ice face, he noted to Robinson, "You've never talked to me like that before." The controlled use of a very directive tone was the right solution in this situation.

As the students and instructors continued down the peak, the weather worsened, confirming Robinson's judgment call near the summit. Their tracks from earlier in the day were totally filled in with blowing snow, so they had to break trail again. While everyone was exhausted, they all made it safely off Mount Tronador. With the less risk and a more familiar environment, the students were again able to take on the primary leadership role for the hike out to the trailhead.

Disagreement on the Rio Grande————

While safety issues do form a constant theme that leaders must address during outdoor activities, many of the problems that arise are interpersonal. Beth Van Oss is a longtime wilderness leader and group facilitator—a former Outward Bound instructor (we once led a trip together) who now teaches at Arizona's Prescott College. Beth's favorite place to lead trips is the Big Bend region on the border of Texas and Mexico. She's particularly partial to paddling on the Rio Grande—the setting for the leadership story related here.

Beth and her co-leader—I'll call him Jeremy—were leading a Prescott College group though the spectacular Santa Elena Canyon, where sheer limestone walls rise 1,500 feet above the river. They had a group of "really good students," Beth reports. The water level the group found in the canyon meant that they faced the challenge of Class III rapids in their open canoes. While the students were skilled paddlers, a couple of the boats did capsize in the most difficult rapid. The group went ashore to bail the boats and reorganize.

With the boats bailed and repacked, they set off downriver below

CONSENTING TO CONSENSUS

Juliana Popper

Over the summer of 2001 I worked as a group facilitator among twenty-five fellow riders biking across the United States from San Francisco to Washington, D.C. We had all volunteered for this adventure to raise money for social change and grassroots community activism. This group, BikeAid, is an experiential education program for the riders, who in turn share what they learn along the way with community groups across the country. Part of what we hoped to learn was how a small group of dedicated individuals can work together and within their community to create social change. As such, we decided that within our COW—as we affectionately called our Community on Wheels—we would make all decisions pertaining to group life by consensus. This included everything from which route we would follow, to what foods we purchased with group funds, to how we divided daily chores.

In any group choosing to use consensus as its mode of decision making, the group must first agree to standards by which the process will occur, such as what percentage of the members constitutes a "majority" or enough to pass a decision that isn't unanimous. The group must also understand that there are certain decisions (depending on the group)—primarily those concerning safety—that are nonnegotiable and transcend group consensus. These rules must be set in place when the group initially comes together.

One of the requisite elements to consensus is setting the stage, with everyone present and taking part in the discussion. Members must understand why they're using consensus and how specifically it will function within their group. Group roles within a consensus meeting include a facilitator, timekeeper, note taker, and vibes watcher/peacekeeper. At our weekly meetings, we rotated these roles, so that by the end of the summer everyone had a chance to take part in the leadership. Again, this spreads responsibility and promotes equality.

One sweltering day in July, our group had planned on riding 70 miles through Utah, where a stay on an Indian reservation in Duschesne had been arranged for us. Each of us planned our day accordingly, in terms of pacing ourselves to arrive in Duschense in time for dinner. A few of us who had been riding ahead, however, learned that the reservation was actually in Fort Duschense, not Duschense—and that Fort Duschense was an additional 37 miles away. At lunchtime, when everyone arrived at our designated stop, we called an impromptu meeting to decide whether to continue riding as planned to our original destination, despite the significant change in mileage, or to come up with an alternative plan. Sure, our smaller group could have told the rest of the group that we must add 37 miles to our already long and hot day, but we hardly considered this an option, knowing it should be a group decision, not ours alone.

Once the group came together, we quickly designated a facilitator, and it became clear that there were varying opinions—a prime time for consensus! Several members of our group were overheated and feeling sick. Others had been looking forward to the visit to the reservation and weren't much concerned about riding an additional 37 miles to get there. Everyone had something to say, and everyone also realized we had only fifteen minutes to make a decision suitable to all. The decision we all finally consented to was to find a place to camp that night in Duschense, allowing us to cook dinner and recuperate. Then we would leave early the next morning so that we could spend a long lunch at the reservation. Initially, many were disappointed about not getting to stay where they'd hoped, but the group's satisfaction was immense, knowing that we had listened to all sides, weighed our options, and decided together on a solution agreeable to all.

Riding 3,600 miles was a small task compared to making all our decisions by consensus. Consensus requires serious commitment on the part of each member of the group—a commitment of time, attention, and collective resources. Because of this, however, the weight of a decision made by consensus sits heavier than one made by an individual and then handed down to the group. When all members of a group have collectively made a decision—sometimes through hours of painstaking compromise—there is a sense of ownership and respect for the outcome. Inclusion, individual growth, and satisfaction can be among the results of this grassroots approach.

To me consensus represents the truest democratic form of decision making. It is qualitative rather than quantitative and requests of group members a significant devotion of attention, time, and compromise. The consensus model thrives in groups where members are mature, intelligent, and motivated. Successful operation of the model demands from its participants as well as the group creativity, cooperation, and flexibility. I have worked in many different types of groups, as a leader as well as a participant, but never have I experienced a feeling as rewarding as when our group succeeded in our commitment to work together to achieve a common vision and goal.

Since pedaling across the United States, Juliana Popper has coordinated the AMC's Mountain Leadership School.

the rapid. It was not until a lunch stop later in the day that they discovered several water jugs had been left below the rapid where the canoes had been bailed out. These five-gallon plastic jugs carried drinking water; the Rio Grande is polluted and heavy with sediment. Jeremy said to the group, "What should we do?" The group reached a consensus that they needed to go back and retrieve the jugs: They needed the water, and leaving the jugs would be littering. That left the question of how to retrieve the water.

It was a good paddle back *upstream* to the jugs. Jeremy agreed to go and asked for a volunteer to go with him, saying, "I want someone really competent." A woman in the group spoke up and said that she wanted to go. Jeremy told this student that he wasn't comfortable with this because he didn't know her well; he'd rather go with one of the students he knew from earlier courses. He proceeded to name three students with whom he'd feel comfortable going. Beth wasn't sure why Jeremy didn't want this woman along—they'd already been on the river for seven days, and she was obviously a competent paddler. Perhaps it was because she was a small woman, and Jeremy wanted someone who he thought would be stronger—Beth just didn't know.

Another woman whom Jeremy knew from previous courses volunteered. The original volunteer continued to say that she felt she could handle the paddle back upriver. Jeremy repeated that he'd rather go with the student he knew. The group was asked to give a thumbs-up, thumbs-down, or in the middle to show how they felt about this decision (this is a great technique for gauging consensus—or lack thereof—in a group). The thumbs all went up, and Jeremy moved to get ready to go.

Beth, however, wasn't comfortable, feeling that Jeremy had pushed through a decision that was unfair toward the original volunteer. It could certainly be a blow to this student's confidence that the group leader didn't trust her with this task. Beth also felt that it was out of character with the participatory leadership style they'd been using with their skilled and motivated students. She spoke up.

Lesson: *Lead by example.* Leaders must always set an example that they want participants to emulate. If a leader's actions are less than ideal, leaders must acknowledge and change this.

◆

This group managed to deal with the situation. In the end both the original volunteer and the second volunteer went up the river. It was not a clear-cut situation with a right and a wrong answer, but the student whom Beth stood up for appreciated her support. Other students later said that they appreciated the discussion; they too hadn't understood why Jeremy made his decision. They also felt that the discussion was a learning experience for them.

Lesson: *Make questioning an expectation.* When people have concerns or questions, they should be heard. Participants should feel like they know what is going on; if they don't, they should know that they may ask. Additional perspectives may help in the decision-making process. Except in the most time-pressed or risky situations, the leader should value this dialogue.

Beth says (not in reference to this trip; she's very clear that she thinks Jeremy is a good leader), "A lot of people have a negative perception of groups because of poor leadership." She continues, "In the outdoor world there is a lot of emphasis on safety issues and hard skills. There is less emphasis on talking to people and resolving conflict when people are at each other's throats. Leaders need to have a bag of tricks and be willing to intervene when necessary."

Over time, Beth has "become a lot more okay with confrontation." Not every issue needs to be taken on, but some are best addressed rather than left to linger. Beth says that challenging people on group process issues can be useful in improving the safety and fun of an activity and "gives them something to think about in life." Some of this is dependent upon the goal of your program—whether it's more focused on education or recreation. In either case the group leader needs to find a way to create an inclusive environment, the road to which can be a learning experience for all involved.

Courage

It took a pinch of courage for Beth to stand up to her co-leader and express her disapproval of his decision. Socially it would have been easier to go along. It took courage for Brady Robinson to turn his group around barely shy of the summit because he knew that going for it could have dire consequences. It probably would have been easier to let the group go for the summit they wanted to climb so badly. As Robert Kennedy said in 1966, "Each time a man stands up for an ideal, or acts to improve the lot of the rest or strikes out against injustice, he sends forth a tiny ripple of hope, and crossing each other from a million different centers of energy and daring, those ripples build a current that can sweep down the mightiest walls of oppression and resistance. . . . Few are willing to brave the disapproval of their fellows, the censure of their colleagues, the wrath of their society. Moral courage is a rarer commodity than bravery in battle or great intelligence. Yet it is the one essential, vital quality for those who seek to change a world that yields most painfully to change." While Kennedy is talking about people who stand up for big ideals, the ideals of a small group take courage to realize as well. Social pressure can be a powerful force that leaders must be able to buck when an important issue or principle is on the line.

Courage is not the absence of fear, but the willingness to act in the face of fear. Those who have no fear in the face of physical or social dangers are not courageous, just foolish. The courageous leader finds the best course of action for the group and acts to implement that. Courage in the face of physical danger—Robert Kennedy mentions bravery in battle—is, in fact, more common than moral courage. Outdoor leaders work from a vision for their program and their group. At times courage—moral, physical, or both—will be required to keep this vision alive. So be afraid, but also be brave and do not let fear prevent you from being an exceptional leader.

RECOMMENDED READING

Drucker, Peter, *The Essential Drucker,* New York: HarperCollins, 2001.

Freedman, David H., *Corps Business: The 30 Management Principles of the U.S. Marines,* New York: HarperBusiness, 2000.

Gookin, John, Molly Doran, and Rachael Green, eds., *2000 NOLS Leadership Education Toolbox,* Lander, Wyoming: National Outdoor Leadership School, 2000.

◆ Hersey, Paul, Kenneth Blanchard, and Dewey Johnson, *Management of Organizational Behavior: Leading Human*

Resources, 8th ed., Upper Saddle River, New Jersey: Prentice Hall, 2001.

Johnson, David W., and Frank P. Johnson, *Joining Together: Group Theory and Group Skills,* 7th ed., Boston: Allyn and Bacon, 2000.

Langmuir, Eric, *Mountaincraft and Leadership,* 3rd ed., West Didsbury, England: The Mountain Leader Training Board, 1995.

McClintock, Mary, "Who's in Charge?: Leadership and Decision-Making Among Peers," *Sea Kayaker,* pp. 28–35 (December 2000).

Petzoldt, Paul. *The New Wilderness Handbook,* New York: W. W. Norton, 1984.

Priest, Simon, and Michael Gass, *Effective Leadership in Adventure Programming,* Champaign, Illinois: Human Kinetics, 1997.

Schimelpfenig, Tod, and Linda Lindsey, *NOLS Wilderness First Aid,* 3rd ed., Mechanicsburg, Pennsylvania: Stackpole Books and National Outdoor Leadership School, 2000.

Tannenbaum, Robert, and Warren H. Schmidt, "How to Choose a Leadership Pattern," *Harvard Business Review* 51, no. 3, pp. 162–180 (May–June 1973).

Useem, Michael, *The Leadership Moment,* New York: Times Books/Random House, 1998.

◆ = Advanced Recommendation

CHAPTER 9

Group

Chapter 6, Participants, raised belonging (social acceptance) as a basic human need. Groups help their members meet this social need. Groups also allow members to achieve goals that would be difficult or impossible individually. This chapter addresses how groups function and how the leader can assist in the development and maintenance of effective groups.

The following two chapters, Communication and Expedition Behavior, focus on the communication and interpersonal skills necessary for leaders and participants to form outdoor communities. All these skills working with groups are central to a leader's fundamental responsibilities—minimizing risk and impact on the environment while maximizing enjoyment and learning—as outlined in chapter 1. For the leader to accomplish any of these objectives, there must be a group that is reasonably willing to work with the leader and with each other. That is what this, and the following two chapters, are about.

Rugged Individualism ————————————

The myth of the rugged individualist is very prevalent in the world of outdoor adventure. Perhaps, in the United States, it is descended from the ideal of the rugged frontiersman who ventured forth and tamed the wilderness single-handedly. The problem is that the rugged individualist ethic doesn't work well in groups, and it defeats the concept of community. While it's possible for the skilled individual to undertake many outdoor activities alone—and I would argue that this presents many opportunities for personal growth—it's a limiting way to live your entire life. Leaders or participants in groups who assume a superwoman or superman mentality cut off many opportunities for their own learning and growth. Individuals who look only to themselves for answers will not be happy in a group or leading a group and will spread unhappiness to others.

> "... The problem—indeed, the total failure—of the 'ethic' of rugged individualism is that it ... incorporates only one half of our humanity. It recognizes that we are called to individualization, power, and wholeness. But it denies entirely the other part of the human story: that we can never fully get there and that we are, of necessity in our uniqueness, weak and imperfect creatures who need each other."
>
> —M. SCOTT PECK, M.D., THE DIFFERENT DRUM

Community ————————————

While the concept of the frontiersman as rugged individualist is a popular one in our society, the history of humanity has been one of community. Small groups, in particular, have dominated human history. First it was nomadic bands, and later the small farming villages in which most humans resided. That most people live in cities is a development of only the past hundred years. What we see in cities is the intense need for people to form small groups—through work, religion, shared interests—in which to interact. Many people, in fact, are partially (perhaps even largely) motivated to participate in outdoor

THE TAO OF LEADERSHIP

The *Tao Te Ching* is a classic Chinese text of wisdom. While its exact origins are debated by scholars, it is traditionally believed to have been written in the fifth century B.C. by the philosopher Lao-tzu. The *Tao Te Ching*'s lessons relate to how events naturally happen and how to lead or educate based on working with this natural process.

There are now many adaptations of this book, but one of the earlier and best ones is John Heider's *The Tao of Leadership: Lao Tzu's Tao Te Ching Adapted for a New Age*. An instructor on the first outdoor leadership course I ever took recommended this book to me. At the time it was out of print, and it took me several years to obtain a copy. I'm glad I persevered. Heider makes Lao-tzu's insights every bit as relevant today as they were twenty-five hundred years ago when they were written. From a foundation in awareness, *The Tao of Leadership* urges the leader to use gentle interventions to move the group process forward. Several quotes from Heider appear in this chapter as well as elsewhere in this book.

activities for the relationships and sense of community it brings.

The true objective of the leader with regard to the group is the development of community. The words *community* and *communicate* share a common root in Latin: *communis,* meaning "common." Communication is about the sharing of information, or making it common. A community is any group of people with some relationship connecting it members. A community in a deeper sense must serve its members by helping them meet some common goals. For this to happen there needs to be a sense of belonging, trust, and some expectation of being understood.

Why should you encourage community? For starters, a sense of community encourages following group rules and norms. It causes members to pull together to support the goals of the trip—and in doing so support each other. Groups with a sense of community and purpose are generally more accepting of all members and have a higher level of participation. A sense of togetherness bolsters confidence and encourages striving for new accomplishments. It provides the safety net often needed for taking risks, moving people to explore things they might otherwise not be provoked to do. It provides the optimal opportunity to make a meaningful difference in those we lead.

Group Behavior

The leader must develop a relationship with each member of the group but must also realize that the group is more than the sum of its parts. The group, in essence, becomes an organism in its own right with its own patterns of behavior. These behaviors would not be present without the unique combination of diversity existing within the group. Thus the leader needs to be aware not only of the individuals but also how the group functions as its own entity.

The importance of group behavior is often underestimated. Imagine a basketball team that did not commit to the goal of winning games. Or an engineering team that did not communicate with each other on their concerns about the structural integrity of a project they were developing. Or a backcountry trip on which a third of the group is stressed by finding it hard to keep up with the others. Group behavior can result in seemingly illogical situations in which the effectiveness of the group is compromised—they are often subtle, but very real. It is the leader's job to assist the group in overcoming these obstacles and paving the way for an effective community to develop.

Assessing Your Group

Assessing your group is really just an extension of your awareness of your group. When you're assessing your group, you consider not only the behavior of the group, but also why this behavior is taking place. Think of the group *process* as the overall health of the group. Good group process is indicated by the harmonious involvement of all group members in tasks and decision making. Disharmony can some-

"The superficial leader cannot see how things happen, even though the evidence is everywhere. The leader is swept up by drama, sensation, and excitement. All this confusion is blinding.

But the leader who returns again and again to awareness-of-process has a deep sense of how things happen. This leader has a simple time of it."

—JOHN HEIDER,
THE TAO OF LEADERSHIP

times be important in a group—nobody ever agrees on everything—
but constant disharmony is not healthy and is a sign of poor group
process. Consider not only harmony or disharmony, but also the causes
of these different states.

In assessing the group, consider these overall questions:

▶ Is the group moving toward accomplishing its goals?

▶ Where is group process working?

▶ Where and how can group process be improved?

There are many cues to the nature of a group's process. The experienced
leader has developed a deep, almost intuitive, sense of how things happen. Some of the kinds of questions you can ask yourself and that may
give you insight into group process are included here. This is not
intended as a checklist to carry into the field (though I suppose you
could) but rather as an outline to provide you with some areas and
questions to consider when assessing your group. There are many other
issues to consider; still, if you can consider at least some of these, you're
off to a good start.

Verbal Participation: This is the most important indicator in the assessment of group process.

▶ Who is most actively participating? Least actively?

▶ Does the group attempt to engage the quieter participants?

▶ Who talks to whom? Whom do people look at when they
   share in the group?

▶ Why are people engaging in the verbal behaviors you
   observe?

Listening: Verbal participation is useful only if the messages people say
are received by others in the group.

▶ Do members appear to be listening to one another? Does what
   they say reflect this?

▶ Who interrupts whom?

▶ Why do people listen or not? Are only certain people listened to?

▶ Does anyone attempt to summarize what has been said?

Physical Participation: Observe any differences in the amount of action taken by participants.

▶ Who takes the initiative in regard to actual physical tasks?

▶ Are tasks evenly distributed among group members?

▶ Are participants' actions consistent with their verbal messages?

▶ Why are participants physically participating? Why not?

Power: Examine which participants are most influential as the group passes through various stages of development.

▶ Are there participants who seem to consistently get their way?

▶ Do other participants appear to have limited influence in the group?

▶ Are there groups that exert influence as a unit?

▶ If there are inequalities in power, why?

Decision Making: Groups are constantly making decisions. It is useful (and interesting) to observe how decisions are made and who makes them. Also consider what decision-making and leadership styles are being used.

▶ How does the group make decisions?

▶ Are decisions made by one participant, several, or the entire group?

▶ Does the group attempt to reach a consensus?

▶ Does the group follow a democratic process based on majority rule?

► Why are decisions made in the way they are and what impact does it have?

► Who follows through and makes sure the decisions are implemented?

Leadership: Look for behaviors that contribute to good and harmonious working relationships among participants.

► Who helps others get into the discussion or involved in a task?

► Who seems to disrupt cooperation?

► Are ideas rejected in a supportive manner?

► Who contributes to group morale?

► Who takes courageous positions?

► Who attempts to keep the group focused?

Norms: These are the obvious or subtle expectations of the majority of group members regarding what behaviors should take place in the group.

► Are feelings openly expressed? If so, what are they?

► Are certain things talked about and others avoided?

► How do participants act toward one another? Are they overly polite or do they challenge one another?

► Have group members assumed set roles in the group? Are these determined by gender?

This list is based, in part, on material in *The Role of the Instructor in the Outward Bound Educational Process* by Kenneth R. Kalisch and *Processing the Experience* by John Luckner and Reldan Nadler. These are both excellent references on group process, group development, and facilitation.

Group Development———

Participants in an outdoor activity generally form a group for a predetermined period of time. It has long been understood that groups typically pass through several stages of development, focusing on specific issues during each stage. The height of the development is when the group becomes a community and is able to work effectively without significant intervention from a leader. Of course, not all groups reach this community stage, nor do they all pass through exactly the same stages. There's enough commonality, however, that you as leader will generally be able to identify the stage a group is in. Awareness of the stage of

The way you present information to a group will depend in part on the level of group development.

group development will enable you to understand and predict the behavior of the group. It also allows you to subtly intervene and guide the group toward community.

Group Life Cycle (Stages of Group Development)

We refer to a group life cycle because we can draw an analogy between the life cycle of an organism and stages we observe in groups. This begins with the formation of the group (birth), moves through several stages including the group's becoming effective (maturity), and ends when the group disbands (death). There are numerous models of group development. In 1972 Bruce Tuckman and Mary Ann Jensen created one of the best-known models, which is commonly used in the outdoor leadership field. The stages Tuckman and Jensen identified are (1) forming, (2) storming, (3) norming, (4) performing, and (5) adjourning.

Forming: Coming together for the first time, individuals will generally be very polite and intensely interested in learning about the future. From the start the leader will usually observe what M. Scott Peck terms "pseudocommunity"—everyone is nice, friendly, and open to one another. True community, Peck points out, is conflict resolving, while pseudocommunity is conflict avoiding. Members of this pseudocommunity are interested in finding out the procedures of the group, how things will work, what to expect. Participants appear to be focused on tasks at hand. They are mastering initial tasks and knowledge that will be helpful throughout the program. At the same time, group members are also forming a relational base with one another. In this stage participants are unlikely to challenge one another as they find their common ground with other group members and feel out whether they can fit in and trust them. Participants at this stage will look for connections with others in the group—where they are from, what school they go to or went to, even what TV shows they watch. For many participants this will be a critical time as they assess whether basic and safety needs will be met and also consider whether their belonging and even esteem needs will be met in the group. There is preoccupation with belonging. If participants are comfortable that the group can meet these needs, the development of the group will progress. If they are not comfortable that their safety and belonging needs are likely to be satisfied in the group, then the group's development will stall—participants will hold back rather than taking the chances necessary to form the group.

    Leaders of groups in the forming stage use the telling leadership style, but selling may be used for a willing group in a low-risk situation, or participating for a skilled group. It is most important to be active during this phase: participants need to develop trust in you.

▶ Provide factual information about the trip.

▶ Make sure everyone understands group goals.

▶ Communicate rules and norms for working together.

▶ Keep your word: breaking it diminishes trust.

▶ Practice skills necessary for groups: good listening and conflict resolution.

▶ Watch for patterns of behavior in individual participants and the group as a whole.

▶ Encourage socialization.

▶ Observe strengths and weaknesses of participants.

Storming: Pseudocommunity falls by the wayside as group members rebel against the leader and challenge each other. This stage is necessary for groups to reach maturity—if it does not occur at least briefly, it is an indication that conflicts remain suppressed. This stage is often triggered as group members discover that the tasks before them are more difficult than they imagined they would be. Storming is necessary for group members to establish their place in the group's hierarchy of influence and decision making and for them to test the validity of the approaches to practical and interpersonal issues the leader has modeled or taught.

> *"Coordinating a group at this stage is like teaching a child to ride a bicycle: One runs alongside to prevent the child from falling, but one must let loose so the child can learn to balance on his or her own."*
> —DAVID AND FRANK JOHNSON, JOINING TOGETHER

The storming stage is not enjoyable, and some participants may become disenchanted with the group at this point. Participants may question whether the group can provide for their belonging and esteem needs even if they previously felt comfortable in these areas. They may feel that the benefits of the group's working effectively together might provide are not worth the effort. Often they will blame the leader and claim that they are not being given enough direction. They are correct that a directive leader using a telling style can eliminate this stage. However, the group that does not pass through a stage of storming will not reach its full potential as an effective community—which may be fine for a shorter activity, when the group may not have time to pass through all the stages of development and achieve its full potential. Here a more directive leadership style that avoids conflict may be the most workable.

Leader of groups in the storming stage must provide gentle guidance during this time of power struggles and confusion about goals and roles. The appropriate leadership style will generally be selling, although sometimes participating or directing styles may apply. This stage is demanding and can be unpleasant. If criticism is directed at you, try not to be defensive. Hear it and try to evaluate it as dispassionately as possible but maintain the distinction between an attack on you as the leader and you as a person.

► Model and encourage conflict resolution skills.

► Take responsibility for errors if need be.

► Pay attention to inclusion of all members.

► Address difficult issues, goals, and expectations.

Norming: A team approach emerges in which people acknowledge their interdependence and establish norms on communicating and coping with conflict. As turbulence fades, friendship reasserts itself and the group will ideally recommit itself to common goals. These goals may be different from those participants had originally envisioned. The group will look less to the leader for direction and may collectively challenge the leader if they want to pursue a path different from the leader's. During this stage the group takes ownership of its experience, and it becomes "our" trip rather than the leader's. Most groups will expect to take an active role in some decision making along with the leader.

In the norming stage of group development members will generally be satisfied in their physiological, safety, and belonging needs. Participants may look to satisfy their esteem needs, their sense of self-worth, as they develop a stable role in the group.

Leaders of groups in the norming stage must assist in the development of an emerging sense of shared leadership. The appropriate leadership style will typically be participating but may also be selling with a less skilled group.

► Provide opportunities for the group to function autonomously.

► Play more of a facilitation role in decision making and conflict resolution.

▶ Negotiate and/or work toward consensus on important issues.

▶ Give feedback.

Performing: Effective community emerges as the group reaches its full potential. Frequently a group will be stable at this level until the end of the trip approaches. The group, as a mature community, will work together to accomplish goals and deal effectively with conflict. Disagreements are tolerated, and members feel well supported. They will try to identify each participant's strengths and make use of them. The group may begin to see the leader as more of a consultant and less of an absolute authority. At this stage most of the participants' basic needs may be reasonably satisfied, and individuals may focus attention on esteem or self-actualization needs.

Leaders of groups in the performing stage are working with a group that is doing a good job of functioning autonomously as a community. You will typically be using a participating or delegating style of leadership. One caveat is to keep in mind that you are still the leader and must remain vigilant regarding the group dynamics (and, of course, safety).

▶ Analyze group process with an eye toward improving overall functioning.

▶ Provide feedback that will allow for improvements in groups function.

▶ Expand opportunities for participants.

Adjourning: Members of a group that has successfully formed a community will find the impending end of the experience unpleasant. While some participants may be eager to return to the "real world," even these individuals are likely to find the separation painful. As a defensive mechanism some participants will withdraw prematurely from their prior level of involvement in the group. The group tends to focus on superlatives at this point, focusing on the best characteristics of the group. While the exact group experience will never be re-created, some participants will attempt to keep some of the experience alive by making plans to communicate or get together in the future.

Alex Kosseff

Members of a performing group will be able to work together to accomplish many tasks.

Leaders of groups in the adjourning stage will typically use the participating or delegating leadership style. As the end of the experience approaches, however, some participants may become less self-motivating and you will need to engage in more task-oriented behavior, perhaps even turning back to a directing style. Continue to monitor—you don't want your success spoiled by some last-minute complication. Don't forget to congratulate yourself and your co-leader on the success you have achieved.

▶ Encourage discussion about the experience.

▶ Give feedback.

▶ Celebrate successes and acknowledge failures.

Because groups are involved in a dynamic process, the stages outlined are not rigid and inflexible. They are guidelines that can assist the leader in facilitating the growth of the group and in assessing the group's ability to manage problems. For example, a group in the performing stage might be expected to independently address a pressing concern, whereas a group in storming would become mired in it. The composition of the group as well as the nature of the activity may affect the evolution of stages. Some research has shown that women tend to enter the storming stage later in group development, after they have formed strong relationships with other members. Confronted with crisis and change, groups can slip back into earlier stages and function less effectively. Also, it's very possible for groups to not achieve all the stages and to become stuck at a particular one. Frequently, there is a back-and-forth quality to development. When the group regresses, emphasize approaches used during the earlier stages. Don't be afraid to gently let group members know that their ability to handle themselves on their own will dictate the level of task, or directive, behavior you engage in.

Facilitation

Facilitation is the art of assisting an individual or group in finding their own understanding of issues or solutions to challenges. It can be used to foster the development of effective group skills and to help participants learn from their experiences. The artful facilitator can guide many groups without ever engaging in the kind of directive behavior many people associate with leadership. The most successful facilitators make themselves superfluous by eventually guiding the group toward the skills and insight to lead themselves.

The leader's approach to facilitation will vary with the length and purpose of the activity she seeks to lead. At a minimum the leader will want to facilitate some discussion on how the activity is going for participants and what could be improved. This can be accomplished in a discussion intentionally called for this purpose or more informally at any time of day. On a longer outdoor program the leader will want the group to develop more into a community. This may necessitate more facilitation. Ultimately, however, leaders find facilitation techniques most helpful in guiding participants to greater learning from their experiences.

The leader may be a strong presence in a group; the facilitator is not. Facilitation means assisting a group or individual through their own process, thus allowing the delivery of experience and learning. While facilitation is the ideal of leadership, it is not appropriate in all situations.

Facilitation is a technique leaders use the most when they are focused on relationship behavior. While task behavior and facilitation are not incompatible, the more the leader is a driving force in the group, the more difficult it is to play the role of facilitator.

Investment

For facilitation to be effective in a leadership perspective, the facilitator-leader must not be seen as having a stake in the outcome of the discussion. This low level of investment in outcome is rarely the case with a leader who has a strong task focus. Facilitation, however, can be used to assist in non-decision-making tasks with all groups. Leaders often use facilitation techniques to aid groups in maximizing their learning from an experience.

Facilitating

The facilitator increases the group's awareness of important issues. The focus is on constructively addressing areas for improvement and areas for new learning. The leader, however, should also be cognizant of the need to reinforce what's being done well and what learning participants are doing without guidance.

The leader employs facilitation to guide the group in becoming more cohesive. For example, you might observe a pattern in the group process of certain members dominating discussions while others remain silent. You could comment directly on your observation; hopefully a group member might provoke discussion. That is your goal: to let the group do as much as possible. The real growth of the group emerges as it addresses its own development—this is the path of the participants' ownership.

If discussion does not ensue, you could repeat your initial observation or choose to engage a particular group member on this topic in private. Alternatively, you might opt to conduct a review of group expectations and ask how people think they are working. Keep working from your basic tenets and observations of the assessment process to step in as gently and minimally as possible to provoke the group to become an educated mirror by which it can observe itself. Step in powerfully only when absolutely necessary. From *The Tao of Leadership:* "Gentle interventions, if they are clear, overcome rigid resistances." Think back to teachers who instructed you well. Chances are the ones you learned the most from guided your learning respectfully with encouragement rather than from a stance of authority and disapproval.

It is difficult to be actively involved with the group and simultaneously conceptualizing about the group process. Of course, you are already doing this and can introduce more techniques and concepts for analyzing and improving the group functioning as your skills increase.

Consider a situation in which your group has been paddling all day. The riverbanks have been too steep to offer even a marginal camping area until you reach a spot where you could squeeze in camp among some trees. Two group members have been on the river before, and they tell everyone that there is a beautiful camping spot on a sandbar 2 miles downstream. "The river turns so you get a great view of the sunset from that spot," one of the paddlers who has been there says. "It's part of the reason I came on this trip again." A debate ensues, and it seems that about half the group wants to stay. One group member is adamant that he is too tired to continue. A couple of group members try to reach a compromise and make several suggestions, including stopping for a break and then continuing to the better camp in an hour. You note some people who are not contributing to the conversation.

Potential Interventions

It is easy to read this and immediately think: *What is the solution to the paddlers' impasse?* Instead think process: *How can I use the information gleaned from my assessment of the situation to guide the group in addressing the problem?* If you can relate to the group that members are taking positions similar to ones they have assumed at other times of disagreement, you encourage them to look at themselves and fellow members in a new light.

Similarly use the assessment to inform other interventions. Let's say the paddler extolling the sunset is generally a good listener and cooperative. You might attempt to engage him or her by beginning your focus on listening. Focus attention on messages that have been expressed but may not have been heard. "Let's stop and summarize the opinions and ideas that have been expressed thus far."

Or you could immediately direct attention to the tired paddler. Here it would be good to know that this participant can tolerate the group focus and have a sense of how he or she is generally regarded by the group. If you're in the storming phase and you know that this member doesn't have much influence, you might not choose this tack. The possibilities are vast. In this anecdote, you might also want to address interventions around verbal and physical participation.

The assessment questions from earlier in this chapter guide and support your interventions. You may not know the driving force behind certain group behaviors, but hopefully you can guide the group to do the explorations.

> "Too much force will backfire. Constant interventions and instigations will not make a good group. They will spoil a group.
> The best group process is delicate. It cannot be pushed around. It cannot be argued over or won in a fight.
> The leader who tries to control the group through force does not understand group process. Force will cost you the support of members."
>
> —JOHN HEIDER, THE TAO OF LEADERSHIP

Facilitation is not an easy role, and it is one that requires trial and error to perfect. Knowing when and how to intervene requires an insightful reading of the group and participants. Sometimes your interventions will succeed and sometimes they will fall flat on their faces—at times you will become the target of the group's ire. The only approach is to keep your head up and try.

RECOMMENDED READING

Heider, John, *The Tao of Leadership,* Atlanta: Humanics Limited, 1985.

Johnson, David W., and Frank P. Johnson, *Joining Together: Group Theory and Group Skills,* 7th ed., Boston: Allyn and Bacon, 2000.

Kalisch, Kenneth R., *The Role of the Instructor in the Outward Bound Educational Process,* Three Lakes, Wisconsin: Author, 1979.

Luckner, John L., and Reldan S. Nadler, *Processing the Experience: Strategies to Enhance and Generalize Learning,* 2nd ed., Dubuque,. Iowa: Kendall/Hunt Publishing, 1997.

Peck, M. Scott, *The Different Drum,* New York: Touchstone, 1987.

Schiller, Linda Yael, "Stages of Development in Women's Groups: A Relational Model," in *Group Work Practice in a Troubled Society: Problems and Opportunities,* edited by Roselle Kurlan and Robert Salmon, New York: Haworth Press, 1995.

◆ Tuckman, Bruce W., "Developmental Sequence in Small Groups," *Psychological Bulletin* 63, no. 6, pp. 384–99 (1965).

◆ Tuckman, Bruce W., and Mary Ann Jensen, "Stages of Small-Group Development Revisited," *Group & Organization Studies* 2, pp. 419–25 (December 1972).

◆ = Advanced Recommendation

CHAPTER 10

Communication

Communication is the exchange of information between two or more people. This exchange can flow in one or more directions and can make use of, among other things, speech, writing, and body language. While our educational system provides us with plentiful instruction in written communication, the critical communication skills for the outdoor leader—listening, speaking, and body language—are not typically the focus of significant instruction. Perhaps as a result of this, many leaders and participants find effective communication challenging.

Caring leadership and awareness, subjects of two earlier chapters, are highly dependent upon communication. The aware and caring leader must effectively communicate plans and other useful information to participants on an almost constant basis. The leader also needs to be on the receiving end of communication from participants in order to understand their needs.

As an outdoor leader, you will often serve as both the chief source of information and the moderator of communication. This can be a challenging role. On one hand, there are times when a leader needs to talk a lot. But the leader must also monitor the quality of communication, ensuring that all voices are being heard and that important messages are getting across.

One difference between the outdoors and our everyday communications lies with the use of technology. In the outdoors our usual mode of communication is not e-mail or cell phone, and information from TV, radio, and the Web isn't easily accessible. Most communication in the outdoors takes place in one fashion—face to face. Making good use of this interface will allow you to bring all your other skills and knowledge to bear on the program you are leading.

Communication Process

Communication is something we all have a tremendous amount of experience with. Using a very simple metaphor, we can think of communication as being similar to a tennis game where messages are volleyed back and forth between participants. This model, however, is really too simple for a complex process of sending and receiving many types of messages that are both verbal and nonverbal. Understanding the subtleties of how communication works (and sometimes does not work) can tell you how best to work with your participants.

Coding and Decoding

This section has nothing to do with espionage, but rather with how we all communicate with one another. Communication begins with an individual who has something to express. The individual encodes that thought into a message, which may include verbal and nonverbal components. Once encoded, the message is then sent to a recipient or recipients using a channel, which may also have verbal and nonverbal (body language) components or be a combination of the two. When the message reaches the recipient or recipients, it is then decoded. Communication takes place on different channels simultaneously, with all participants constantly encoding and decoding messages—many of them quite subtle.

Much of the communication in which leaders are involved during an outdoor activity is verbal, but nonverbal communications are very

Katherine E. Jones

Effective communication involves verbal and nonverbal messages.

important. While writing is usually a small component of the outdoor leader's role, and there are hand signals for paddling and rope tugs for climbing, the predominant nonverbal communication is body language. Some examples include facial expression, eye contact, body posture, and the personal space individuals keep between themselves and others. Researchers have found that these physical cues contribute more to our communication than does actual speech. Body language is often a useful hint regarding a participant's or co-leader's unstated feelings.

Consider, for example, a participant who drops to the ground without even taking off his large pack. Frowning, he wipes his brow and lets out a sigh. You could assume that he's hot and tired. You might also think that he's frustrated, or even upset with the leaders of the trip over its difficulty. When he says, "That was a beast of a pass we climbed," he might be indicating pride at the group's accomplishments or a sense of being at the limits of his endurance. The messages this participant is sending may or may not be of major importance. It's up to the recipient to decode them, decide on their importance, and decide if further clarification is necessary. Obviously there's a lot of room for confusion and misinterpretation. This chapter focuses on effective coding and decoding of messages—which is helpful in all circumstances and critical in others, such as dealing with safety issues.

Communication Tools

Three Foundations of Effective Communication

Effective communication is more than exchanging simple messages. The key to communication is the attitude with which people approach each other. A positive attitude can open the door to effective communication and understanding one another on a deeper level. An attitude that is less than open to all communication will limit the messages that can be received and will also probably be perceived by others in the group. There are three foundations of communication—empathy, acceptance, and realness (or being yourself)—that form the basis of an effective attitude. The three foundations serve three purposes in communication:

▶ establishing that you, the listener, are interested in understanding the speaker's message,

▶ aiding you in truly understanding the intent of the speaker's message, and

▶ ensuring that your messages will be caring and sincere—and thus effective.

The foundations described here are based on the work of pioneering psychotherapist Carl Rogers.

Empathy: As discussed in chapter 4, empathy means understanding people well enough that their true feelings and motivations are apparent: It is the hallmark of an effective leader. Stated another way, it's the ability to walk a mile in another person's shoes. While many effective workplace managers employ empathy, the intense nature of outdoor activities makes this a particularly critical ability for the outdoor leader. Empathy allows you to better support group members and is particularly valuable on challenging excursions or when working with beginners.

Acceptance: As a leader, it is important to accept others as they are. This does not imply that you should agree with everything someone says, but you must listen with an open mind. People are more accepting of themselves, and more willing to discuss their feelings, when you listen without imposing your own perspective. If you listen without prejudice to someone you are more likely to be able to empathize, and you might even learn something. The skills useful for acceptance are detailed later in this chapter in the Listening section.

Realness: Be yourself. Noted author and therapist Virginia Satir puts it this way: "Successfully hiding your feelings . . . takes a kind of skill most people don't really have. So their efforts often turn out to be like the traditional ostrich with its head in the sand. It thinks it's safely hidden, but of course it is not. We who delude ourselves like the ostrich often feel misunderstood and betrayed by others." Your manner will appear more natural and people will be more at ease with you if you express yourself honestly and with openness. Remember how important nonverbal cues are in communication, and how difficult it can be to control all those channels if you are not reasonably open with your feelings. People will simply place more trust in leaders who appear comfortable with and accepting of themselves.

Successful leaders use these foundational approaches and the other communication techniques described in this chapter to develop rapport with those they are speaking with. Rapport is a relationship of respect and understanding that allows people to communicate effectively together. Though it is more difficult to develop, rapport can exist even between those with opposing views. The leader, in a power position in the group, can develop this type of relationship only through an honest commitment to empathy, acceptance, and realness. Participants, given enough time, will see through anything less.

Setting the Tone

In addition to enabling leaders to communicate effectively with their groups, good communication on the leader's part also sets the tone for all communication in the group. Effective communication among group members is often vital for safety reasons. It can also enhance participants' enjoyment and learning. On an extended or challenging trip, good communication among group members isn't just nice—it's a necessity. For this reason the following chapter, Expedition Behavior, addresses approaches to cultivating good communication skills and group dynamics within your group. The leader's behavior and effective communication skills, however, will be what really define the communication behavior of the group. The more effective you are, the higher the bar you set for your group to aspire to.

Noise

The term *noise* is used here to refer to anything that interferes with the accurate coding, transmission, and decoding of a message. The roar of the river, two people talking at the same time, or mosquitoes flying around your head are examples of *external noise*. *Internal noise* is the dialogue that takes place within your head. Listening to someone occupies only a fraction of our incredible brainpower—the rest of that mental capacity is free to wander to other subjects. You might employ your brain to consider all the verbal and nonverbal cues you are receiving, or you might let noise slip in and think about the view, lunch, or the next thing you're going to say. The trouble with the human brain is that it isn't terribly good at multitasking. Once you stop directing 100 percent of your attention to the sender's message, you're going to miss out on messages, particularly the important, nonverbal ones. *Semantic noise* is the final type of noise, and it interferes with accurate decoding of messages. This third type of noise occurs because the words, symbols, and nonverbal cues the sender uses may be decoded to mean a variety of different things to the listener. Virginia Satir places some of the blame for inaccurately decoded messages on the sender and some with listeners who guess at meanings instead of clarifying them. In *The New Peoplemaking,* Satir writes:

> I believe this guessing procedure is responsible for a great deal of unnecessary estrangement between people. Part of the problem is that we are such sloppy talkers! We use words such as it, that, and this without clarifying them. . . . Any listener in this situation is in an impossible bind if the rules require that he act as though he understood.

Many of the techniques in this chapter are designed to counteract all three forms of noise and enable senders to code clearer messages and listeners to correctly decode them.

Listening

Communication is more than sending messages; the effective leader must also be skilled at receiving messages. Attentive listening combined with verbal engagement—often called active listening—is a communication and a group awareness skill. Like the seasoned outdoorsperson who notices sights and sounds that the newcomer will miss, outdoor leaders need to develop a similar skill with people. These verbal and nonverbal communication cues that others may miss help a leader understand the members of the group.

The active listener is invested in understanding and accepting the intent of the speaker as fully as possible. The concept for these active listening guidelines is drawn from the work of Carl Rogers and Virginia Satir.

Full Attention: Eliminate the noise—be free of your own internal dialogue, as well as other distractions. Multitasking results in missed messages. Guessing to fill in this missed information may result in an inaccurate understanding of the speaker's message.

Listen, Don't Assume: This is a complex task that entails listening to the speaker without overlaying your own attitudes and preconceived ideas. The ability to listen without making assumptions is more difficult when you, as the recipient, have an emotional response to the message. A high degree of self-awareness will aid you in keeping your response separate from the speaker's message.

Be Aware of Verbal and Nonverbal Cues: These cues give critical context to words. Think of verbal and nonverbal messages as pieces of a jigsaw puzzle—the more pieces you have, the clearer your picture of the sender's message. Awareness of these cues can also help the listener understand the meaning of a message even when it lacks clarity.

Confirm the Message: Respond to the speaker in a way that reflects your best understanding of his or her communication. This need not be complex but should confirm that the speaker has been heard and that the message has been correctly understood. Allow the sender to clarify the message if needed.

Consciousness of these four points will aid your active listening skills. These skills can also be improved by observing others whose communication skills you respect and through listening skills training. Listening is one half of the communication process—ask questions to clarify the intent of the speaker but be careful not to complicate this part of the process by injecting your bias. The listening process is where you truly put your empathy and acceptance abilities to use. Successful listening is greatly appreciated by others and opens the door to improving your leadership with the new insight you will gain.

Sending Messages

What people often think of as communicating is sending messages. Messages, or course, may be sent to one person or a group of people. The same concepts apply, though you may have to speak louder with a larger audience. Remember the concept of realness, or being yourself, and find ways to put any of the following concepts that work for you to use.

Own Your Messages: In any communication situation you should take ownership of your opinions by using "I-messages" and feelings by expressing yourself using *I, me,* or *my* (the first-person singular pronoun). As a leader your statements wield significant power—don't state your personal perspectives as broad truths. Avoid saying, "You don't understand"; instead say, "I don't feel you understand." The first statement leaves no room for debate. The latter statement—*I don't feel you understand*—expresses your personal opinion and does not attempt to present this opinion as fact. This is a subtle difference, however; when approaching difficult issues with participants (or co-leaders), exactly how you express yourself can mean the difference between a constructive conversation and an argument.

Shying away from phrases such as *the group thinks* or *people say* is advisable. As a leader you should take ownership of your opinions without generalizing them as others' opinions; nor should you state them as fact. If the group really thinks something, let the group members express this to the participant. Don't do their work for them. Attention to how you are expressing yourself can have a profound effect on how the message is received.

Carefully Craft Your Message: While it can be challenging, effective outdoor leaders work hard to keep important communications organized and individual messages concise. Make sure you're finished with one subject and have answered any questions before moving on to another. We have all interrupted another discussion to say something like, "Oh, I forgot to tell you before when we were discussing the crevasse rescue . . . and don't forget because this is really important." This is not the most effective means of communicating your message and can be avoided by roughly outlining your communications before you speak. By presenting your information and instructions in a structured manner, you not only ensure optimal attention from your participants but also reinforce your role as the knowledgeable and trustworthy leader.

Filter Information: As a leader you should *filter information,* disseminating a steady stream (sometimes a trickle is enough) of relevant information—avoid damming the flow or releasing a flood. Ask yourself the question "What's important now?" and remember this pertinent question by the acronym *WIN.* When leading trips, I'm often tempted to enthusiastically impart all of my wisdom at once, but check myself by remembering WIN. Extraneous information can overwhelm the channels of communication. On the flip side, too little communication can leave people feeling disenfranchised or with insufficient information to safely engage in an activity. The proper level of filtering is a judgment call you make with every new group and in every stage of a group's development.

Repeat Yourself: This is advice you won't often hear, especially when you're communicating to a group. Not everyone may receive and decode your message successfully on the first try. Repetition can run the risk of annoying people, but some messages, especially those related to safety, are too important for people to miss. Keep repeating the message until you can confirm that it's understood.

Change Channels: If you're on the verbal channel telling the group about why they should unbuckle the hip belt on their pack to cross a river, switch channels by giving a visual demonstration (this can also inject a little humor into a serious issue). Another way to change channels is by allowing others to have a significant voice or teach something whenever possible. Varying what channels messages are sent on is an effective way to get them to participants. With creativity, alternating channels can make the process of repeating yourself less annoying and more effective.

Alex Kosseff

Leaders sometimes struggle to maintain the attention of the entire group—
the position of individuals can be very important.

Fit Your Message to the Recipient: A message needs to be understand-able to its listener. Outdoor recreation is loaded with jargon. Don't use terms such as *belay, bivy, expedition behavior, active listening,* or *AMC* unless you're absolutely sure those the message is intended for will understand. Likewise, fit the message to the age of the recipient. Not only are messages that cannot be decoded useless, they also set up a barrier between the sender and the recipient. This barrier can be exac-erbated when only some of the recipients can understand the message; the others may feel excluded or even act as if they understand when they really don't.

Physical Position

When a group of outdoor leaders gathers, you'll notice that they always form a circle for discussion. It's automatic. Likewise, participants often get used to "circling up" very quickly. Why sit or stand in a circle? It gives everyone equal standing. It allows each member of the group to see the faces and expressions of the other group members. It's inclusive in a way that no other formation can be. If you're interested in the one-way delivery of information in a lecture style, you might choose some other arrangement. For any other situation the circle is ideal.

When communicating one on one, but also in a group, eye contact is important. People have varying tolerance for eye contact. When speaking directly to an individual, or when listening to one individual, try looking directly at him or her. If this makes the individual uncomfortable, avert your eyes a little. Again, the circle is key to allowing for eye contact.

Within a circle there are still inequalities. Height is the major one. If some people are standing and some sitting, it creates a different dynamic and makes it harder to see each person's face. Those higher up will tend to be more dominant in this situation. Even if people are sitting down and one person is perched atop a convenient boulder, it creates a different dynamic. The best place for a group discussion is a level and comfortable area where everyone can sit. Of course, this is not always possible. This is why outdoor leaders are adept at the art of making do.

A Note on Manners

Part of effective communication is being polite or using old-fashioned good manners. Good manners call for respect for those speaking to you or those to whom you're speaking. By setting the tone and using common courtesy, you'll encourage your group to do the same with each other. Say *please* and *thank you* when appropriate. Compliment people and refrain

> *"Bright people—especially bright young people—often do not understand that manners are the 'lubricating oil' of an organization."*
>
> —PETER DRUCKER, THE ESSENTIAL DRUCKER

from unnecessary criticism. Use sarcasm with extreme caution; some people may not understand your humor and will take it personally. Use appropriate language. Swearing can be common in the outdoors, but it's unnecessary and is offensive or off-putting to many people. Sometimes the old stuff is the good stuff—if nothing else from this chapter sticks with you, remembering to mind your manners will get you a long way.

Good Communication

Like many aspects of outdoor leadership, good communication is an art. The formative moments of good communication come early on the trip, when leaders must both state a commitment to good communication and model the skills themselves. As leaders—brimming with empathy, acceptance, and realness—engage in easy conversation, participants become more at ease. In order for communication to be effective in a group situation and for rapport to develop, those communicating must know something about one another. Once rapport develops, the leader must remain committed to the principles and techniques of this chapter—although there is some more freedom. The leader who has developed a rapport with one or more participants can be freer to lead the communications in new directions. Before rapport develops, it may be difficult for the leader to get participants to discuss their true reasons for participating in the trip, especially if they are emotional in nature. Once rapport develops, there is a relationship and trust. Participants will be more open to discussing their reasons for participation.

Good communication begins with listening and depends on your confidence. Knowing when to accept your own decoding of a message and when to seek confirmation takes confidence. It also takes confidence to speak with authority when that's what's needed. It takes confidence to be real and project some of who you are without knowing how your participants will receive you. Although effective communication demands hard work on the part of the leader, the model of communication it provides for participants offers the opportunity for sharing among all members.

RECOMMENDED READING

Hersey, Paul, Kenneth Blanchard, and Dewey Johnson, *Management of Organizational Behavior: Leading Human Resources,* 8th ed., Upper Saddle River, New Jersey: Prentice-Hall, 2001.

Johnson, David W., and Frank P. Johnson, *Joining Together: Group Theory and Group Skills,* 7th ed., Boston: Allyn and Bacon, 2000.

Kalisch, Kenneth R., *The Role of the Instructor in the Outward Bound Educational Process,* Three Lakes, Wisconsin: Author, 1979.

◆ Rogers, Carl R., *On Becoming a Person: A Therapist's View of Psychotherapy,* New York: Houghton Mifflin, 1989.

◆ Satir, Virginia, *The New Peoplemaking,* Mountain View, California: Science and Behavior Books, 1988.

◆ = Advanced Recommendation

CHAPTER II

Expedition Behavior

*E*xpedition behavior, referred to simply as EB by outdoor leaders, is a term used to describe all of the interpersonal relationships and interactions on an outdoor program. When everyone gets along and helps each other out we say there's good EB. When the skies are cloudy all day and people are grumpy, mean, and selfish, we have poor EB. This book is founded on the assumption, introduced in the first chapter, that leadership has caring at its core. Good expedition behavior involves the transfer of this ideal from the leader to the members of the group. This is more than a rosy ideal—it's a practical approach to helping group members work together to accomplish shared objectives.

The term *expedition behavior* originated with the late Paul Petzoldt, founder of the National Outdoor Leadership School and the Wilderness Education Association, climber, and general wilderness guru. Petzoldt writes in *The New Wilderness Handbook*:

> Human nature influences the success or failure, comfort or discomfort, safety or danger of an outdoor experience as much as equipment, logistics, trail techniques, rations, and other basic organizational concerns.

Although a breakdown in personal relations between individuals is encouraged by poor pre-planning, even the well-thought-out and well-equipped outing might face failure, injury, or death if good Expedition Behavior practices are missing. In high altitudes or during adventure-some, energy-draining endeavors, outdoorsmen must make a concerted effort for the consideration of companions in addition to securing their own personal comfort and safety.

Petzoldt was concerned that the emphasis in outdoor leadership was on choosing leaders with an impressive-looking record of peaks bagged or rivers run and that interpersonal skills were being ignored. With the development of the expedition behavior concept, Petzoldt set out to correct the imbalance he had perceived in the leaders' skills.

When Petzoldt writes of potential repercussions of poor EB, he is direct and backs up his points with numerous real-life examples. Further defining the root of the issue, Petzoldt says: "Simply, poor Expedition Behavior is a breakdown in human relations caused by self-ishness, rationalization, ignorance of personal faults, dodging blame or responsibility, physical weakness, and, in extreme cases, not being able to risk one's own survival to insure that of a companion." In writing and practice Petzoldt did not stop there but went on to make expedition behavior a pivotal concept to outdoor leadership in the United States and around the world.

Scott Smalley, the education coordinator for Vermont's Green Mountain Club and a former NOLS instructor, can bag peaks and run rivers with the best of them, but in the Petzoldt tradition he also has a serious dedication to good group dynamics. "A student on one of my NOLS courses changed the way I think about EB," relates Smalley. "He said to the group 'Do you know that *EB* backward is *BE?*'" That convenient language trick reconfigured the way Smalley teaches and thinks about EB: "I tell people that EB is BE, or being—a whole way of interacting with others." He continues, "At its ideal, EB probably shares some common elements with Buddhism and is about being mindful and aware in relationships. Like being a good Buddhist, good expedition behavior is almost subconscious and requires many years of practice." For a simple perspective, Smalley suggests thinking of each member of the group as a petal, with EB being what makes the flower whole. While the petals are pretty in and of themselves, the whole flower is truly the thing of beauty. Expedition behavior melds individuals into a beautiful

At the heart of good EB is respectful communication.

group—because it allows people to work together; they achieve lofty goals that would be impossible for any individual acting alone.

Expedition behavior skills are a basic element of your caring leadership, but to be effective EB must be an objective of the entire group. Development of the relationships and skills necessary for good expedition behavior takes time. The leader must plant the seeds of good EB early in a trip and then provide frequent watering. The seeds are much more likely to fully germinate over the duration of an extended trip than they are in the course of a weekend outing. Once the seeds you have planted germinate, you will need to nurture, mulch, and prune. Even the best groups have conflicts and issues that must be brought into the open and given attention. Only if concerns continue to be addressed throughout the life of the group will it be able to grow into a more cohesive unit.

Good Expedition Behavior

Each leader who is dedicated to good expedition behavior will have his or her own perspective on what its key components are. The ten principles of good EB listed below are one attempt at defining the concept. These principles will guide new leaders for whom EB is not yet second nature, and they provide a way to guide participants. It cannot be overstated that the best way to guide a group toward working well together is to establish some type of expedition behavior principles early on. You might use this list as a starting point in discussions with your participants. While these principles are focused on interactions within the group, good EB also extends to interactions with other groups you encounter, to land managers, and to the land itself through dedication to Leave No Trace principles.

> *" When the pursuit of natural harmony is a shared journey, great heights can be attained. "*
>
> —LYNN HILL, FIRST PERSON TO FREE-CLIMB THE NOSE OF EL CAPITAN

Ten Principles of Good Expedition Behavior

1. **Self-Awareness:** This constant theme in this book means that you are aware of your own needs, physical and mental state, and the effect you have on the rest of the group. Be aware of who you are and do not act in a manner that you are uncomfortable with or does not fit your personality.

2. **Self-Leadership:** To be an integral part of a group, you must take care of yourself and not impose avoidable demands on the group. Self-awareness is about identifying needs, while self-leadership means you take the initiative to address them. Eating regularly, keeping yourself hydrated with water you treat properly, preventing blisters, using sunscreen as needed, and keeping your gear organized so you don't hold up the group are examples of self-leadership.

3. **Selflessness:** Ask not what your group can do for you—ask what you can do for your group. While we are unlikely to hear another president utter words to this effect in the near future, this unselfish attitude can function on a smaller stage.

4. **Commitment:** *EB* is just a backcountry name for "teamwork," and like a sports team the wilderness expedition functions best when there is commitment to common goals. The group should do its utmost to ensure that these are goals benefiting all group members and that all group members meet them.

AMC file photo

Self-leadership means taking care of yourself so you do not create problems for the group. Here a participant addresses hot spots before they become blisters.

5. **Tolerance:** You don't have to be lifelong friends with everyone in the group, but you do need to accept them for who they are. Work to not take offense easily.

6. **Consideration:** Be polite and avoid testing the tolerance of others. Sarcasm or remarks that others find offensive can be very damaging to relationships in a small group. Respect the time and personal space of others.

7. **Trust:** Be relatively confident that the others will successfully fulfill any specific roles they are given and that they will practice good EB—this trust is often self-fulfilling, as people step up to the roles they have been given responsibility for. Trust, whether it's letting someone else pack the food or sharing your most intimate fears, means making yourself vulnerable, because benefit or harm is in the hands of another.

8. **Communication:** One of the basic tools that makes good EB possible is open and honest communication. Make use of the tools outlined in the previous chapter. Always consider what information you have and what would be useful to others.

AMC file photo

Expedition behavior involves selflessness and always being willing to help others. Here a participant helps another across a stream.

9. **Humility:** Even if you're a great and famous outdoor leader, approach all situations and individuals knowing that you may still be able to learn. Learn to rely not only on yourself, but also on others in the group, especially turning to those with more skill in certain areas than you have.

10. **Sense of Humor:** Have fun and be playful! Even in the worst of circumstances an active sense of humor can be invaluable in lifting the sprits of the group. In the most unpleasant weather or when tension in the group is high, a silly song or a funny observation can improve everyone's mood. But use caution in poking fun at individuals— even if someone laughs at his or her own expense, it may still be hurtful on a more personal level.

Says Scott Smalley, "Good EB is about straightening out the tent's guylines at night, saving the last tea bag for someone else, making hot drinks before the rest of the group emerges from their tents, or figuring out which way to go but then letting someone else do it for themselves." These sound like genuinely nice things to do that don't require much effort, but reality is that making expedition behavior work requires constant attention. There is also another side to good EB that the group

> " *It's good to have an end to journey toward; but it's the journey that matters in the end.* "
>
> —URSULA K. LE GUIN

has to buy in to in order for it to work. Scott states it simply: "Fully committing to good EB lowers the group potential in terms of peak ascents." Instead of focusing on getting yourself to the summit, good EB dictates that you should focus on getting your entire, well-functioning group there. Individuals who could have made the summit—or accomplished the goal, whatever it is—will sometimes be held back by the group. As more and more people venture outside with specific lists of peaks to climb, rivers to run, or records to break, this needs to be taken into consideration before a trip so people come into an experience with common expectations.

Poor Expedition Behavior

An individual's basic needs, as identified in chapter 6—food, water, shelter, sleep, and a sense of security—provide a psychological and physiological foundation for good expedition behavior. Participants, used to having these needs met, may have a very difficult time coping if they are deprived, even for a short time. Paul Petzoldt says people can become like "animals in the jungle" when put into a situation of deprivation or potential deprivation.

Deprivation of basic needs leads to decreased mental function and irritability, both of which lead to friction among group members. This friction is the enemy of good EB. Other potential sources of individual and group frustration and unease that can lead to friction among group members include:

▶ Lack of agreement on shared goals.

▶ Different attitudes and expectations.

▶ Varied skill and energy levels.

▶ Unequal tolerance for risk and adversity.

▶ Anxiety about ability to perform required skills.

▶ Individual behavior patterns.

► Apprehension about the future.

► Feelings of dependence on the leader and others.

► Nervousness about being in a new environment.

Scott Smalley points out that we often go on outdoor trips to "get away from it all," but once there we wind up in closer proximity to a group of people, sometimes strangers, than we would ever be at home. "Tents, snow shelters, cooking areas, belay ledges, and even hiking together put people in a cramped space," says Smalley. These close living conditions persist, with little refuge, for the duration of the trip. It would be difficult to craft a better recipe for friction among group members than coping with these many unusual and challenging conditions.

The road to good EB can be a long one, and for many leaders and participants it often starts with identifying poor EB. For Scott Smalley, an understanding of EB came during a monthlong wilderness leadership course after he had already been in outdoor leadership positions for several years. "I wound up in a tent with a friend, Jeff, from college; we were both twenty-one or twenty-two years old," says Smalley. "The third person in the tent was a woman, Simone, whom we had just met." He continues, "Jeff and I were clicking, we were excited to be there, and it seemed the course was going well for us." Scott and Jeff were openly very confident and excited to be on the course, but Simone was not very engaged with them. "Looking back I see that we were pretty exclusive," admits Smalley. "We didn't do a good job of including her or teaching things that we knew but that were new to her."

Compounding a tense relationship, Simone developed serious blisters several days into the course. This meant that Scott and Jeff grudgingly had to carry more of the gear for their small group. After ten sometimes frustrating days sharing the tent, the groups were switched around and Scott wound up with new tentmates. "It wasn't until several days later, during an individual check-in with the instructors, that I realized there was an ongoing problem," he admits. "The instructors pointed out to me that I still was not getting along with Simone and they encouraged me to talk to her." Scott thought things over, and on day twenty he took the advice and went and apologized to Simone for excluding her. This, he recalls, "broke down a wall between us." Scott thought Simone was just a quiet person, but this turned out not to be true: "She told me that she had been intimidated by us." Scott realized the unintentional impact of his and Jeff's behavior had been more serious than he had imagined.

Once Scott and Simone had opened up a dialogue, he found that she was more interesting and likable than he had imagined. She also turned out to be the best rock climber in the group. Near the end of the course Scott and Simone chose to partner for a daylong multipitch climb, leaving their instructors impressed with the improvement they were able to realize in their relationship. While EB can get a lot worse than what Smalley was involved with here (there are stories of expedition members attacking each other with ice axes), this was a major learning experience for him, and probably for Simone as well. This experience also proved important when, six years later, Scott and Simone wound up leading a rock climbing course together.

Symptoms of Poor Expedition Behavior

Many different types of behavior are indicative of poor EB. Detailed here are a few of the more common symptoms seen on outdoor programs. Often people resort to these behaviors when they're frustrated and there's friction among group members. At the same time, these behaviors can be a sign of participants trying to preserve their self-esteem in a situation where they are not comfortable.

1. **Rationalization** occurs when individuals do not accept personal responsibility for the role they played in failures. They say things such as, "I didn't really care about that climb anyway" or "I wouldn't have burned the rice if we had a good stove."

2. **Scapegoating** refers to the practice of blaming another for one's own or the group's frustrations or failures. These people might say, "If Suzy hadn't kept me up all night snoring, I would have had enough energy to paddle the entire route" or "We would have made it up the peak, but Jason was too slow." Because it's contrary to the ideal of working together toward common goals and polarizes individuals against one another, scapegoating can be very damaging to expedition behavior in a group.

3. **Regression** occurs when an individual behaves in the manner of

someone less mature. The participant who kicks the kayak after failing to successfully run a rapid can be said to be regressing.

Individuals who rationalize, scapegoat, or regress tend to become isolated in the group. While it's not ideal to have an individual isolated in the group, even more damaging is the effect the poor expedition behavior of one can have on everyone else. Small groups tend to develop ingrained patterns of behavior, or splinter into cliques that find some common element to bond around. In *Management of Organizational Behavior,* Hersey, Blanchard, and Johnson write: "Misery does not love just any company; it loves other miserable company." People who are unhappy tend to gravitate toward each other. Happy and positive people tend to flock together as well, but the effect may not be as strong. A group of miserable people commiserating with one another is also uniquely—I have to put it this way—miserable. The effect of small subgroups or cliques in an already small group can be strong and may make others feel as if they need to go along or they will be ostracized. The leader, as we will see, needs to be proactive in efforts to address poor expedition behavior in the group.

Making Expedition Behavior Work

Adversity is one of the greatest threats to good expedition behavior, but simultaneously it's the one factor that will push a group to achieve good EB. Some form of adversity is actually a prerequisite for the development of highly effective groups in any setting.

If you're running trips with a low level of adversity, you're unlikely to get your group to gel and fully adopt good EB, but your group also has less need for working together in this manner. This is also the case for short trips, where participants have less commitment to harmonious relations—they know they'll be going home soon. We are, after all, talking about *expedition* behavior, and if you lead relatively mellow adventure travel programs or daylong cross-country ski trips, the concepts are useful but somewhat less valuable than they are for a ten-day backpacking trip. It will be up to you to decide how much to focus on

EB, but as the rigors and length of the trip increase, so will the level of adversity, which increases the applicability of EB.

Adversity is a highly subjective concept, and a grueling slog for one may be a figurative (and literal) walk in the park for another. This may result in a group that has difficulty progressing among the levels of group development covered in chapter 6, but it also impedes the group from adopting good EB. The participant who feels the trip is a "walk in the park" may perceive little incentive—benevolence aside—for the kind of mutual support and respect that good EB entails. To make EB work, then, the leader must ensure that the goals of that group are just that—group goals. For example, instead of each individual focusing on hiking a full 10-mile hike, the goal of every group member becomes making sure the entire group hikes the 10 miles.

Introduce Expedition Behavior Early On: Again, Scott Smalley: "You need to start early with EB. Once we're under way on a longer trip, I ask the group to come up with a mission statement." He helps set up the discussion and lets people know that the mission statement should be inclusive of the entire group, but then he allows the group to commit to a mission statement they believe in. His example from a trip: "We agree to work together to climb six peaks, each catch a fish, eat good food, and return without injury" is succinct and commits the group to assisting each other in reaching their goals. Living up to this mission statement, Smalley says, "requires real commitment." If you're leading a trip for friends, a club, or another situation in which it's possible to meet in advance of the trip, you may want to develop a mission statement then. This avoids any controversy on the trip and the potential for "buyer's regret" if people feel the trip isn't what they expected.

Though I will try it in the future, I've yet to have a group come up with a mission statement like Scott suggests, but I have had groups develop their own list of EB-type principles that they commit to live by. It's much more valuable for the group to do this exercise and express how they would like to be treated than to deliver a list of principles that may be viewed as "rules." This is one way that EB can be addressed very early in a trip, which is critical for setting the tone and helping to prevent friction from developing. Don't wait to talk about EB until you perceive problems developing in the group or your introduction of EB will be perceived as an attempt to remedy problems in the group, not a fundamental expectation. Even on a short trip, take the time to do some sort of tone setting on how you expect people to work together.

Use Teachable Moments: As EB-related issues arise during your trip, do not ignore them; use them as teachable moments and reinforce the original agreement you reached with the group. Don't preach, but make observations that may lead to greater insight among group members. You may notice, for instance, that members of the group need a break but aren't saying anything—violating the self-leadership and communication principles of good EB. You might let the group keep going until the situation becomes more acute and let them learn from that, or you can ask the group if anyone needs to stop and get them to again talk about good EB. Alternatively, you might just mention, "I'm really hungry; anyone else interested in breaking for a snack soon?" When you do this you are teaching and, importantly, you are modeling good EB.

Model Good Expedition Behavior: EB will not work for you or your groups if it exists only in theory, and leader modeling is very helpful. When inattention leads to a spilled dinner pot, spicing up your mac and cheese with a pinch of grit and a few pine needles, you don't want to scroll down the EB list until you hit upon "tolerance." You should be first to say, "Don't worry, it's no big deal—let us help you pick up the pasta." Participants will follow your lead. EB must become the way you act, not a list of appropriate behaviors to demonstrate. When you've accomplished this, you're ready to start your participants along the same path. Good EB for your group begins with your modeling of it, and doing so in a manner that makes it seem natural, not forced. If good EB is perceived by participants as the way you lead your life, not something you do when you're the "leader," they'll be most likely to see you as a role model.

Cultivation

Consistent cultivation of expedition behavior will yield the most successful groups. The seed is best planted early and nurtured through careful example. When problems arise, don't be shy about dealing with them immediately. Nothing can spoil a group like a problem that's allowed to fester while people pretend nothing is wrong. Ultimately the objective is to pull all the participants together into something unique and special—like the petals of a flower forming a more perfect whole.

RECOMMENDED READING

◆ Gookin, John, Molly Doran, and Rachael Green, eds., *2000 NOLS Leadership Education Toolbox,* Lander, Wyoming: National Outdoor Leadership School, 2000.

Harvey, Mark, *The National Outdoor Leadership School's Wilderness Guide: The Classic Handbook,* New York: Simon & Schuster, 1999.

Johnson, David W., *Reaching Out: Interpersonal Effectiveness and Self-Actualization,* 5th ed., Boston: Allyn and Bacon, 1993.

Johnson, David W., and Frank P. Johnson, *Joining Together: Group Theory and Group Skills,* 7th ed., Boston: Allyn and Bacon, 2000.

Kalisch, Kenneth R., *The Role of the Instructor in the Outward Bound Educational Process,* Three Lakes, Wisconsin: Author, 1979.

National Outdoor Leadership School, *NOLS Wilderness Educator Notebook,* 1999 ed., Lander, Wyoming: The National Outdoor Leadership School, 1999.

Petzoldt, Paul, *The New Wilderness Handbook,* New York: W. W. Norton, 1984.

◆ = Advanced Recommendation

CHAPTER 12

Risk

We define *risk* as the potential for suffering some harm or loss. *Risk management* attempts to reduce the potential for harm or loss and minimize the effect of any harm or loss that does occur on leaders, organizations, and those associated with them. The harm or loss referred to can be physical, such as an injury or illness; psychological (mental trauma or social discomfort); or financial (as the result of a lawsuit or damage to property). Risk management is what we do to control the probability of loss in order to allow leaders and organizations to continue carrying out their missions. Ethically, as an outdoor leader or a program manager, you have an obligation to your participants and fellow leaders to minimize—whenever feasible—the danger of harm or loss they face on your trips. Outdoor leaders and organizations also have to be mindful of liability issues. However, the duty to minimize risk must always be balanced against the meaningful gain a program provides.

Corporate risk management often works to ensure that a corporation will not go bankrupt if sales are slow or a physical asset is lost (a factory burns down, for example). Outdoor leaders typically work with one tremendously precious asset—people. The tools we work with typically are not very valuable. If a backpacking stove, a climbing rope, or even a whitewater raft is damaged or destroyed, it's just not a major issue. We focus on protecting people, and to do this we attempt to improve safety practices in our programs. Secondary to protecting people is protecting the assets and interests of the organization. This is secondary because it is less important than people's health and well-being, but also because if we can avoid harm to participants, the assets and interests of the organization aren't threatened.

This chapter addresses some basic concepts of risk management, how leaders manage risk in the field, and briefly touches on risk management on an organizational level. An additional resource is found in appendix B, where attorney Catherine Hansen-Stamp covers the basics of risk management from a legal perspective.

Risk-Management Concepts————

Inherent Risk: Every field of human endeavor has some level of risk associated with it. This risk can be minimized, but every activity has *inherent risk* that is difficult to eradicate. This is actually useful for us, as some level of risk is central to the experience we provide for our participants. The outdoors it not a video game where you just press RESET and everything's okay. Part of the challenge and educational value of outdoor recreation rests in its reality—actions in the outdoors have direct repercussions. Typically these repercussions are minor—hunger, fatigue, failure to reach some predetermined objective—but at times they can be more serious.

Risk can and should be minimized to an acceptable level, but it's impossible to completely eliminate—that is why we speak in terms of managing, but not eliminating, risk. The best way to think about risk is on a sliding scale—the level of risk can be increased or decreased in small degrees. Each degree of variation is the result of small actions taken (or not taken) by the leader and any sponsoring organization. The definition of *acceptable risk* tells us that there's some room for programs to operate on different parts of this scale. The goal, however, must always be to reduce the levels of risk whenever it is possible to do so without excessively compromising the mission and the objectives of the program.

Acceptable Risk: The maximum level of risk that is ethically and socially acceptable is *acceptable risk*. This is a simple definition for a slippery concept. One argument is that activities have an acceptable level of risk when people are willing to engage in them. This is ethically suspect because sometimes participants may not have sufficient information and perspective to make an informed decision on the risk involved in the activity. Attempting to define *acceptable risk* thus falls on those engaged in outdoor leadership. There is an obvious ethical incentive to manage risk at an acceptable level, but there is a practical one as well. The better we are able to manage risk and justify those risks we do take, the less control will slip into the hands of insurance companies, courts, and the media—institutions with less dedication to outdoor recreation and education than most leaders.

Programs have different levels of acceptable risk. The level of acceptable risk in an environmental education program for schoolkids is less than that for a mountaineering training program for adults. It is difficult to quantify the level of risk, so for practical purposes leaders and programs should strive for a level of risk that is consistent with the program's mission and goals, as well as the age and expectations of the participants. In seeking to understand acceptable risk, leaders and trip-sponsoring organizations must also look to the practices and level of risk that exist on similar activities run by different leaders and organizations.

Actual and Perceived Risk: This book, and this chapter in particular, focuses on reducing the risk of harm to participants. A skilled outdoor leader can reduce the likelihood of serious harm in most activities to a negligible level. In rock climbing we minimize risk through the careful selection of routes, the use of proper technical gear in a belay system, and training participants in procedures. When done correctly, these steps reduce the *actual risk* in instructional climbing programs to a very low level. Participants well informed about the safety systems still face the challenge posed by *perceived risk,* which comes with the exposure and the need to trust oneself, others, and the technical system. Rock climbing is a dramatic example, but perceived risks exist in all outdoor pursuits and present challenges important to many programs and participants as we effectively minimize the actual risk.

PARTICIPANT SCREENING

Successful participant screening is a challenge for outdoor organizations. In some organizations, screening is performed by designated staff; however, in other organizations—particularly small or volunteer ones—it may be carried out by leaders. Participants are screened to attempt to determine if they are physically, medically, or emotionally fit or appropriate to participate in a program. Screening may also consider whether participants have an appropriate level of skills for the activity, and in some situations if they have the appropriate clothing or equipment. Looking at risk factors effective screening might possibly help prevent medical problems such as heart attacks during programs. This process should also identify issues for leaders to be aware of in the field—prior injuries, allergies, illnesses, and the like. Screening can help programs run more smoothly by considering physical fitness, emotional issues, and skill level—issues that can also have a major effect on the safety of the individual and the rest of the group in a backcountry situation. In the ideal scenario a program will be able to screen participants by finding the right trip for each individual; however, this is not always possible when the range of offerings is limited.

Screening is often accomplished with the aid of a medical and health history form that participants or their medical provider complete, and may also involve gathering additional information. There are many different levels of detail and scrutiny that an organization can delve into. The highest level of scrutiny is certainly appropriate for extended programs venturing into remote regions. While there's considerable room for discretion on most programs, until a consensus emerges in the industry some level of participant screening is generally appropriate.

Telling applicants that they cannot engage in a program can be a delicate proposition. There are legal obligations, including the Americans with Disabilities Act, under which your program must make "reasonable accommodations" or modifications, if appropriate, for those with disabilities. Consult an attorney with knowledge in this area for guidance on the legal do's and don'ts of screening. A set of guidelines for screening is helpful from a practical standpoint and may also help address some of the legal concerns.

Risk Management in the Field——————

The safety of the group, and the value of all other risk-management efforts, hinges on the critical yet often subjective decisions leaders make in the field. Participant and leader safety—themes that pervade this book—comprise field risk management. Trip planning, awareness, and expedition behavior are all elements of risk management—and major elements of risk management are included in almost every chapter of this book. The relevant guidance from each of these chapters is not repeated here. Instead, the focus of this chapter is on incorporating safety into your decision making as a leader and weighing the relative risks of different options.

Risk Assessment and Management System

The premise is simple: To maintain risk at an acceptable level you must assess what risks there are and the threat they pose. This assessment must often be accomplished on the go, in a narrow sliver of time, with only a portion of the necessary information. Once the assessment is completed, your task is to manage these risks to maintain them at a minimal level. Sometimes circumstances will eliminate options—if, for instance, your only choices are to cross an unstable avalanche slope or reascend the peak you're coming down from in a blizzard, you can no longer avoid the risk by spending the day in camp. While good planning and constant awareness can help eliminate many risks, some will always remain. Risk is part of outdoor adventure. The leader's role is to keep risks to a minimum while at the same time allowing participants to enjoy and learn from the experience they signed up for.

Assessing Risk in the Field

Part of the challenge of assessing risk in the field is that it originates with dangers that, in isolation, may not be significant concerns. Dangers are individual sources of risk. Take, for example, a trip participant who is swept downstream during an afternoon crossing of a river swollen with snowmelt; she emerges in the shallows downstream hypothermic and missing her pack. This incident resulted from the

Rock hopping across a stream can be very dangerous, involving numerous human and environmental dangers.

interplay of two broad types of dangers—human and environmental. Human dangers are ones we often have some control over—those involved in this accident might include inexperience, improper technique, excessive haste, and fatigue. Instructor judgment may itself, at times, be a human danger, but it is also what we most often rely upon to reduce or eliminate the human dangers presented in the group. On the other hand, environmental dangers, although they can often be avoided, are usually out of the leader's control. In this case the environmental dangers might include high water levels, poor footing, and cold water. None of the individual environmental or human dangers would have been likely to cause this incident on its own, however, putting them all together raises the risk greatly.

An accident is anything that happens that we hoped would not happen. They are typically the result of an interaction of environmental and human dangers. The risk of an accident is minimal if only human or only environmental dangers are present. Because there are almost always environmental dangers present, we can consider human dangers the trigger factors. The solution, however, is not just to reduce human dangers, but to reduce all dangers. To better understand this, let's consider how environmental and human dangers interact.

Returning to the example of the river crossing, consider how an

Holly Anderson

Human limitations, such as a lack of swimming ability, play a major part in determining the level of risk in this situation.

experienced, well-rested team taking its time might be able to cross the river safely even given the existing environmental dangers. After the incident the group could have waited until the following morning, and reviewed their technique. This could have eliminated the environmental danger of high water (the river had been swollen with afternoon snowmelt) and the human dangers of fatigue, haste, and improper technique. Consider the remaining human danger—inexperience—and the environmental dangers—poor footing and cold water. It is reasonable to assume that the level of risk would be greatly reduced. While it's impossible to assess this situation adequately on paper, I would be much more comfortable leading the group that had waited to cross.

Quantifying Relative Risk: While it's virtually impossible to accurately assess the relative risk of the different options an outdoor leader may face, it is possible to do a crude analysis: Multiply the number of environmental dangers by the number of human dangers. The result is your relative level of risk. Even if you never use this analysis tool in the field, it serves as an awareness-raising illustration of how environmental and human risks magnify each other.

Going back again to the river crossing, consider the four human dangers involved in the incident (inexperience, improper technique, excessive haste, and fatigue) and the three environmental factors (extremely high water, poor footing, and cold water). Multiply these dangers and we get a figure of twelve. Now consider a group that waited until the following morning—eliminating all the human dangers except inexperience, and eliminating one of the environmental dangers, leaving poor footing and cold water. The danger level the next morning would be a two. I have taken inexperienced groups across rivers with poor footing and cold water. The level of risk was reasonable—and our calculations indicate this.

Equation

TOTAL HUMAN DANGERS × TOTAL ENVIRONMENTAL DANGERS = RISK

Original River Crossing Attempt

4 HUMAN DANGERS × 3 ENVIRONMENTAL DANGERS = RISK LEVEL OF 12

Crossing the Following Morning

1 HUMAN DANGER × 2 ENVIRONMENTAL DANGERS = RISK LEVEL OF 2

Let's continue with the river crossing example and imagine that the group hiked in the area for another two weeks, gaining extensive practice at crossing rivers. They might come back to the original river and have no human dangers, because they are rested, not hurried, and no longer inexperienced. Zero human dangers multiplied by the remaining two environmental dangers leave us with a risk as close to zero as we can get. A group experienced in river crossing and properly employing their skills should be able to deal with poor footing and cold water. Remember, however, that nothing we ever do has a risk of zero—something can always go wrong. Two factors—judgment and awareness—can be flawed and lead you to believe there are no human risks, when, in fact, this is rarely the case. For this reason it is best to always consider that there is at least one lurking, but unidentified, danger.

Awareness and Judgment: Even leaders with incredible awareness of their groups will not be aware of everything. The group might return to the river crossing after two weeks. As a leader you might imagine there are no human risks at that point, but they creep in. The sneaky new human risk is called carelessness, and it has snuck in because the group thinks it has everything under control. Furthermore, three members of the group might be having a quiet feud—in jumps poor expedition behavior that may cause these group members to work poorly together. You might not be aware of the EB issue or you might incorrectly judge it not to be a problem. All of a sudden you have two human risk factors instead of none and your risk level is back up to four—worse than the morning after the initial incident.

Along with the human risk factors that a leader might be unaware of or judge unimportant, there might be additional environmental dangers as well. The tremendous afternoon snowmelt might have rearranged the

Avalanches, such as these in the Alaska Range, present a serious environmental danger, even in less rugged terrain.

Alex Kosseff

river bottom over the course of the two weeks since the group had last crossed the river. In addition to poor footing there are now dangerous drop-offs where the water goes from 2 feet to 6 feet deep. Even if you are aware of the drop-off you may not judge it important. The point of this is not to make you completely paranoid but to indicate that awareness is never complete; as leaders we must always be alert to unknown danger.

Severity: Identifying environmental and human dangers helps us understand the likelihood of a problem. The severity of risk is another factor that must be considered in decision making. The environmental hazard might be poison ivy or it might be avalanche potential. As a leader you might be willing to risk poison ivy in order to hike a certain route. Poison ivy has a range of severity—I once had a participant who had to be hospitalized with it—but for the most part it holds no potential for long-term harm. Being caught in an avalanche also has a range of severity, though it tends toward the more intense end of the spectrum. You might risk the poison ivy but not the avalanche.

Returning to our river crossing example, in the initial attempt a participant fell and was swept downstream, but was able to reach a shallow area and scramble out. Though she did lose her pack, she was essentially unharmed. Had the river crossing been just above a major waterfall or a deep stretch of dangerous rapids, the outcome could have been much worse. Establishing and understanding severity is an important component of risk assessment.

Equipment: Along with environmental and human hazards, we can also consider equipment as a danger. Equipment we trust our lives with can fail us. Climbing ropes can (rarely) be cut over sharp edges, kayak paddles can break, and camping stoves can flare up in dangerous fireballs. Improper equipment and people who don't know how to use their equipment are more frequent causes of problems than equipment failure. These equipment dangers are really just a subset of human dangers. In December 2000 a group from an "adventure" school in Vermont set out for a hike above treeline along Franconia Ridge in New Hampshire. They were equipped with a hand-drawn map and minimal clothing; one participant wore sneakers. The group became lost in whiteout conditions and wandered past several trails—not marked on the sketched map—that could have led them to safety. Eventually the group bivouacked at a spot 3 easy miles from a major road—but no one knew the road was there. In the morning they retraced their route over the exposed ridge, again passing several trails leading to safety, and descended the way they came in. A thirteen- and a fifteen-year-old on the trip suffered serious frostbite. The hand-drawn map and improper clothing could be considered equipment dangers, but they are ultimately human dangers that resulted from a flawed decision-making process. Modern equipment—when properly used—is so unlikely to cause serious harm that equipment failure or malfunction does not carry nearly the same weight as human or environmental dangers.

Managing Risk in the Field

Once you've assessed the level of risk, the remaining challenge is deter-mining what an appropriate level of risk should be. In most circum-stances you will be guided by prior experience and knowledge of com-mon practices in the activity. Still, there will always be situations where the appropriate course is less well defined. Here you must have a little more understanding about the place of risk in outdoor activities and the level of risk leaders attempt to maintain through field risk management.

In *Mountaincraft and Leadership,* Eric Langmuir expresses the leader's dilemma this way:

> The leader has an ever present practical problem—to maintain the right balance between apparent danger and safety. This requires finding the balance between, on the one hand, excitement, pleasure, interest, spon-taneity, enjoyment and freedom; and on the other hand, excessive disci-pline, regimentation, monotony and the sterile rigidity that comes from over-planning and over-preparation. The leader should always try to be aware if the balance is being tipped in one direction or another—either through over confident arrogance, optimistic inexperience or anxious lack of self confidence.

This balance of apparent risk (Langmuir calls it *danger*) versus safety is the challenge for leaders in situations with unclear risk management. Before we can address this issue, however, it's important to consider the tools leaders have for managing risks in the field.

Tools: The tools you use to manage risk in the field are as limitless as your creativity. We can, however, define the general concepts with which leaders typically work. Under ideal circumstances the leader will have the following three general options:

1. Proceeding with the activity as planned.

2. Modifying the activity in order to reduce risk.

3. Avoiding the risk by not doing an activity.

Circumstances may eliminate an option. You cannot proceed with your planned activity if the river you intended to cross is in a raging flood and carrying logs that could knock over a whole group. However, in general, after assessment of the risk, you will have these three options.

Option one, proceeding with the activity as planned, is done when you assess that there's not significant risk or that there's an acceptable level of risk and no appropriate way to reduce it.

Option two, modifying the activity in order to reduce risk, is done when you assess the risk level to be unacceptable and there is an available approach to reduce it. This approach is also used when the original risk is acceptable but there is a readily implemented way to lower it. Risk can be modified in many ways. You might choose a different route for a river crossing; take extra safety precautions, such as using spotters or helmets on a steep and rocky trail; stop and teach your participants a new skill, such as how to prevent blisters; cross a potential avalanche slope one at a time (rather than as a group), so that if anyone is caught the rest of the group is available to assist. There are many, many ways to modify activities.

Option three, avoiding the risk by not doing the activity, is a simple option. If the risk is unacceptable and there are no reasonable ways to reduce it, don't do the activity—that is, if the activity can be avoided. A simple example is skiing a questionable slope when the forecast is for "extreme" avalanche hazard. Given this forecast it makes sense to avoid skiing any terrain with even slight avalanche risk. Of course, if you are already out there and have no viable options but to cross avalanche terrain you must cross the slope after considering any available options to reduce the risk.

Balance: This is the fine art of finding the correct path between too much risk and not enough. We are aided here by *perceived* risk. Participants can feel as if they are having an adventuresome experience without being exposed to significant *actual* risk—for example, with new rock climbers on a relatively low-risk top-rope setup. Actual risk, however, is always a part of outdoor activity. Attempting to eliminate risk entirely (which is, of course, impossible) would mean that helmets and some sort of body armor would be worn at all times; rafters would not raft in whitewater; and skiers would be restricted to the gentlest slopes; perhaps use of a compass would be banned, because Global Positioning System units might result in fewer lost groups. There's a point at which the attempt to eliminate all risk leaves activities too boring or cumbersome to be worthwhile.

Any actions that result in additional risk must be justifiable, based on the program's mission objectives. For instance, consider a mountain biking trip leader who's presented with two route options. Both offer wonderful scenery and challenging riding, as participants have been promised. One route traverses the top of a dangerous rock drop-off that riders could fall from, while the other doesn't. The route with the lesser danger is the obvious choice, regardless of any personal preference the leader may have. This preferred route fufills the participants' expectations and program goals without adding unnecessary risk.

At a minimum you should employ basic practices that reduce risk. Examples include wearing an appropriate helmet when climbing, biking, or whitewater paddling or wearing a personal floatation device when sea kayaking. The effect on a participant's experience is minimal, but these practices can result in significantly decreased risk. Leaders must also take opportunities to reduce risk in ways that don't affect an activity significantly, even if these are not recognized practices. For instance, if members of a particular group seem prone to walking through the cooking area, nearly knocking over stoves topped with pots of boiling water, you might mark off a "kitchen" by laying a rope on the ground and prohibiting anyone from walking inside it.

Certain conditions may result in risk levels that are simply too high —even on advertised activities. Avalanche danger might be too great to ski a slope, a river might be too flooded to run, the chance of a thunderstorm might be too great to set off on a peak ascent. These calls must be made, often in the field, when you determine that the risk has become significantly out of line with the norm for that activity.

Attitude: Our perception of risk greatly influences our attitude toward it. Paul Slovic, Baruch Fischoff, and Sarah Lichtenstein studied how the manner in which seat belt use is presented to people influences whether they wear them. People who considered wearing a seat belt for only one trip knew that there was a very low likelihood of an accident. However, the risk of an injury-producing accident over fifty years of driving is much higher, and those who considered the lifetime perspective were far more likely to buckle up.

Outdoor leaders too need to look at the long haul. In a situation with a one-in-a-hundred chance of something going wrong, for instance, instead of thinking *I can probably get through this safely,* consider how many times you'll be in similar situations in the future. Taking that one-in-a-hundred risk once every trip means that your risk-taking leadership will likely catch up with you someday. If you're accurate in your risk assessment, odds of one in a hundred aren't very good for someone who might lead fifty, two hundred, or five hundred trips in a lifetime.

Sometimes one of the most challenging parts of a proactive and long-term view of safety and risk is that your participants may not share it with you. They may view their experience as a one-shot deal; if you say, "I don't feel climbing is safe under these conditions," they may still want to go. The lesson from this is to avoid making decisions based on prior investment. Modern outdoorspeople often have tight schedules and are very motivated to meet their goals. The whitewater paddler who pays to fly across the country may be willing to take more risks in a flood-stage river than someone who lives nearby. The climber dedicated to ascending a tick list of summits may also be willing to take additional risks to put a checkmark next to another one. Neither justifies increasing the level of risk to an unacceptable level.

I spoke with one leader who has spent several thousand days in the field in outdoor leadership roles. She said that she used to think it was just luck that kept her from ever having anything go seriously wrong on a trip. Having led with many leaders and seen things go wrong on other trips, however, she's now convinced that there's more involved, including maintaining a conservative attitude toward safety and encouraging others to share it—making safety everyone's job, not just the leader's.

Organizational Risk Management———

The goal of organizational risk management is to limit the occurrence of accidents and incidents, and, if they do occur, to minimize the effect on participants, leaders, and the organization. A complete description of organizational risk management is beyond the scope of this book, nevertheless it is important for field leaders to have a basic understanding of this subject. Ultimately, field leaders are responsible for managing

LEADER CERTIFICATION

By long-standing tradition anyone can call him- or herself a guide or outdoor leader in most parts of the United States. In New York State and Maine, outdoor leaders must obtain a guide's license, though the requirements are minimal. In some western states river guides or outfitters must be licensed, and a Coast Guard captain's license is required for those leading groups in small boats in coastal waters.

Certification has been touted as the best route to creating leaders who can provide consistent quality in leading or instructing programs. Beyond any government-mandated programs the American Canoe Association, American Mountain Guides Association, and Professional Ski Instructors of America certify people as skills instructors or leaders. Certification in the various levels of wilderness medicine or in water safety skills (such as those provided by Lifeguard or Water Safety Instructor training) have become broadly accepted for outdoor leaders. Yet training has not become expected or even broadly accepted in many other areas.

To understand leader certification we need to look at its two different components: hard skills and soft skills. As discussed in chapter 2, hard skills are the physical-activity- and knowledge-based skills necessary to engage in a given outdoor pursuit. Soft skills are more difficult to train and evaluate than hard skills. Soft skills such as teaching, awareness, and judgment require psychological and intellectual abilities that take experience and time to develop. It is far easier to train and assess leaders on their hard skills, and thus to certify them, than it is to certify them on soft skills.

One argument against certification, particularly against certification in soft skills, is that it stifles creativity. Why should every leader teach or facilitate in the manner prescribed by a certification course? Certification may also exclude those with talent and experience who don't have the time or money to take the certification course and examination.

On the plus side, certification would mean that all outdoor leaders approached their tasks with a similar set of basic skills. Some accidents have been the result of leaders who lacked fundamental skills—certified leaders would, presumably, have these skills. Certification thus has some potential to increase public confidence in outdoor leaders and even the potential to reduce insurance rates if programs actually were able to demonstrate reduced incidents. However, like all steps taken to manage risk, certification offers no guarantee participants won't be injured or otherwise harmed.

much of the risk an organization faces. It is critical that, as a leader, you understand how and why the organization you lead for approaches risk in the manner it does.

Typically a written risk-management plan is used to document how an organization addresses risk management in its activities. This plan is usually compiled by knowledgeable individuals associated with the organization, and ideally it is updated and modified on a regular basis. There must also be a system within the organization for assisting with proper implementation of the plan—typically this is done by an individual who serves as risk manager.

No packaged risk-management plan will work for every program. Each risk-management plan will share common elements with other organizations but will need to fit your mission, activities, operating area, and many other variables. The implementation of a risk-management plan need not extinguish quirks or sentence an organization to homogenization, as there are often many ways to reach any desired outcome.

Risk-management plans often feature two major sections. The first is focused on prevention of accidents and incidents, and the second addresses minimizing the impact of accidents and incidents that do occur. The prevention section typically seeks to minimize to the lowest feasible level the risk of fatalities and disabling injuries and reduce all other injuries, illnesses, and property loss. While there are many approaches to preventing accidents and injuries on outdoor programs, a number of elements are typical to this section of a risk-management plan.

Prevention may be addressed in the risk-management plan through written procedures for field leaders and other staff. Procedures may cover how a specific activity is conducted in the field or they may be more general—establishing training standards for field leaders, for example. Field procedures can be limiting to leaders, but can also be a helpful guide for leaders making critical decisions. The risk-management plan will also likely cover how participants are screened to determine whether they are appropriate for a given trip and if any accommodations will need to be made for them. Incident reporting is also an important component of prevention—while this may seem confusing, it is well established that patterns of more minor incidents can warn of more serious potential incidents. Only through consistent incident reporting and analysis can an organization detect these patterns.

Minimizing the impact of accidents and incidents is accomplished

PROGRAM ACCREDITATION

When it comes to improving consistency in program quality and risk management, program accreditation has emerged as the preferred alternative to leader certification. Unlike certification, accreditation is not program based but rather founded on the idea that outdoor programs should establish documented standards for their operations. Part of most accreditation schemes is some form of peer review in which expert reviewers provide feedback and recommendations on risk management, but also on other aspects of program philosophy, educational practices, ethics, and more. These peer reviews are typically based on field observations and review of relevant procedures, policies, and other documentation.

Accreditation programs have been growing in recent years. The Association for Experiential Education (AEE) accredits a broad array of outdoor and experiential education programs. The long-standing American Camping Association (ACA) continues to develop more standards for accreditation of outdoor programs at the summer camps and similar youth programs it accredits. The American Mountain Guides Association (AMGA) accredits many of the nation's climbing guide services.

Compared with leader certification, accreditation can be less onerous for leaders and organizations. Accreditation standards typically do not dictate one approach to accomplishing a given objective—instead leaving this to the judgment of the individual organization. The peer-review process gives an independent perspective on what is and what it not working in a given organization. This helps programs meet minimum standards, while also allowing organizations to improve their programs through the introduction of new ideas and practices.

On the downside, accreditation can be costly and time consuming and it may require the development of a lot of written documentation. Especially for a smaller organization, this can be a significant imposition. Programs with volunteer leaders such as those run by the AMC and other mountain clubs as well as organizations such as the Boy and Girl Scouts have, for the most part, not been accredited. Some college outdoor programs with volunteer leaders have been accredited by the AEE; this may be the road to the future. Effective accreditation programs may present a path toward advancing the standards of adventure activities on the organizational level.

primarily through proper emergency planning and measures taken to protect against loss through legal action. An emergency action plan, addressing issues such as patient care in the field, emergency communications, and available rescue resources might—in a serious emergency—make the difference between life and death. The other component of minimizing the impact of incidents is legal, financial, and, to a lesser degree, public relations. Appropriate insurance, participant agreements, and other steps are outlined in appendix B by attorney Catherine Hansen-Stamp.

One particularly important component of any risk-management plan is a form of safety review. A review will address both preventing and minimizing the impact of incidents. Periodic safety reviews assess a program's compliance with its own risk-management plan, may point to potential improvements in that plan, or recommend other operational changes. A safety review is conducted by one or more knowledgeable individuals and is based on observation of a program's operations, review of paperwork, and discussions with staff, leaders, and even participants. The spread of valuable risk-management practices is greatly aided by the opportunity for cross-fertilization among various outdoor organizations that reviews offer.

Risk-management plans are important because they may make more consistent the risk level in programs for participants. Without any organizational guidance the risk involved in an activity may vary widely from leader to leader. By attempting to maintain the risk in activities at an acceptable level, the plan may also help to prevent accidents and injuries. This minimizes the risk of harm to participants and leaders and also helps the organization to maintain its reputation and avoid financial losses due to lawsuits. In a situation where an injury or other harm does occur, the risk-management plan seeks to guide the best response to the incident. As a leader you need to understand the critical importance of a risk-management plan to ongoing operations of the organization for which you lead. More information on organizational risk management can be obtained through reading, conferences, industry associations, peers in other organizations, and consultants.

RECOMMENDED READING

Ajango, Deborah, ed., *Lessons Learned: A Guide to Accident Prevention and Crisis Response,* Anchorage: University of Alaska

Anchorage, 2000.

Ford, Phyllis, and Jim Blanchard, *Leadership and Administration of Outdoor Pursuits,* 2nd ed., State College, Pennsylvania: Venture Publishing, 1993.

◆ Garvey, Daniel, Drew Leemon, John E. Williamson, and William Zimmerman, *Manual of Accreditation Standards for Adventure Programs,* 3rd ed., Boulder, Colorado: Association for Experiential Education, 1999.

◆ Geller, E. Scott, *The Psychology of Safety Handbook,* 2nd ed., Boca Raton, Florida: CRC Press, 2001.

Haddock, Cathye, *Managing Risks in Outdoor Activities,* Wellington: New Zealand Mountain Safety Council, 1993.

Hunt, Jasper S., Jr., *Ethical Issues in Experiential Education,* Dubuque, Iowa: Kendall/Hunt Publishing, 1990.

Langmuir, Eric, *Mountaincraft and Leadership,* 3rd ed., West Didsbury, England: The Mountain Leader Training Board, 1995.

Priest, Simon, and Michael Gass, *Effective Leadership in Adventure Programming,* Champaign, Illinois: Human Kinetics, 1997.

◆ Slovic, Paul, Baruch Fischhoff, and Sarah Lichtenstein, "Facts versus Fears: Understanding Perceived Risk," in *Judgment Under Uncertainty: Heuristics and Biases,* edited by Daniel Kahneman, Paul Slovic, and Amos Tversky, Cambridge, England: Cambridge University Press, 1982.

Wade, Ian, and Mike Fischesser, *The Outward Bound Safety Review Manual,* Garrison, New York: Outward Bound USA.

◆ Wilde, Gerald J. S., *Target Risk 2,* 2nd ed., Toronto: PDE Publications, 2001.

◆ Wurdinger, Scott D., and Tom G. Potter, *Controversial Issues in Adventure Education: A Critical Examination,* Dubuque, Iowa: Kendall/Hunt Publishing, 1999.

◆ = Advanced Recommendation

CHAPTER 13

Crisis

A *crisis* can be defined as any unstable situation that has the potential for a harmful outcome. This chapter is about stepping back and managing an overall crisis situation as an outdoor leader. The skill to handle an emotional situation while managing people in a number of different tasks isn't easy to come by. Those who are best at crisis response do it on a regular basis—few outdoor leaders are in this situation. Understanding the management of a crisis and training go a long way if you find yourself in the unfortunate situation of handling a crisis in the wild.

What this chapter doesn't do is serve as a guide to wilderness first aid. Chapter 3 details the excellent and strongly recommended courses offered on Wilderness First Aid. There are also good books on wilderness first aid and medicine—several of the best are listed in the recommended readings at the end of this chapter. Instead of focusing on wilderness first aid, a topic well covered elsewhere, this chapter addresses the outdoor leader's role as overall crisis manager.

One Responder

Jeff Hogan is the guy you want around in a backcountry crisis. An active adventure racer, he's one of the fittest human beings I know. Jeff regularly lends his talents as a volunteer leader to AMC outings around the country and currently serves as director of the AMC's Mountain Leadership School, a five-day backcountry training program. Jeff is a Wilderness Emergency Medical Technician and a captain in the Farmington, Connecticut, Volunteer Fire Department. In 2001 his resourcefulness in the cold-water rescue of two intoxicated canoeists saved their lives and perhaps those of two fellow rescuers, earning him a Hero Award from the governor of Connecticut. Hogan also manages the regional division of a major insurance company, yet still finds time to climb and hike with his wife and two children. Sleep does not play a major role in Hogan's schedule.

One of Jeff Hogan's most challenging outdoor experiences, recounted below, involved what all would clearly recognize as a medical crisis. Other crisis situations may involve missing group members, extreme weather conditions, shortage of water or supplies, or anything else you can dream up (plus some scenarios impossible to conjure).

Jeff Hogan was mountain biking with two friends in icy conditions, and they had stopped to walk their bikes up a hill. On the ascent, one of his friends, an accomplished triathlete, slipped and tumbled, hitting his head on the embankment. This fallen friend went into a seizure, so Hogan cradled him in his lap, trying to protect him from further injuring himself. He sent his other biking companion off to call 911. Now alone, Hogan realized that his friend's airway had become obstructed by the seizure—he could not breathe. Hogan wasn't sure what would be the best thing to do in this situation, but he knew he had to take action so he used his fingers to pry open his friend's mouth and establish an airway. This crisis, which Hogan counts as one of his most intense in the "backcountry," occurred an eighth of a mile from the road in suburban Connecticut.

While Hogan was struggling to maintain his friend's grip on life the other group member had made it to the trailhead. He then drove home to call 911, bypassing many houses near the trailhead. In speaking with the 911 dispatcher, he did not give Hogan's exact location over the phone but instead drove back to the trailhead to guide the waiting EMTs to Hogan and his patient. The whole process took almost half an hour, during which time Hogan held his friend in his lap, struggling to maintain an airway and desperately yelling to try to get him to regain consciousness. His friend later related that he had seen himself floating out of his body toward a white light at the end of a tunnel. Then he heard Hogan screaming at him, which brought him back to consciousness. When he was admitted to the hospital he had a heart arrhythmia due to the trauma but suffered no long-term ill effects.

Jeff Hogan says it took ten years of experience for him to develop his approach and some sense of comfort in dealing with backcountry emergencies. Practice is key to speeding up the development and can come through good wilderness medicine courses or specific training and practice in crisis management. Many outdoor organizations, including the AMC, offer this type of training for their outdoor leaders. When he teaches crisis management for the AMC, Hogan focuses on two concepts: prevention and self-reliance. Over time he feels that self-reliance has become the more important of the two concepts to him in the outdoors. His no-nonsense message for outdoor leaders is: "You are responsible for your outcomes." As his story from the trails of suburban Connecticut proves, this is almost equally true close to the highway as it is in the remote Himalaya.

Prevention ————————————————

If an ounce of prevention is worth a pound of cure elsewhere, in the backcountry that same ounce is worth ten pounds of cure. Cure is that much harder to come by in the wilderness. "Anticipate what can go wrong and how to avoid those problems," writes Mike Lanza in the AMC's *Ultimate Guide to Backcountry Travel*. "Avoiding trouble is the best strategy in the backcountry, where the seriousness of any injury or problem automatically magnifies because of your distance from medical care; a dry, heated shelter; etc." Had Jeff Hogan's triathlete friend fallen a mile from the road, the likelihood of his survival would have been much lower. The additional time needed to obtain assistance and for emergency personnel to arrive on the scene might have made the difference between life and death. Similarly, a case of hypothermia that could be cured with a hot shower has the potential to deteriorate into something much more serious if that shower is a 10-mile trek away. Prevention is a constant theme throughout this book, but the message is critical enough to merit repetition.

Self-Reliance

When you venture into the outdoors, especially as a group leader, you must be prepared to cope with whatever is thrown at you. There's a current trend to go light (sometimes this includes not just equipment, but also skills) and perhaps rely more on outside help when trouble comes. The wise leader knows that good prevention makes a crisis unlikely but nonetheless undertakes every outing assuming that one will occur. Anything less allows complacency to fester. Proximity to a road or, even worse, carrying a cell phone does not absolve the leaders and their group of the need to be self-reliant. If Jeff Hogan had not been prepared to act and had instead waited for help to arrive, his friend, in all likelihood, would have continued on into that white light. The first and best line of assistance in any kind of crisis is the people right there. Additional help, even if the cell phone or radio does work, may be many hours or even days away.

Self-reliance has three components. In decreasing order of importance, they are (1) competence, (2) planning, and (3) equipment. Competence is about putting your strongest tool—your brain—to good use. Wilderness first aid and other skills are important, but clear, systematic, and rational thought are the biggest keys to competence. Planning means that your original plan was viable, but you have also developed backup options. When a crisis comes, you already know the answers to many pressing questions—the shortest way to the road, for instance, and who in the group has medical skills. Equipment is the third and final component of self-reliance, and perhaps the most easily understood. You would not be a self-reliant group if you didn't have sufficient clothes and equipment to keep an injured party member warm or if you forgot the first-aid kit or the duct tape (which has uses—crisis or no— that are too innumerable to relate).

COMMUNICATIONS TECHNOLOGY

Within the past few years it has become possible to place a phone call from almost anyplace on the planet. Compact mobile phones that switch to transmitting via satellite when ground-based transmission is unavailable now cost no more than a thousand dollars—less than what a participant would pay to participate in many outdoor programs. Ground-to-ground and ground-to-air radios that are useful in many backcountry areas have been available for some time. Cost and reliability in remote areas were once frequently cited together in arguments against the use of these radios. These issues are much less valid today (though dead batteries remain a common source of trouble with all these devices). Many well-respected outdoor programs now routinely carry radios or phones into the backcountry and view them as a critical part of their emergency-response plan.

The argument most frequently made against carrying communications technology is that is will encourage people to take greater risks and be less self-reliant. The theory is that people will feel that help is only a phone call away instead of hours or days. The reality is that leaders need to understand that even if communication is possible—the batteries are good, the phone did not get wet, and there is a signal—help may still be a long way away. Rescuers need to be rounded up, sometimes from far away, and travel into your location; this may take many hours or days. Helicopters, under the best circumstances, can provide rapid assistance, but they typically don't do night rescues or fly in bad weather.

There have been problems with users calling for unnecessary assistance on cell phones. The caller who wanted a helicopter because he was late for a meeting and the numerous calls from backcountry travelers with a phone but no map have been widely covered by the outdoor press and even mainstream general interest publications such as *Newsweek* and the *New York*

The Six-Step Process to Crisis Resolution

Responding to any crisis, from a trauma to a missing group member, is complex and can be stressful. The six-step process is not a scientific procedure you must follow exactly, but it does provide a rational decision-making framework for managing a crisis situation. It's best to

Times. Such incidents involve individuals or casual groups of recreationists, however, not organized programs.

I know several instances in which leaders of organized groups borrowed phones or radios from other individuals or groups in true crisis situations. Some of these same leaders and the organizations they lead for have continued to advocate against carrying communications devices because it will inspire decreased self-reliance. The message that it is acceptable to rely on the cell phones of others in an emergency but not to carry our own seems to me to be hollow.

This does represent capitulating to the slow creep of new technology into the backcountry. The important issue is one of preserving the wilderness experience both as a state of mind and a state of quiet. A key aspect of the wilderness experience has typically been the self-reliance and accompanying sense of accomplishment that it's possible to achieve in the backcountry. The solution to all these issues seems to be careful management of the use of communications technology. It should be made clear that it is not there to make things easier, but to assist when there is the potential for loss of life or serious injury.

Groups that have communications devices should have a clear policy on their use. They should not be used to make plans for after the trip or even to change the location of a pickup to another trailhead (except perhaps once the group is at the trailhead). On the one hand, I'd hate to tell someone that a child, spouse, or other loved one could not get help because there was no nearby cell phone to borrow and I was philosophically opposed to carrying one. On the other, I do believe that there's still a line to be drawn. An evacuation that may be inconvenient or uncomfortable but does not pose any dangers to the patient should still be accomplished using group resources. Leaders and the organizations they work with should be willing and able to justify this. Not every situation needs a helicopter of an army or rescuers.

have an *incident commander* who assigns tasks to individuals and receives information back from them. The incident commander is typically a leader, but should be a person who combines the most experience in crisis response with a knowledge of how to accomplish things in the area. The incident commander should, if possible, avoid becoming too involved in the hands-on work. Having an incident commander allows the leader to have an overall perspective of the situation, follow the six steps, and ensure all needed tasks get done. If

MAKING THINGS WORSE, PART I

We were on a narrow ledge 100 feet up a cliff in New York's Shawangunk Mountains, tending to a climber who had fallen 20 feet, landing on her head. She was not someone I knew, but I was in the area so I responded to the calls for help. Thankfully, the rescue cache maintained at the climbing area meant that we were able to get our patient backboarded, on oxygen, and secured in a litter. I was coordinating medical care, and a ranger was managing setup of the litter lower. As we began to ease the litter off the ledge to be lowered down the cliff, we could hear a life flight helicopter landing in the road half a mile away. Just as the litter was almost off the ledge, one of the other rescuers suddenly let go of it. The additional weight jerked me off balance, sending me off the edge of the cliff. I should have been tied directly to the cliff with a length of rope, but I wasn't. I was tied, with a good dose of slack, to another rescuer who, in turn, was loosely tied to another rescuer; only then was the rope connected to the cliff (again, lots of slack, which allowed us to move about the ledge with a maximum of ease). A totally foolish system, but we had been busy with a rescue and it was a big ledge. As I started to fall I knew that I'd pull the others over with me. Instinctively, I grabbed for the guy nearest me and got a handful of his shorts. It was enough to stabilize me, and quickly another rescuer grabbed me, allowing me to fully regain balance. Had I fallen, all three of us would probably have been injured given the long and awkward fall. In the worst-case scenario the three of us falling simultaneously onto the anchor in the cliff could have caused it to fail. The rescue of our initial patient, who went on to a full recovery, would have been delayed, and resources would have had to be devoted to three new victims.

Samantha, a hypothetical leader, is rendering medical care, it's hard for her to simultaneously ensure that proper steps are being taken to prepare a litter, ensure that the rest of the group is safe, and locate the easiest evacuation route. If Samantha is both the obvious leader and the only one with medical training, she can still take steps to maintain a command and less of a hands-on role. She might delegate tasks, saying things such as, "Can you please put pressure on this wound like this and *do not* let up," or "Get all his warm clothes out of the pack and help him get them on." Through the confusion of a crisis situation, the

MAKING THINGS WORSE, PART II

It was a busy spring weekend in Mount Washington's Tuckerman Ravine, which typically involves hundreds, if not thousands, of skiers and snowboarders. I was there to ski with some friends but instead wound up responding to an injured skier on a steep slope that was especially icy on the day in question. I was creating a snow anchor so that the litter the victim was placed into could be lowered on a rope down the steep slope when a shout went up. A snowboarder was literally cartwheeling toward us, repeatedly hitting his head and board at a high velocity. When his head hit the snow it left a smear of blood, but that wasn't our main concern—we were focused on getting out of the way. One rescuer stayed with the skier we were tending in an attempt to shield him from the hurtling snowboarder and yelled at the rest of us to do the same. Ignoring his directions, the rest of us hustled out of the snowboarder's path. We would have been of little assistance trying to use our bodies to protect the fallen skier from the hurtling snowboarder—and we could have been seriously injured. As it was, we were going to have to split our limited rescue team between two patients—there was no sense in allowing ourselves to become additional victims. Thankfully, the snowboarder missed everyone. Both the original patient and the snowboarder were transported by litter sliding and lowering, snow machine, and finally ambulance to the hospital where they eventually recovered.

six-step process helps leaders ensure that every necessary action is taken.

Depending on many variables, your initial run through this six-step process might take anywhere from a few seconds to several days. High-altitude cerebral edema on a remote Andean peak will necessitate a long crisis-resolution process. Jeff Hogan's initial review of how to handle the crisis he faced in Connecticut lasted only a minute or two. Likewise, the process in the Andes will likely involve effort and input by the entire group, while Hogan's assessment was largely his own. Thankfully, it's rare to have an outdoor emergency in which seconds count, but when this does happen it may be necessary to move quickly though some steps that would normally occupy time for careful consideration.

The role of incident commander is different from the role of the caregiver you learn during most first-aid courses, and the thinking you do has a different orientation. As the incident commander you're responsible for overall plans and well-being of the group, but in an ideal situation you aren't directly providing medical care or other direct assistance to individuals. This allows you, as the incident commander, to step back and view the big picture. The six steps to crisis resolution listed below are the keys to the incident-command system.

1. Don't make things worse.

2. Initial delegation.

3. Assess.

4. Plan.

5. Implement.

6. Reassess.

The six steps weren't intended to form an acronym, but actually spell out DIAPIR (for those who are interested, a diapir is an anticlinal fold in which a mobile core has pierced through the more brittle overlying rock). For most nongeologists it will be easier to remember as a misspelling of an infant's infamous undergarment.

Step One: *Don't make things worse.* Seem obvious? It should be, but in the adrenaline rush that comes with responding to a crisis, believe me, it isn't. The potential for additional woe will be there. Your interventions should not do additional harm to anyone, especially you and the other responders. In the case of a medical crisis this means not causing your patient additional harm. However, the most common way to make things worse is for those assisting in a crisis to become victims instead of rescuers. Any first-aid course will teach you about "scene safety" and the need to make sure you aren't exposing yourself to danger as you attempt to help out.

When rescuers become victims themselves, they cannot help the original victim and resources must be diverted from the original victims. On cliffs, in avalanche or rockfall zones, at the scene of car accidents—whatever the situation—make sure the original problem is not going to repeat itself and be alert to new hazards. Aquatic rescues, such as the one Jeff Hogan received his Hero Award for, are particularly prone to turning would-be rescuers into additional victims. These two scenarios described in "Making Things Worse, Parts I and II," also hint at another lesson—despite the best prevention in your group, you may wind up assisting another individual or group who has not been as cautious or lucky.

Step Two: *Initial delegation.* If you're dealing with a medical emergency, make sure someone is providing initial first aid. For a missing person, assign someone to determine when the person was last seen. In case of an avalanche, assign a person or people to do an initial search. In every situation where it's possible—this is important—assign someone to document in writing what's going on. This scribe keeps facts, assessments, plans, and implementation steps organized, which can be invaluable during the crisis, vital for sending along if you need outside assistance, and useful in documenting the incident afterward. You will already have an initial sense of what needs to be done even if you haven't made a full assessment and committed to a plan. Keep everyone occupied, allowing them to feel productive even if they're performing insignificant tasks. Get important activities going so you have time for steps three, four, and five, which are critically important.

Step Three: *Assess.* Determine, as best you can, the nature of the crisis. Does the injury seem to be a profusely bleeding but otherwise mild scalp wound, or might it involve a head injury? Was the person caught in the avalanche wearing a transponder, and are you receiving a signal? Make certain you know where you are, especially if you anticipate evacuating someone or sending for help. Finally, consider what human and equipment resources you have with you—if you've planned well, you should already know this. Assign people to determine the answers to your questions if they have the expertise or can free you for other tasks.

A medical assessment will reveal one of four situations:

▶ **Life Threatening:** Patients who are in obvious need of modern medical facilities or patients whose lives may be endangered. This would include such conditions as femur fractures, severe hypothermia, heart attacks, or extensive burns.

▶ **Cannot Continue:** These patients don't have a condition that's immediately life threatening but are incapable of continuing with the planned trip. Examples would include diarrhea or vomiting that cannot be quickly remedied, serious ankle sprains, or fractures in smaller bones.

▶ **Can Continue:** These patients have a medical problem, but if it's monitored carefully they can continue with the planned activity. Some accommodations may be required to make continued participation possible. Examples would include some minor sprains, blisters, and mild to moderate sunburn.

▶ **Ambiguous:** These are the difficult judgment calls that keep you up worrying at night. Medical conditions (as opposed to trauma), such as abdominal pain, can be particularly difficult to assess in the field. Generally it is advisable to err on the side of caution.

Assessment of nonmedical issues will vary with the situation. If someone was rappelling and caught his or her hair in the belay device, you're dealing with issues different from if you're stuck on an open ridgeline in a fierce lightning storm. In each case you need to determine the seriousness of the problem and identify potential options to resolve it.

Step Four: *Plan.* Apply the judgment and decision-making skills that are addressed in chapter 10 to the problem or problems you have identified. If you have sufficient time, start with the options identified in the assessment phase, weigh the benefits and risks of each option, and finally settle on the best one. Include as many others in the process as time and your situation permit—multiple minds will result in a better plan and better cooperation from the group in the next stage. Some crisis situations require fast action and a directive approach from leaders who are able to rapidly apply their experience to developing a plan and moving to implement it rapidly. A good plan, however, is critical if there are elements of it that cannot be changed once it's set in motion.

Step Five: *Implement.* "The leader controls the scene; the scene does not control the leader," says Jeff Hogan. You may have a plan thirty sec-

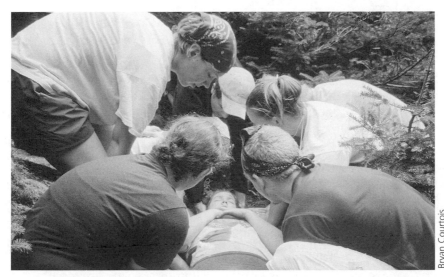

Bryan Courtois

Many hands may be required to successfully undertake a backcountry rescue.

onds into a crisis or it might take a day to develop. Once you have that plan, it's your job to make it occur, but this doesn't mean taking on all the details yourself. Assign tasks to group members, not only to have more hands and minds working on the challenges at hand, but also to keep people positively occupied. Idle minds occupied with thoughts of the worst possible outcomes are not helpful in a crisis situation. If you have absolutely nothing for people to do, try to get them out of the immediate vicinity of the problem. Ideally you'll be part of a leader pair. This allows one leader to serve as the incident commander while the other deals with the more hands-on issues such as first aid. Some issues that must be considered during the implementation phase:

▶ **Medical Care:** Assign one person to be the lead on providing medical care. This will generally be the person with the most training. Earlier, I related a story of assisting with a cliff rescue in the Shawangunks. Because I was a Wilderness EMT and the climber assisting me was a Wilderness First Responder, we had more medical expertise than the ranger who arrived on the scene. The ranger listened to our summary of our initial patient survey and then became the incident commander, supervising the setup of the litter lower and maintaining radio communication.

▶ **Victim's Needs:** Be sensitive to physical and psychological needs. Consider appointing one person just to communicate with the victim in a reassuring manner. The communicator can help ascertain the victim's needs and at the same time isolate the victim from the commotion as the group pulls together for their response. Imagine if you were injured, had no sense of how severe your injury was, and had several different frantic people asking you questions, some of them repetitive. It might not be too comforting.

▶ **Group Needs:** Safety of the group, as addressed in step one, is paramount. This includes addressing concerns such as a group that is becoming hypothermic, dehydrated, or soaked by rain as they stand around. A secondary concern is ensuring that people are not standing around feeling useless and potentially moving toward panic. Perhaps they can set up camp, or even boil some water. Maybe you can have people take a look at the map even if you know exactly where you are or know that you will have to recheck everything they tell you. In a crisis you can usually expect the best from people. Delegate tasks that are appropriate to individuals' experience levels and expect that they will be carried out to the best of their ability.

▶ **Scribe:** This individual, mentioned in the initial implementation stage, records the details of what's going on and keeps track of the decisions made.

There may be other issues that you need to address in the implementation stage. In the Shawangunks crisis mentioned in the sidebar the incident commander had to supervise the setup of technical systems and maintain communication with rescuers on the ground. There are many other potential aspects to implementation, depending on the . nature of the crisis and the plan you've developed.

Step Six: *Reassess.* Keep going back and repeating the first five steps. Situations change and new information becomes available. You might be looking for someone missing from camp, realize that the cook pot is missing, and determine that you should focus your search on the route to the nearest water. Don't keep changing your plan without good reason—this wastes time and frustrates people—but remain flexible enough to adjust to changing circumstances. Do finish what you've started, whether it be getting someone to medical care or finding a missing group member.

Outcome

How a group responds to a crisis has everything to do with the actions that members observe their leaders taking—this basic point has already been made, but it bears reiteration. Leaders cannot control the reaction of every group member, but they should focus on what can be done and the potential for a positive outcome. Realistic optimism will help fill a group's tank with morale, while pessimism will rapidly suck it dry. No matter how small the contribution, every positive effort in a crisis should be commended. Every little thing can help, and, if nothing else, people making contributions are not panicking and getting in the way.

Again I will turn to Jeff Hogan to provide an example of a crisis situation. Jeff was leading a student group for the AMC's Mountain Leadership School in New Hampshire's White Mountains. The group ranged from eighteen to forty years old and also had a range of experience levels. They were two days into the five-day program, and it had been raining and very windy the whole time. As Jeff relates it, the group was tired and low spirited when they made a decision to divert from their original plan and stay below treeline due to the inclement weather. Descending into the valley, the group crossed a shallow river, with both Jeff and his co-leader, Frank, hiking near the front. Just after reentering the woods, the lead hikers heard a scream.

Jeff and the others with him quickly retraced their steps to the river. They found one of the younger students—I'll call her Susan—in significant pain. Susan had slipped down a muddy riverbank, slamming her foot into the riverbed at the bottom. One of the students in the group, Becky, a freshly minted EMT, was already at Susan's side.

A quick assessment by Becky and Jeff revealed the probability of a tib-fib fracture—they felt Susan had broken her lower leg. Darkness was quickly approaching, and Frank and Jeff had a quick huddle with their group to settle on what plan to implement. They decided that

Frank would work with the students to find and set up camp nearby while Jeff and Becky continued to tend to Susan. By this point their assessment indicated that Susan fell into the "cannot continue" category of field medical conditions, but, thankfully, her situation was not life threatening. Jeff and Becky worked to splint Susan's leg, and the rest of the group set up camp.

Following their plan, in the morning the group split up. Frank led a small group that went to obtain help while Jeff and the rest of the group committed to attempting to move toward the road with Susan. Both groups got an early start. With her leg splinted, Susan was initially able to hop along the rugged trail with the support of two others. Slow progress came to a halt after about 3 miles when Susan was too exhausted to continue on one leg. Jeff and his group had a complex situation to resolve. They could estimate when Frank would reach the trailhead but were unsure how long it would take for him to get more assistance. Then the rescue party would have to start walking in. Jeff was concerned that Susan was still too far in for a rescue party to reach her and carry her out during daylight hours, so he was determined to keep moving toward the trailhead.

The group considered constructing a litter, but decided not to invest time in this project, because they had doubts about their small group's ability to move a litter through the rugged terrain. Instead they employed a more arduous approach for such a long evacuation—Susan rode piggyback on Jeff's back. The rest of the group carried Jeff's and Susan's packs, assisted her in getting positioned on his back, and then spotted them in difficult stretches. Unfortunately for the health of Jeff's back, he was the only one who was able to carry Susan for any extended period of time. They would move for about twenty minutes and then rest, but, remarkably, they made progress.

About a mile and a half from the trailhead Jeff, Becky, Susan, and their team met Frank and his part of the group coming back in with a litter and more people to help carry it. Those who stayed with her had been focused on getting Susan out of the woods for twenty-four hours, however, they still insisted on carrying the litter out to the trailhead. As we learned in chapter 11, Expedition Behavior, most groups require adversity to achieve their highest level of functioning, as displayed by this group. For Jeff this was a defining moment and an experience that remains vivid in his mind five years later. Susan's injury, once in a hospital setting, was easily addressed. For Susan, the leaders, and the group, this crisis had a positive outcome.

It can be an incredible experience to be a member of a group that rises to the occasion and resolves a crisis together. A group addressing this situation deserves tremendous credit. It should also be recognized that not all outcomes can be controlled with even the most valiant group efforts. These groups deserve praise for their efforts and support as well. When the outcome is not positive, Jeff Hogan warns, "Group members, and particularly leaders, will have feelings of guilt." This can be especially acute if leaders feel they didn't do all they could have to prepare. My own experience, dealing with the aftermath of crises with results ranging from minor inconvenience to fatalities, bears this out. Regardless of the seriousness of the outcome and even when leaders and group members bear no rational blame for the incident, feelings of guilt, frustration, and anger can remain.

Jeff Hogan had a profound personal experience involving inability to effectively assist with a crisis. "Early on September 12, 2001, I got to the site of the World Trade Center disaster as part of a medical rescue team from Yale–New Haven Hospital. We were so prepared to help, but there was nothing to do. I spent that day with some of the world's best trauma surgeons picking up body parts. It was by far the most awful and frustrating experience of my life." People want to help, and they want to find some glimmer of hope even when confronted with epic-scale disaster. Do all you can to keep people's hopes alive in the field. After a serious accident or fatality, consider a group debriefing with a facilitator trained to deal with post-traumatic stress and make sure you and others involved consider individual counseling.

Most leaders, if they are cautious, will never face a life-or-death crisis in the outdoors. But all leaders must go into the field assuming they will face such a situation on their trip. Outdoor leaders are not like emergency personnel who have frequent practice in responding to crisis situations. In a crisis even the best-trained leader must rise to the occasion. By planning and training for self-reliance and keeping your guard up, you will have a critical edge when a problem does come your way.

RECOMMENDED READING

Ajango, Deborah, ed., *Lessons Learned: A Guide to Accident Prevention and Crisis Response,* Anchorage: University of Alaska Anchorage, 2000.

Lanza, Michael, *The Ultimate Guide to Backcountry Travel,* Boston: Appalachian Mountain Club, 1999.

Schimelpfenig, Tod, and Linda Lindsey, *NOLS Wilderness First Aid,* 3rd ed., Mechanicsburg, Pennsylvania: Stackpole Books and National Outdoor Leadership School, 2000.

Tilton, Buck, and Frank Hubble, *Medicine for the Backcountry,* 3rd ed., Guilford, Connecticut: Globe Pequot Press, 1999.

Wilkerson, James A., ed., *Medicine for Mountaineering,* 5th ed., Seattle: Mountaineers, 2001.

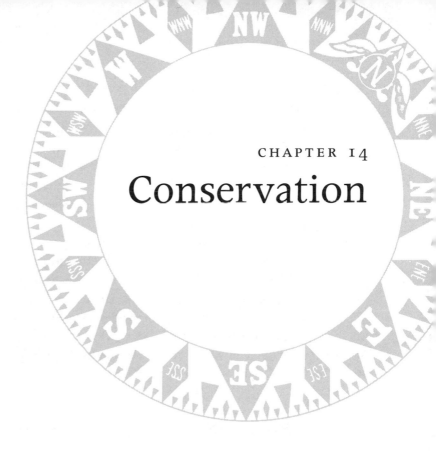

CHAPTER 14

Conservation

Conservation is the natural partner of outdoor recreation. It's hard to venture into the wild outdoors without developing a commitment—though its intensity may vary—to the protection of our remaining wild lands. Outdoor leaders are in an excellent position to assist participants in developing a sense of respect for the land and educating them as to how they can have a positive impact on conservation of these areas.

Outdoor leaders today deal with two components of conservation. The first component of conservation is the reduction of impact. Identified in chapter 1 of this book as one of the four fundamental responsibilities of the outdoor leader, the instruction and implementation of Leave No Trace practices is increasingly critical as more and more people seek to enjoy our outdoor resources. The second aspect of conservation as it relates to outdoor leaders is the education of participants on ecological principles and conservation issues. Conservation issues affect all of us, and issues such as logging, hydropower, mining, road building, and air pollution often impact the experience of outdoor recreationists.

A natural progression exists that allows leaders to introduce Leave No Trace principles early in a program. These concepts provide a good introduction to broader issues such as natural history, basic ecological concepts, and conservation issues. Many participants are interested in learning about the areas where they recreate and the issues these areas are facing. While it's possible for participants to feel they're being indoctrinated, there are also plenty of low-key, unobtrusive approaches.

In addition to teaching Leave No Trace, natural history, or conservation issues, outdoor leaders can involve participants in hands-on stewardship work. This could include small efforts in the context of a longer activity—say, doing some trail work, dismantling an inappropriate fire ring, or even picking up litter. Or stewardship might be the focus on an entire outing. A group might be organized to do trail work, fix up a shelter, clean up a river, or work to eradicate an invasive species. Such hands-on work can be very rewarding for participants—and a learning experience in its own right.

Leave No Trace

"Wilderness management is eighty to ninety percent education and information and ten percent regulation."

—MAX PETERSON, CHIEF OF THE U.S. FOREST SERVICE, 1985

In addition to serving as director of the AMC's Teen Wilderness Adventures program, Dara Houdek coordinates Leave No Trace (LNT) education efforts for the organization. She explains why LNT is so important for outdoor recreationists: "It has to do with statistics I can't rattle off about the increasing number of visitors." I checked the figures. More than 136 million Americans age sixteen and over participated in outdoor recreation activities in 2000. This latest numbers reflect a steady increase—though there have been occasional ups and downs—since the 1950s. "Land mangers," Houdek continues, "discovered that for a variety of reasons regulations don't work to diminish impact. Inability to enforce regulations is a major issue, especially in the backcountry."

Houdek cites additional reasons why regulations don't work well—people may not understand them, or may construe them as limiting the freedom to enjoy public lands as they choose. Houdek speaks like a believer when she says, "Education is the best, most productive way to reduce human impact." Unfortunately, some participants consider LNT principles as regulations in disguise—but they are not, and part of the job of outdoor leaders is to convince participants of this and help them understand Leave No Trace concepts so the participants will want to comply. LNT, Houdek explains, "is very dependent on judgment—there are gray areas. Everyone needs to understand the principles of LNT and make their own decisions on how to act responsibly."

The real selling point of LNT education is that it works. Both research and anecdotal evidence tells us that educating people about impact issues causes them to change their behavior. Sometimes called low-impact or minimum-impact practices, the "travel lightly on the backcountry" movement has been given a significant boost with the establishment of Leave No Trace, Incorporated. With roots as a joint education effort between the National Outdoor Leadership School and federal land management agencies, LNT, Inc., is now a full-blown nonprofit organization in its own right. As an organization, Leave No Trace educates backcountry users on best practices through the development of educational materials and course curricula, many interactive or experiential in nature, with activities to suit all age levels. LNT, Inc., also conducts research on optimal practices, impact issues, and educational effectiveness. Such efforts have been and will continue to be critical in the protection of backcountry physical environment and the spirit of wildness.

The seven Leave No Trace principles of outdoor ethics form the framework of Leave No Trace's message:

1. Plan ahead and prepare

2. Travel and camp on durable surfaces

3. Dispose of waste properly

4. Leave what you find

5. Minimize campfire impacts

6. Respect wildlife

7. Be considerate of other visitors

Many excellent LNT references can provide more details on these critical practices, including the group's Skills and Ethics booklets, offered in both a North American version and regional editions that adapt the information to specific conditions. You can also visit the group's website, lnt.org, and see the list of references at the end of this chapter.

1. Plan Ahead and Prepare

▶ Know the regulations and special concerns for the area you'll visit.

▶ Prepare for extreme weather, hazards, and emergencies.

▶ Schedule your trip to avoid times of high use.

▶ Visit in small groups. Split larger parties into groups of four to six people.

▶ Repackage food to minimize waste.

▶ Use a map and compass to eliminate the use of marking paint, rock cairns, or flagging.

2. Travel and Camp on Durable Surfaces

▶ Durable surfaces include established trails and campsites, rock, gravel, dry grasses, or snow.

▶ Protect riparian areas by camping at least 200 feet from lakes and streams.

▶ Good campsites are found, not made. Altering a site is not necessary.

▶ In popular areas:
Concentrate use on existing trails and campsites.
Walk single file in the middle of the trail, even when it's wet or muddy.
Keep campsites small. Focus activity in areas where vegetation is absent.

▶ In pristine areas:
  Disperse use to prevent the creation of campsites and trails.
  Avoid places where impacts are just beginning.

3. Dispose of Waste Properly

▶ Pack it in, pack it out. Inspect your campsite and rest areas
  for trash or spilled foods. Pack out all trash, leftover food, and
  litter.

▶ Deposit solid human waste in cat holes dug 6 to 8 inches deep
  at least 200 feet from water, camp, and trails. Cover and disguise the cat hole when finished.

▶ Pack out toilet paper and hygiene products.

▶ To wash yourself or your dishes, carry water 200 feet away
  from streams or lakes and use small amounts of biodegradable
  soap.

▶ Scatter strained dishwater.

4. Leave What You Find

▶ Preserve the past: examine, but do not touch, cultural or his-
  toric structures and artifacts.

▶ Leave rocks, plants, and other natural objects as you find
  them.

▶ Avoid introducing or transporting non-native species.

▶ Do not build structures, furniture, or dig trenches.

5. Minimize Campfire Impacts

▶ Campfires can cause lasting impacts on the backcountry. Use a
  lightweight stove for cooking and enjoy a candle lantern for
  light.

Alex Kosseff

Preserving cultural artifacts is just as much a part of LNT as protecting the natural environment. A little-known location has helped protect this Native American rock art from vandalism and other damage.

▶ Where fires are permitted, use established fire rings, fire pans, or mound fires.

▶ Keep fires small. Use only sticks from the ground that can be broken by hand.

▶ Burn all wood and coals to ash, put out campfires completely, and then scatter cool ashes.

6. Respect Wildlife

▶ Observe wildlife from a distance. Do not follow or approach it.

▶ Never feed animals. Feeding wildlife damages the animals' health, alters natural behaviors, and exposes them to predators and other dangers.

▶ Protect wildlife and your food by storing rations and trash securely.

▶ Control pets at all times, or leave them at home.

▶ Avoid wildlife during sensitive times: mating, nesting, raising young, or winter.

7. Be Considerate of Other Visitors

▶ Respect other visitors and protect the quality of their experience.

▶ Be courteous. Yield to other users on the trail.

▶ Step to the downhill side of the trail when encountering pack stock.

▶ Take breaks and camp away from trails and other visitors.

▶ Let nature's sounds prevail. Avoid loud voices and noises.

These seven principles form the backbone of the LNT curriculum. They're easy to remember and can be interpreted by the individual user. Outdoor leaders play a critical role in introducing these concepts to trip participants and in modeling conscientious decision making based on the principles. Teach by explaining why you're doing what you do—it may not be obvious to a participant who sees nothing wrong with tossing some leftovers in a stream or building a roaring fire every night.

In addition to educational materials, LNT also offers formal training programs. The two-day Trainer course is designed for those who will be teaching others LNT skills. This is a valuable opportunity for outdoor leaders to hone their impact and teaching skills on this subject. The Trainer courses are offered by organizations and individuals around the country. Those who instruct the Trainer courses have completed a LNT Masters course, a five-day training program offered only through the National Outdoor Leadership School or the Appalachian Mountain Club. Typically, Masters courses are taught by one instructor from the training organization and one from a land-management agency.

OVERCROWDING

While there remain many relatively unvisited wild areas, these tend to be remote from population centers, poorly known, or perceived as particularly inhospitable. Other areas tend to be quite popular.

When pressure builds to decrease overcrowding, organized groups are usually the first to be regulated. All commercial programs on federal land are already required to obtain some form of permit so that appropriate fees can be collected. It's fairly easy to restrict where and when these groups can go into areas. Management of informal groups is much more difficult—although this happens through permit systems in many areas.

To some degree this is a tragedy of the commons. Many organized groups attract people by offering to take them places the participants have heard of. Leaders, as well, may not know of other areas to take their groups. Use builds and builds until land managers or users begin to push for a solution—usually regulation. Some forward-thinking outdoor leaders steer away from the most heavily used areas, which raises new issues. Some people go to these less trafficked areas to get away from the crowds. Organized groups, which tend to be on the larger side, seem like crowds to many outdoor recreationists. Also, people who attend outdoor programs often return to the same areas they visited on the program—increasing use even further.

How much use is too much is a highly individual issue. Do you wish to

Conservation Education ——————

My favorite approach to conservation education is the teachable moment. This occurs when a topic serendipitously comes up. This might be because the group passes by a dam, a rare plant, an interesting critter, or a clearcut. Or it might be a subject someone brings up in conversation—someone asking about a canyon formed or an offhand remark about the glacier you passed the day before. Leaders who want their participants to understand their surroundings and the conservation issues that are important in an area jump on these opportunities. Use them to teach what you know, as a way to get someone else to share their knowledge, or as a jumping-off point for a discussion.

One valuable lesson for all participants to understand is land man-

encounter no other groups in the backcountry? What if you encounter a group of ten (or fifty) when you get to the summit? How about passing people every few minutes all day? Or paddling a river where boats are practically "bumper to bumper," and local authorities use jet boats to enforce laws and regulations and assist paddlers in distress? While some people who venture outdoors enjoy a social atmosphere once they get there, most set out to find some peace and solitude. Often the only way land managers feel they are able to provide for more solitude is through limiting users via a permit system. This approach turns off many users who feel it is antithetical to the nature of the "wilderness" experience they seek. Recent efforts by land managers to provide for more solitude on Oregon's Mount Hood, for instance, were thwarted by users who resented limits on their right to visit the area.

Unregulated use and users who do not employ Leave No Trace skills can turn a backcountry experience into something entirely unexpected. "I had no idea what I was getting into," Vanessa Tomasic told me. Tomasic, an instructor for the AMC's Mountain Leadership School, had just gotten back from a canoe camping trip on the Saco River through New Hampshire and Maine. "People left bags of trash in the campsites—bags. There was loud music all night, and during the day it was like playing bumper boats with a bunch of drunk canoeists—they would just run into you." Clearly, Vanessa's experience is not the norm in many areas, but the backcountry users she encountered will go elsewhere. We all need to lend a hand in determining how areas should be used and how many people should use them.

agement. Many people assume that the land they are recreating on is a park and as such is protected from logging, development, mining, and other human intrusion. This is not always the case. Recreational activities in the United States take place on national park, national forest, Bureau of Land Management, national wildlife refuge, state park, state forest, and private lands—to name just some of the more common situations. Each government management agency, and even each unit within that agency, has different regulations and priorities. It is interesting to participants to understand this, particularly if the explanation can tie into the regulations the group must observe, a clearcut in the distance, or cows grazing nearby.

National parks are managed for conservation and public enjoyment. National forests are managed for conservation and multiple use, including recreation, timber harvesting, grazing, and mining. These are just

An outdoor leader instructs participants in a stewardship project.

two examples. The participant who leaves a program understanding some of these basics will be a more informed citizen with regard to land use and land protection issues. In complex issues, a few informed individuals who feel a strong connection with the issue can have a lot of influence.

Stewardship

One of the greatest ways to incorporate conservation into the programs we lead is by using our own hands to give something back to the areas we love. Trails need work to prevent erosion and maintain a passable route, rivers and other areas often benefit from trash cleanups, and invasive species that threaten the stability of ecosystems are sometimes removed by hand. Land managers rarely have the funds to perform all of this work, and the extra hands of volunteers are often appreciated.

Stewardship might consist of a period of service with a longer program, or it may be the express purpose of an outing. The AMC's *Complete Guide to Trail Building and Maintenance* is a good primer on trail projects. Many organizations, the AMC included, and trail clubs offer training opportunities for volunteers to learn trail or other stewardship skills. Government agencies are often willing to provide free training for groups of volunteers willing to come and labor for the land. The Student Conservation Association is another great resource for those interested in all aspects of land stewardship.

RECOMMENDED READING

Demrow, Carl, and David Salisbury, *The Complete Guide to Trail Building and Maintenance,* Boston: Appalachian Mountain Club, 1998.

Hampton, Bruce, and David Cole, *Soft Paths: How to Enjoy the Wilderness without Harming It,* Mechanicsburg, Pennsylvania: Stackpolc Books, 1995.

Leave No Trace, *Outdoor Skills & Ethics,* Boulder, Colorado: Leave No Trace and National Outdoor Leadership School, n.d.

Reid, Scott, ed., *The Leave No Trace Training Cookbook,* Boulder, Colorado: Leave No Trace, 2001.

Waterman, Laura, and Guy Waterman, *Backwoods Ethics,* 2nd ed., Woodstock, Vermont: Countryman Press, 1993.

Waterman, Laura, and Guy Waterman, *Wilderness Ethics,* Woodstock, Vermont: Countryman Press, 1993.

CHAPTER 15
Don't Forget to Have Fun!

I can juggle—I taught myself from a book in high school. I can keep three beanbags in the air and even do a few tricks. But I'm not a juggler—I can't juggle more than three objects, and I haven't advanced on to knives, torches, or the like. Nor can I juggle while on a unicycle—in fact, I've never been on a unicycle. I firmly believe that trying to ride one while juggling would be a bad place to start.

As an outdoor leader you are a juggler—there are always several things to remain aware of and involved in at once. Outdoor leadership and juggling are most enjoyable when you can meet with some success without having to try too hard. Neither activity is much fun if things are supposed to be in the air but instead you're picking them up off the ground. Even worse than dropping everything and rushing around to pick it all up is grabbing the wrong end of the knife or torch.

Picking everything up off the ground all the time, grabbing the wrong end of knives and torches, and falling off unicycles doesn't sound like much fun? You're right—it isn't. That's why jugglers work their way up to these skills, and it's why as an outdoor leader you should start small too.

My very first outdoor leadership experience, before I ever had a summer job doing it, was leading a college outing club group winter camping in Minnesota. I'd never been winter camping before. The last time my co-leader had been snow camping, she'd frozen her feet. Our lack of planning meant that we had to switch destinations due to camping restrictions at the first park we went to; then, once we skied in and set up camp, our stoves didn't work well, most of our water bottles froze, and our van got stuck in the snow as we were trying to leave. Had a helpful man with a big 4X4 not happened by to tow us out, we would've been stuck 15 miles from a main road—and nobody knew where we were. Clearly, I would've been better off starting with something more manageable—like a summer day hike.

Put everything you've read in this book in the back of your mind and get out and lead something. On my first juggling venture, I used one soft beanbag. If it's your first outdoor leadership experience, make it a day trip somewhere familiar doing something relatively simple and sane. In no time I moved up to two beanbags, pushing myself just enough to keep things interesting. Soon I tried three bags, but I couldn't remember what the book said about moving your hands back and forth so the balls didn't hit each other, so I went back to two. You'll find that when you're out leading, you won't remember much of what this book says either. You'll have the most fun if you don't struggle by undertaking too much at once; instead, slowly develop your talents. That way you can have fun instead of having to worry and think too much.

Many of the AMC's volunteer leaders start out by participating in trips. Then they move on to take a weekend-long leadership training program. The next step is becoming an assistant to a more experienced leader. Finally, they become full-blown leaders—often only on a day hike. This approach builds skills, develops confidence, and lets both leader and participants have fun.

With time and commitment you will develop the talent and skills to enjoy more ambitious outings. Tasks that once seemed difficult will become second nature—you won't even have to actively think about them. Then, and only then, will you have fun leading the first ascent of Mount Precipitous in the northern reaches of Outer Backofbeyondistan. Until then, have fun on Mount More Familiar, closer (if only slightly) to home.

Humor

In case you haven't realized it, a sense of humor and an upbeat attitude are key to enjoying outdoor leadership. Even when you start small, you can be pretty sure everything is *not* always going to go perfectly. When things go wrong, smile. Figure out how to fix whatever it is (*still* smiling). Return to juggling all that's going well.

Even if you're still smiling, everybody else may not be. Joking can be your best friend. When the pot is boiling over and nobody seems to know what to do—just when you're trying to find your left shoe and the seals you came to see haven't said "boo"—this is when having fun is entirely up to you. It really (usually) isn't all that bad. In hindsight, you will probably reflect on your worst moments as an outdoor leader as some of the most memorable (or even the best) of your life.

Being confused as to where you are can be stressful to some group members. Whenever I'm in this situation (hardly ever, really) I break out my "homing spatula." Acting very seriously, and holding the $1.99 device by its pancake-flipping end, I claim that I can feel a pull on the handle that shows me the right direction. I have eventually had to explain to a few people that I am not serious, but for most people having a little laugh and seeing the leader be relaxed breaks any tension. Then we can get back to figuring out where we're going.

Why Is It Fun (and Rewarding)?

While there are many answers to this question, here are a few of my ideas:

People: Working with and getting to know people is fun and rewarding. This is especially true when they enjoy and compliment your efforts. Knowing you're doing something important for other people can offer tremendous personal fulfillment.

The smiles on people's faces, the appreciation at the end of a trip, and even the ongoing thanks that people may express years later are all fun and rewarding. When you hear a story from a trip you led, you can have the pleasure of thinking *I helped build that*—even if you publicly give the participants all the credit, you deserve some too.

Sharing: Most outdoor leaders are passionate about the outdoors and the activities they lead. Beyond getting to be in the places you love and doing the activities you want to do, it's fun and fulfilling to see people develop some of the same connections that you have.

Sharing has its immediate rewards, but it's also nice to see the long term. I know many people who've developed a lifelong involvement with the outdoors following trips or training programs I led them on.

Learning: You are guaranteed never to lead *any* activity in the outdoors in which you don't learn something and grow as a person. There's always something a little different about the environment, the people, or yourself. Nothing beats experiential learning—every experience you have as an outdoor leader expands your horizons just a little more.

I don't think there are any leaders out there who don't feel they're better people for the leadership roles they've take on. There's the better understanding you might reach of an alpine ecosystem and the appreciation you gain for its weather. There are skills in working closely with groups that are in huge demand by society, but so hard to develop—some employers put extra value on outdoor leadership experiences for just this reason. And there's the better understanding of yourself you'll come to—how you work best with others, what your strengths and weaknesses really are, and how you respond in a crisis.

Flow: When everything comes together perfectly—the people, the activity, your leadership—there is a profound sense of mastery, focus, and accomplishment. The concept of flow is explained in a little more detail in chapter 6. Perhaps for some this is the moment of self-actualization.

Because of all the variables that need to be in alignment, flow is difficult to achieve during an outdoor activity. When it does happen, it can be a powerful experience. I recall struggling as a group post-holed through deep snow on one of the earlier trips I led. The teamwork, the brilliant blue skies, and the physical effort were a remarkable experience that I will remember with fondness for the rest of my life.

Belonging: To some degree this may be found in a group, but many leaders gain a sense of belonging within a community of other leaders. Some of the best moments of my life and my greatest experiences have been shared with fellow outdoor leaders—both on trips and elsewhere

The Reward

"*It is more important to tell the simple, blunt truth than it is to say things that sound good. The group is not a contest of eloquence.*

It is more important to act in behalf of everyone than it is to win arguments. The group is not a debating society.

It is more important to react wisely to what is happening than it is to be able to explain everything in terms of certain theories. The group is not a final examination for a college course.

The wise leader is not collecting a string of successes. The leader is helping others to find their own success. There is plenty to go around. Sharing success with others is very successful.

The single principle behind all creation teaches us that true benefit blesses everyone and diminishes no one.

The wise leader knows that the reward for doing the work arises naturally out of the work."

—JOHN HEIDER, THE TAO OF LEADERSHIP

in life. Outdoor leaders are a great community of people and a lot of fun to be around.

As this book makes clear, caring leadership requires a lot of effort. The best way to remain motivated for this effort is to make sure the leadership experience remains fun and rewarding for you. When you start to lose this sense of enjoyment and reward, it's time to make some kind of change in your approach or what you're leading.

Dealing with Stress

If everything you're trying to juggle falls to the floor and you can't move fast enough to pick it all up, outdoor leadership can be stressful. First, remember the "sense of humor" stuff. If that doesn't help, smile anyway and remember all the positive reasons you have for taking on

AMC file photo

A smile can make the whole experience fun—even under cold, damp, and cramped conditions.

your leadership role. After things get worse, they will get better, and you'll be rewarded for your patience.

Remember that you aren't alone. Much of this book talks about the leader as a lone actor. Sometimes this is the case, but not that often. Co-leaders are invaluable for sharing the burden of a stressful situation (they can also, on occasion, be the cause of stress). Also look to your group for strength and support (within appropriate bounds)—do not try to do everything yourself. Remember the story about Jane Imholte, the uber-guide with the injured knee, and know that offering real participation to the participants is beneficial to them as well as helpful to you.

If you routinely find yourself stressed in your outdoor leadership role, something's wrong. Try backing off and leading an easier group or an easier activity—there are outdoor leadership roles to match almost every aspiring leader. Get some more hands-on training or review a few relevant sections of this book. Talk to experienced leaders and ask for their advice. If things still don't seem to work out, do realize that outdoor leadership is not a good fit for everyone in every stage of their lives. There are many other rewarding things to do in life.

In Closing ———————————————————

Outdoor leadership should be enjoyable. The outdoor leader's definition of *wages* must be broader than the numbers that appear on any paycheck that may happen to come your way. If you're not having fun, it's probably not worth it. There are easier ways to visit wild places and travel the world. I'm not saying that outdoor leadership isn't hard work some of the time—it certainly isn't play. But the best of what we do and who we are emerges when we can enjoy it even during the rough stretches. As you juggle all the responsibilities of outdoor leadership, may your beanbags stay airborne, and may you remember at least a few of the things you read in this book.

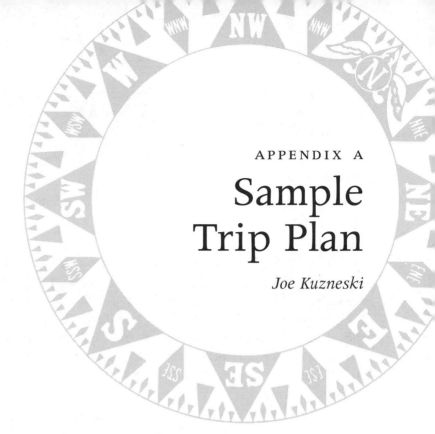

Sample Trip Plan

Joe Kuzneski

A MC leader and master trip planner Joe Kuzneski graciously contributed one of his detailed trip plans. This plan is for a three-day backpacking trip, run by two volunteer leaders and open to AMC members.

Activity Type: Backpack in the White Mountain National Forest in NH. Area of backpack is in the Baldfaces and the Wild River Valley.

Dates: July 11–14, 2002.

Skill/Experience Level: Novice (some previous backpacking experience).

Objectives: (1) Manage backcountry risks.
(2) All in group enjoy the experience and the great views (if the weather cooperates).
(3) Participants learn or improve map and compass skills.
(4) Introduce participants to bushwhacking by doing a short one.

Co-leader: Jeff Hogan. Jeff's skills complement my own. He has very strong leadership skills and is adept at route finding and teaching outdoor skills.

Group Size: Eight participants maximum and two leaders.

Brief Description

Thursday, July 11. Group will stay at the AMC Pinkham Notch Joe Dodge Lodge. Review map and compass skills with group at 7:00 A.M. in parlor.

Friday, July 12. Spot cars at parking lot near Wild River campground. Backpack will start from Baldface Circle Trailhead on NH Rt. 113. Group will hike to jct. of Slippery Brook, Baldface Knob, and Eastman Mt. Trails via Baldface Circle and Slippery Brook Trails and camp in this vicinity. First-day mileage and elevation gain are approx. 3.5 miles and 2,050 ft. Before dinner, bushwhack from brook crossing south of trail jct. to summit of Eastman Mt. (approx 0.5 mile). Return to camp via trails.

Saturday, July 13. Hike to summit of South Baldface Mt. via Baldface Knob and Baldface Circle Trails. This is mostly an open ridge. Take a break on the open summit of South Baldface, which has excellent views in all directions, and practice map and compass skills by taking bearings on the Wildcats and Carters and identifying these peaks on the map. Continue hike on Baldface Circle Trail over mostly open ridge to North Baldface Mt. Again, practice map and compass skills. Continue hike on Baldface Circle Trail to Eagle Crag. Turn west onto Eagle Link Trail, which quickly drops below the trees and heads into the Wild River Valley, to a point about 0.25 mile east of Wild River. Camp in this vicinity. Second-day mileage and elevation gain are approx. 6 miles and 1,550 ft.

Sunday, July 14. Hike west on Eagle Link Trail, cross Wild River, and continue on to Wild River Trail. Hike north on Wild River Trail to its terminus at the parking lot near the Wild River campground. Third-day mileage is approx. 5.3 miles with no elevation gain.

Permits: White Mountain National Forest Outfitter-Guide Card

Bailout Routes: All of the below are to get off the exposed Baldface Ridge.

Back down Slippery Brook Trail

South leg of Baldface Circle Trail (has steep ledges that require care and can be dangerous when wet)

Bicknell Ridge Trail

North leg of Baldface Circle Trail (has steep ledges that require care and can be dangerous when wet)

Eagle Link Trail

Evacuation Considerations: If assisted evacuation is required, call should be made to NH State Police (800-852-3411), who will coordinate with NH Fish and Game. Phone available at the AMC Cold River Camp near Baldface Circle Trailhead.

Time Management Plan: Times are approximate and are for guidance only.

Thursday, July 11

7:00 P.M.—Introductions and review trip plan.

7:30 P.M.—Review map and compass skills.
Joe discusses reading topo maps.
Jeff discusses use of compass.
Jeff discusses use of map and compass together.
Joe discusses declination.

9:30 P.M.—Distribute group gear and group food.

Friday, July 12

7:00 A.M.—Breakfast.

8:30 A.M.—Leave the AMC Pinkham Notch parking lot, drive to Wild River Campground to spot cars, then continue on to parking lot near Baldface Circle Trailhead.

10:00 A.M.—Begin hiking.

10:35 A.M.—Reach Slippery Brook Trail.

1:30 P.M.—Arrive at area of campsite. Set up camp, get water from stream that crosses trail to south.

3:00 P.M.—Hike south on Slippery Brook Trail to stream crossing. Start bushwhack from this point. Bearing = 90 deg. true, 107 deg. magnetic.

4:15 P.M.—Reach summit of Eastman Mt.

4:45 P.M.—Start back to camp.

5:15 P.M.—Arrive at campsite, begin dinner.

Saturday, July 13

6:00 A.M.—Wake up.

8:00 A.M.—Start hiking.

9:45 A.M.—Arrive summit South Baldface.

10:45 A.M.—Leave summit South Baldface.

11:30 A.M.—Arrive summit North Baldface.

12:45 P.M.—Leave summit North Baldface.

2:00 P.M.—Start hiking on Eagle Link Trail.

3:30 P.M.—Arrive at area of campsite.

Sunday, July 14

8:00 A.M.—Wake up.

10:00 A.M.—Start hiking.

11:00 A.M.—Cross Spider Bridge.

12:30 P.M.—Arrive at parking lot.

Potential Hazards

Baldface Ridge in thunderstorm.

Bailout routes available.

Stream crossings in high water: Wild River, Spruce Brook, Red Brook.

Carry rope to allow rigging for a safe crossing. Use only if necessary.

Water: Two water filters, belonging to the leaders, will be carried. If any participants have reliable filters that they want to bring, these can be substituted for those of the leaders. Chemical treatment will also be available as a backup.

Friday

Fill water bottles at Joe Dodge Lodge. Each person start out carrying 2 qts.

Closest reliable water to campsite is about 0.5 mile south of campsite on Slippery Brook Trail.

Saturday

> Fill water bottles from Slippery Brook. Since next reliable water is about 4.5 miles from campsite, on Eagle Link Trail, each person will carry 2 qts. minimum.

> Water for dinner is available from the Wild River, about 0.25 mile away from campsite.

Sunday

> Wild River is water source.

Since this day's hike is only about 5 miles, with no elevation gain, and we will be hiking beside a river, only 1 qt. of water per person need be carried.

Food: The leaders will provide backcountry breakfasts and dinners (cost included in price of trip). Each person is responsible for their own trail snacks and lunch. Dinner Thursday at the Joe Dodge Lodge is not included in price of trip, but Friday breakfast is included. Backcountry meals are vegetarian, but not vegan.

Backcountry breakfasts

> Choice of various flavors of instant oatmeal

Backcountry dinners

Friday

> Tomato-basil soup

> Pasta with roasted garlic and sun-dried tomatoes

> Blueberry tart prepared in field

Saturday

> Cream of leek soup

> Couscous with olive oil, garlic, sun-dried tomatoes, and green olives

> Cherry tart prepared in field

Backcountry beverages

> Prior to the trip, each person will be polled to select his/her choice of coffee, tea, herb tea, cocoa, or milk

Group Gear

Tents: After registering participants, leaders will select which participants bring tents. The leader team will bring one tent for their own use.

Stoves: Two stoves will be carried, both butane/propane. Two fuel canisters will be carried. The leaders will supply the stoves, unless participants have similar stoves and would like to bring them. Fuel canisters will be purchased from trip funds.

Cooking Gear: Joe's group cooking gear will be used (8-qt. pot, 3-qt. pot, potholders, ladles, stirring spoons).

First-Aid Kit: Jeff will bring his group first-aid kit.

Water Bag: Joe will bring his 2-gal bag.

Rope: Jeff will bring rope and hardware to assist with stream crossings.

Cost: Assumes 10 persons total

Lodging & breakfast	390	Published rates
Camping food	100	Based on actuals for last year's trip
Setup expenses	20	Phone calls, postage, etc.
Contingency	40	
Total	550	
Per person	55	

Note: Refund any excess funds at closure event.

Closure Event

Pizza at restaurant on Rt. 16 south of Conway.

Communication Plan

Activity announcement to appear in the June issue of *AMC Outdoors.*

July 11–14: Backpack With Map and Compass Theme. This fun backpack for novices (some bkpkng exp reqd) in the Baldface Range and Wild River Valley will focus on improving map and compass skills. A short bushwhack is included. Cost of $55 incls. one night lodging, one restaurant bkfst, backcountry bkfsts and dinners. For info send SASE to P.O. Box 9876, Sometown, MA 02345. Leaders Joe Kuzneski (401-555-1234) and Jeff Hogan (617-555-5678).

Prospectus will be sent to interested persons who call in response to the announcement in *AMC Outdoors*. Convey important information and set expectations.

Objectives

Trip plans

Map and compass theme, including short bushwhack

Skills required

Individual gear required (comprehensive list)

Plan for group gear

Emphasis on group dynamics/teamwork

Hiking pace

Keeping group together

Shared chores

Emphasis on Leave No Trace

Leaders' qualifications

Cost

Items specifically covered by trip cost

Items not covered by trip cost

Cancellation policy

Refund policy

Risk disclosure

Liability waiver form

Registration form with req.'d medical history

Legal Issues

Catherine Hansen-Stamp

This section is intended to provide outdoor leaders with general information on legal and risk-management issues. It is not intended to provide specific legal advice. Laws can vary significantly from jurisdiction to jurisdiction, and outdoor leaders should consult with legal counsel, experienced in recreational law and familiar with the laws in their jurisdiction, regarding matters specific to their work.

Catherine Hansen-Stamp is an attorney in private practice in Golden, Colorado. She consults with and advises recreation providers, recreational product manufacturers and sellers, and related organizations on risk-management and legal liability issues. She speaks and writes on these issues and is coeditor (with Charles "Reb" Gregg) of the *Outdoor Education and Recreation Law Quarterly,* published by the Outdoor Network (lawquarterly.com). She is a member of the Wyoming, Colorado, and American Bar Associations.

Introduction

It's valuable for any outdoor leader to have some understanding of legal liability issues, in the context of risk management. Recreational activities from outdoor hiking to whitewater rafting involve inherent and other risks that provide challenge and excitement, enticing individuals to participate. These risks provide the challenge to participate and the opportunity for growth. The inherently risky nature of recreational activities, our litigious society, and individuals' frequent failure to accept responsibility for themselves are all factors that have made overall risk-management practices critical to the viability of any recreational business. Conducting responsible risk-management practices (including enlightenment on some basic legal issues) is key to assisting organizations and their leaders in minimizing legal exposure.

As you have learned, risk management for recreation and adventure organizations spans all aspects of a business: hiring and training employees, structuring and following emergency protocols, drafting releases and similar documents, using and maintaining equipment, and a host of other things. Outdoor leaders are key players in the risk-management equation, because they're the ones on the ground—instructing and supervising students, making judgments in the field, implementing and maintaining equipment, filling out accident reports, and activating emergency plans. Unfortunately, thinking about legal liability and risk management can be scary. Organizations and their leaders can be overcome with the fear of potential injury and death, and, in thinking about these issues, focus exclusively on how to avoid a lawsuit. If organizations and leaders can change their focus and view these issues in a more positive way, the approach can be different. If you are an outdoor leader, keep your focus on operating professionally—getting the necessary training, honing your skills, acting responsibly, and exercising good judgment. Ultimately your conduct and actions may minimize or reduce actual injuries or accidents, and potentially the occurrence of claims or lawsuits. This results in a proactive, rather than reactive, approach, and a win–win situation for everyone.

What risks are we talking about, and who are we managing them for? From an organization's perspective, there are really two sets of risks. The first set includes those risks or hazards inherent in recreational activities—the who, what, where, and how. These risks can result in injury, death, or loss to participants. Second is the risk of loss (monetary or otherwise) to the operation (or its leaders) often resulting from a participant's injury, death, or loss. By examining risk management, an organization can attempt to manage these various risks. One key in the recreation and adventure field is to remember that risks can be managed, but not necessarily eliminated. An organization and its leaders can run a professional operation and engage in responsible practices, but they cannot guarantee safety. Accidents or injuries can and do occur, and litigation can be an end result. Following is a snapshot.

Civil Law

There are two basic types of law—criminal and civil. And while criminal law is very important, we will focus here on civil law—the most common source of liability for outdoor organizations and their leaders. Civil law is generally divided into two categories: contract law, or "enforceable" promises, and torts—"wrongs" to a person or his or her property, our focus here.

The most common tort is negligence, generally defined under the law as the failure to use ordinary care; that is, failing to do what a person of ordinary prudence would have done under the same or similar circumstances. ("Gross" negligence or other more egregious conduct can form the basis for a separate tort—a claim that the organization or its leader acted recklessly or with an intent to harm.) A person (plaintiff) bringing a legal claim for negligence against another (defendant) must prove four elements: The defendant owed the plaintiff a duty of care under the circumstances, the defendant breached that duty, the defendant's breach was the legal cause of the plaintiff's injury, and this breach resulted in damage to the plaintiff. The judge determines whether the defendant owes a duty of care in a particular set of circumstances; if so, a fact finder (judge or jury) determines whether the defendant has breached that duty and whether the defendant's breach caused the plaintiff's injuries.

Defenses against a claim of negligence vary. The plaintiff may fail to prove one of the four elements of negligence, the plaintiff may be found to have assumed the risk of injuries, or the plaintiff's conduct may be found to have contributed to the injuries. Maybe the plaintiff signed a release of the right to sue for negligence (some type of participant agreement). As a result some lawsuits are dismissed before they go to a jury or judge—but some aren't.

The bottom line is that once a lawsuit is filed, it can take many months or years, and a huge financial outlay, to resolve the dispute. Lawsuits can also take an emotional toll on an organization and its employees, as well as complicating ongoing operations. Alternatives to a lawsuit can include some form of alternative dispute resolution (ADR), in which the parties agree to resolve the dispute outside the confines of the traditional legal system. Forms of alternative dispute resolution can include arbitration and mediation. These more informal means to resolve disputes have become popular in recent years because they often lead to quicker results and do less damage to the parties' relationship.

Ideally, of course, an organization (and its leaders) are in the best position if they can avoid a lawsuit altogether. This isn't always possible, but a positive approach to risk management can go a long way toward it.

Leader's Duty of Care

What are the precise "duties of care" that outdoor leaders owe to their participants? Will an outdoor leader, employed by an organization, be named in a lawsuit? When will an outdoor leader be found to have breached a duty of care and ultimately found responsible for injuring a student? These are some of the questions I'm often asked.

It's impossible to precisely define the duties that outdoor leaders may owe in different circumstances. In addition, duties can vary depending upon the law of the particular jurisdiction or facts of the case. Some general duties of care may include a duty to exercise care to maintain equipment and instruct on its proper use and supervise participants and instruct them on skills. A good concept to remember is that duties can arise in a variety of ways. For example, duties can: be outlined by statutes or case law, established by an organization's own internal documents, shifted through the use of written agreements, defined by the type of individual involved, highlighted by standards or practices in the industry, or expanded by a leader's words or conduct.

In determining whether a duty has been breached, a judge or jury may consider, among other things, expert testimony, statutes, and evidence of standards or practices in the industry. Experts may testify about the standards or practices (if any exist) in the industry. They may look to other organizations for examples of "reasonable" conduct, or look to other evidence of reasonable behavior. State or federal licensing or statutory requirements may be reviewed for compliance. Did the organization have relevant internal policies or procedures—and were these followed?

The judge or jury will compare a leader's conduct with what a "reasonably prudent person" would have done in the same or similar circumstances. A leader's conduct will generally be compared to that of a reasonably prudent leader instructing or leading that particular activity. In other words, a leader is generally required to exercise the care commensurate with someone teaching *those particular skills*. This would probably address the type of equipment used, the way it was used, technical techniques used to engage in or teach an activity, and so forth. The process applies to paid leaders as well as volunteers. (Although a volunteer may have protection, or immunity, from liability under the Federal Volunteer Protection Act and/or a companion state statute, the organization would generally not share that immunity.) If the leader's conduct fell below those standards or practices, he or she could be considered negligent.

The court or jury determination can be very fact-specific and dependent upon the circumstances of the case and the law in the particular jurisdiction. Ultimately, even if the leader is found to have breached a duty, that breach must be proved to be the cause of the plaintiff's injuries.

An organization will be responsible for the acts of its employee (even volunteer) leaders committed within the scope of their employment ("vicarious" liability). If an injured student files a lawsuit alleging leader wrongdoing, the organization may be named as a defendant. In addition, the individual leader, whether employee, volunteer, or otherwise, may also be named as a defendant in the lawsuit (although this is less common). The viability and nature of these types of claims vary from state to state. Again, volunteers themselves may have some immunity from liability.

Note that if a leader is found liable to an injured party for more egregious conduct—gross negligence, willful and wanton misconduct, or criminal misconduct—there can be additional issues. In many cases, an employer will not be vicariously liable to an injured party for this more egregious conduct. Further, a leader may be subject to additional liability (punitive damages) if he or she is proven to have engaged in such conduct. There may also be no insurance coverage (many policies will not cover this type of conduct), and any participant release is usually not enforceable to shield the wrongdoer.

The Inherent Risk Doctrine
and State Safety Acts

In the context of recreational activities, *inherent risks* are those risks that are integral to the activities and cannot be eliminated without destroying the unique character of the activities. Risks may be desirable (moguls, whitewater) or undesirable (falling rocks, sudden and severe weather changes). Common law (that defined by court decisions) generally provides that participants may not recover from providers for injuries that result from the inherent risks of recreational activities. In other words, the provider has no duty to protect participants from these risks and no resulting liability to participants for injuries resulting from those risks.

Courts' confusion over these principles have prompted many states to enact statutes better defining the law. Many statutes cover just one activity. For example, Colorado has a Ski Act and an Equine Act, each of which attempts to define the types of inherent risks specific to the activity, as well as the duties that providers owe to participants. Wyoming, Vermont, and a few other states, on the other hand, have one act covering all recreational activities.

Nevertheless, as discussed above, organizations and their leaders can be held responsible if a court or jury finds that their negligence caused the participant's injuries. Unfortunately, the line between inherent risks and negligence is often fuzzy. Instructor judgment is a common gray area. The argument can be made that a leader's judgment in the context of leading wilderness or other recreational activities is an inherent risk of the activity—some courts have supported this, and others have not. An offshoot is a leader's judgment in an instructional context. Some courts have ruled that the very essence of teaching new skills involves the need to legitimately push students beyond what they have already mastered—an inherent risk of the activity. As a result, some courts have said that instructors are only responsible for somehow increasing the risks beyond those inherent in the activity. Other courts have found that instructors owe a higher degree of care to their students. The waters are muddy. The bottom line: leaders should endeavor to exercise good judgment and use common sense.

The Information Exchange

While it's unconventional, I've found that the information exchange—that critical information flowing from provider to participant and participant to provider—can play an important role before, during, and after an accident. This flow of information (good or bad) can influence whether accidents occur, and if they do, whether a suit is filed.

A provider imparts information to participants through, for instance, brochures, phone calls, releases, and pretrip talks (disclosure). A participant imparts information to the provider through applications, medical information forms and phone calls (screening), and so forth. Information is powerful, regardless of which way it's flowing. It allows individuals to make informed choices about whether and how they would like to participate in the activities. Likewise, the organization needs information to make choices about its participants. The type of information exchanged, when it's exchanged, and the manner in which it's exchanged can have a profound impact upon the activity, particularly if an accident or injury occurs. When the organization and its leaders have taken the time to exchange valuable information, there is a better chance of building good rapport with participants. Furthermore, well-informed participants may be more psychologically prepared to deal with discomforts, injuries, and accidents and less inclined to take legal action.

Written Agreements

Many organizations use some form of written participant agreement with their students. These written agreements (often referred to as a "release," "waiver," and/or "acknowledgment and assumption of risks") serve several purposes. First of all, the document can seek to protect the organization (and its leaders) from liability for their negligent conduct (these documents do not generally extend to protect an entity or individual from liability for gross negligence or other more serious misconduct). Importantly, these documents can provide participants with specific information concerning the activities and their associated risks. Participants can then make informed choices about whether to participate. If they choose to participate, they do so with knowledge of the risks involved and with the understanding that they will be responsible for injuries or death resulting from such risks, and resulting from providers' ordinary negligence, if that language is also included in the document.

These types of documents can serve to deter a party from filing a claim. If a lawsuit is filed, the document can also provide the potential for early dismissal of a case. If that is unsuccessful, the document can serve as evidence in trial that the participant was warned of the risks before engaging in the activity, assumed those risks, and thus is partially or wholly responsible for the resulting injury or damage. The bottom line on these documents is that they are not foolproof—courts will generally review them with a fine-tooth comb (because they attempt to extinguish liability for negligence) and will only enforce them on a case-by-case basis. Certainly the presence of a signed release or waiver should never give an organization or instructor a feeling of comfort that it's "okay to be negligent."

Internal Policies and Industry Standards

An organization often develops its own practices, standards, or procedures for operation. These can cover everything from hiring and training staff, to conducting classes or activities, to how to handle emergencies. Organizations and their leaders need to be careful about what and how something is written. If a lawsuit is ever filed, attorneys for the plaintiff (complaining party) can seek, through the discovery process, to review an organization's written documents. Those documents can be reviewed by the opposing counsel, unless there is sufficient reason to prevent disclosure (for example, the documents are protected by a privilege). If the organization's own internal policies have not been followed or have been ignored in the particular case, and the document is sought and reviewed by the opposing lawyer, it can cause serious problems in litigation.

Standards can include those established by law (such as statutes), internal standards developed by an organization, standards or practices developed by an accrediting organization, or simply the accepted "way to do things" in a particular industry. Standards can include generally accepted practices. Finally, guidelines can include just that: guidelines. They can also potentially include accepted practices, depending upon how the guidelines are interpreted within the organization. Standards can be rigid and exact or general and flexible. The bottom line is: Whether it's termed a *standard, practice, guideline,* or something else, it will probably be interpreted in a way consistent with the context in which it's used. For example, if it's called a guideline, but people are told that it must be followed—a "required guideline"—it may be viewed as a mandatory requirement. Talk with your organization if you feel that internal written standards or policies are too rigid, inaccurate, or simply too voluminous for leaders to comprehend or follow. Proactive actions such as this can assist in avoiding future problems.

Caution: Consider carefully what you may consider to be a standard in the industry. Courts have sometimes found an entire industry negligent in the conduct of a practice. Therefore, the way "everybody is doing it" may not always be the best way.

Words or Conduct

An individual leader can, by words or conduct, expand their duty of care or create a duty where one did not previously exist. For example, a leader may have made a statement that is inconsistent with the organization's position or policies. This can muddy the waters of litigation. In one case, a woman brought a claim against an equine provider. She was injured during a riding lesson when the horse bucked and threw her. Among other things, she argued that the release she had signed should not be enforced against her because she'd relied on the riding instructor's statement that she should . . . *go ahead and sign it—it doesn't mean anything anyway.* The court disagreed and enforced the release against her, dismissing the case. The judge found that the woman, *a practicing attorney,* could not have realistically relied on the statement. However, in another case, this type of claim could have been successful.

Equipment

Equipment is integral to most recreational and wilderness activities. Leaders are key players in storage, maintenance, and retirement of equipment, as well as instructions to students on its proper use. Appropriate and regular equipment maintenance, repair, and replacement are critical. Storage of equipment should be carefully considered, and records should be kept of all these activities. Equipment should be used in accordance with manufacturers' instructions and not misused or altered. Students should be instructed on the proper use of equipment and appropriately supervised

Note that different types of laws and doctrines—products liability—apply to sellers of products, including recreational products. Sellers are those individuals or entities in a product's chain of distribution, including product manufacturers, distributors, retailers, lessors, and dealers. All those within this chain of distribution are considered sellers of the product, because they have dealt with the product in the chain of commerce leading to the ultimate consumer.

Although an outdoor organization may not be considered a "seller" and thus liable under products liability laws, use of a product may be involved in an injury to a student. It's possible that a defect in the product somehow caused or contributed to the injury. Or it may be that an inherent risk caused the injury, and the organization and/or leader are not liable for the student's injuries. However, if the equipment is poorly maintained, altered, or misused, it may increase potential liability exposure (for instance, liability for negligently maintaining equipment) for the organization and/or leader and make it difficult to prove some alternate basis for liability. Again, it can muddy the waters in terms of potential liability—especially if the organization, its leader, and a product manufacturer are all named in a lawsuit.

Conclusion

Remember, try to look at legal issues with a positive focus and in a proactive way. Understanding some fundamental legal and risk-management concepts, and how those concepts can assist you in being a more professional and responsible leader, will likely translate into minimizing injuries and accidents, or, possibly, avoiding claims or lawsuits. If a lawsuit is filed, you and your organization will be more prepared to deal with the issues at hand. Bottom line: Take your training seriously, hone your skills, and exercise good judgment. Be tuned in to your organization's risk-management efforts in all areas. If you see a problem, speak up. The collective efforts of each member of an organization, including its leaders, play a vital role in addressing the legal and risk-management issues integral to recreation and adventure programming.

Catherine Hansen-Stamp can be reached at 303-232-7079; e-mail: reclaw@hansenstampattorney.com; website: hansenstampattorney.com.

Training Resources

Following is a list of some of the organizations that offer high-quality leadership and hard skills training that focuses on the needs of outdoor leaders. This is not a comprehensive list, rather a representative selection of some of the best-known programs. There are many other excellent sources of training—unfortunately space does not permit them all to be included here.

American Canoe Association, Springfield, Virginia: Nationwide training and certification programs in canoeing, kayaking, and whitewater rafting. **Website:** acanet.org **Phone:** 703-451-0141

American Mountain Guides Association, Golden, Colorado: Nationwide training and certification programs for rock, alpine, and ski-mountaineering guides. **Website:** amga.com **Phone:** 303-271-.1377

Appalachian Mountain Club, Boston, Massachusetts: In the eastern United States, the AMC offers outdoor leadership and skills-training opportunities for adults and teenagers, with special programs for youth workers and teachers. **Website:** outdoors.org   **Phone:** 617-523-0636

Alaska Mountain Saftey Center, Anchorage, Alaska: Moutain-safety skills courses with a focus on avalanche education. **Website:** alaskaavalanche.com   **Phone:** 907-345-3566

Association for Experimental Education, Boulder, Colorado: International and regional conferences on many aspects of experimental and outdoor education. **Website:** aee.edu   **Phone:** 303-440-8844

Colorado Outward Bound, Golden, Colorado: Backcountry courses in the Rocky Mountain states and beyond with personal growth, outdoor skills, and instructor-training options (merging with Pacific Crest Outward Bound). **Website:** cobs.org   **Phone:** 800-477-2627

Hurricane Island Outward Bound School, Rockland, Maine: Backcountry and marine courses at sites in the eastern United States with personal growth, outdoor skills, and instructor-training options. **Website:** hurricaneisland.com   **Phone:** 866-746-9771

Minnesota State University at Mankato, Mankato, Minnesota: Offers a master's degree program in experiential education that allows students to focus on adventure education. **Website:** mankato.msus.edu **Phone:** 800-722-0544

National Outdoor Leadership School (NOLS), Lander, Wyoming: Extended expedition-style outdoor leadership and skills courses in western United States, Alaska, and numerous international locations. **Website:** nols.edu   **Phone:** 307-332-5300

North Carolina Outward Bound School, Asheville, North Carolina: Backcountry courses in the southeast states and beyond with personal growth, outdoor skills, and instructor-training options. **Website:** ncobs.edu   **Phone:** 888-756-2627

Pacific Crest Outward Bound School, Golden, Colorado: Backcountry courses in the West Coast states and beyond with personal growth, outdoor skills, and instructor-training options (merging with Colorado Outward Bound).   **Website:** pcobs.org   **Phone:** 800-477-2627

Prescott College, Prescott, Arizona: On campus undergraduate and remote-learning graduate degrees in adventure education and related fields.   **Website:** prescott.edu   **Phone:** 928-778-2090

Sterling College, Craftsbury Common, Vermont: Undergraduate degree programs in outdoor education and leadership.
Website: sterlingcollege.edu   **Phone:** 800-648-3591

Stonehearth Open Learning Opportunities (SOLO), Conway, New Hampshire: The full spectrum of standard courses in wilderness medicine and more.   **Website:** stonehearth.com   **Phone:** 603-447-6711

University of New Hampshire, Durham, New Hampshire: The department of Kinesiology offers master's and bachelor's degrees with a focus on outdoor education.   **Website:** unh.edu   **Phone:** 603-862-2070

Voyageur Outward Bound School, Ely, Minnesota: Backcountry courses in Boundary Waters, northern Rockies, Canada, Texas, and Mexico with personal growth, outdoor skills, and instructor-training options.
Website: vobs.com   **Phone:** 800-321-4453

Wilderness Medical Associates, Bryant Pond, Maine: A full array of wilderness medicine courses offered across the United States and internationally.   **Website:** wildmed.com   **Phone:** 888-945-3633.

Wilderness Medicine Institute of NOLS, Lander, Wyoming: Offers all of the standard courses in wilderness medicine, located primarily in the western United States.   **Website:** wmi.nols.edu   **Phone:** 307-332-7800

Wilderness Risk Managers Conference, Lander, Wyoming: Annual conference addressing management, field, legal, ethical, and medical aspects of risk management; held at a different location each year.
Website: wrmc.nols.edu   **Phone:** 307-332-8800

References and Recommended Reading

Ajango, Deborah, ed., *Lessons Learned: A Guide to Accident Prevention and Crisis Response.* Anchorage: University of Alaska Anchorage, 2000.

Baird, Brian, *Are We Having Fun Yet?: Enjoying the Outdoors with Partners, Families, and Groups,* Seattle: The Mountaineers, 1995.

Blagg, Deborah, and Susan Young, "What Makes a Good Leader?" *Harvard Business School Bulletin,* pp. 31–36 (February 2001).

Blum, Arlene, *Annapurna: A Woman's Place,* San Francisco: Sierra Club Books, 1980.

Bonney, Bruce F., and Jack K. Drury, *The Backcountry Classroom: Lesson Plans for Teaching in the Wilderness,* Merrillville, Indiana: ICS Books, 1992.

Broze, Matt, and George Gronseth, *Sea Kayaker's Deep Trouble: True Stories and Their Lessons from* Sea Kayaker *Magazine,* edited by Christopher Cunningham, Camden, Maine: Ragged Mountain Press, 1997.

Clement, Kent, "The Psychology and Sociology of Judgment for Outdoor Leaders," in *2000 Wilderness Risk Management Conference Proceedings,* Lander, Wyoming: National Outdoor Leadership School, 2001, pp. 28–31.

Cockrell, David, ed., *The Wilderness Educator: The Wilderness Education Association Curriculum Guide,* Merrillville, Indiana: ICS Books, 1991.

Csikszentmihalyi, Mihaly, *Flow: The Psychology of Optimal Experience,* New York: Harper & Row, 1990.

Csikszentmihalyi, Mihaly, and Isabella Csikszentmihalyi, "Adventure and the Flow Experience," in *Adventure Programming,* edited by John C. Miles and Simon Priest, State College, Pennsylvania: Venture Publishing, 1999.

Curtis, Rick, *The Backpacker's Field Manual: A Comprehensive Guide to Mastering Backcountry Skills,* New York: Three Rivers Press, 1998.

Daniel, Lucille, ed., *Appalachia,* Boston: Appalachian Mountain Club, biannual.

Daniell, Gene, "Notes/Accidents, Lost Hikers in Wild River Valley," *Appalachia* LII, no. 3, pp. 117–19 (July 1999).

Demrow, Carl, and David Salisbury, *The Complete Guide to Trail Building and Maintenance,* Boston: Appalachian Mountain Club, 1998.

Drucker, Peter, *The Essential Drucker,* New York: HarperCollins, 2001.

Ford, Phyllis, and Jim Blanchard, *Leadership and Administration of Outdoor Pursuits,* 2nd ed., State College, Pennsylvania: Venture Publishing, 1993.

Fredson, Jill A., and Doug Fesler, *Snow Sense: A Guide to Evaluating Snow Avalanche Hazard,* Anchorage: Alaska Mountain Safety Center, 1994.

Freedman, David H., *Corps Business: The 30 Management Principles of the U.S. Marines,* New York: HarperBusiness, 2000.

Garrett, Jim, "When Judgment Is Crucial: Outward Bound USA's Instructor Judgment Training Curriculum," in *2001 Wilderness Risk Management Conference Proceedings,* Lander, Wyoming: National Outdoor Leadership School, 2001, pp. 30–35.

Garvey, Daniel, Drew Leemon, John E. Williamson, and William Zimmerman, *Manual of Accreditation Standards for Adventure Programs,* 3rd ed., Boulder, Colorado: Association for Experiential Education, 1999.

Geller, E. Scott, *The Psychology of Safety Handbook,* 2nd ed., Boca Raton, Florida: CRC Press, 2001.

Glick, Daniel, "Cell Phones: A Call from the Wild," *Newsweek,* p. 59 (July 28, 1997).

Gookin, John, Molly Doran, and Rachael Green, eds., *2000 NOLS Leadership Education Toolbox,* Lander, Wyoming: National Outdoor Leadership School, 2000.

Gorman, James, "The Call in the Wild: Cell Phones Hit the Trail," *New York Times* (August 30, 2001).

Gorman, Stephen, *Winter Camping,* 2nd ed., Boston: Appalachian Mountain Club, 1999.

Graham, John. *Outdoor Leadership: Technique, Common Sense, and Self Confidence,* Seattle: Mountaineers, 1997.

Haddock, Cathye, *Managing Risks in Outdoor Activities,* Wellington: New Zealand Mountain Safety Council, 1993.

Hampton, Bruce, and David Cole, *Soft Paths: How to Enjoy the Wilderness Without Harming It,* Mechanicsburg, Pennsylvania: Stackpole Books, 1995.

Hansen-Stamp, Catherine and Charles R. Gregg, eds., *Outdoor Education and Recreation Law Quarterly,* Boulder, Colorado: Institute for Creative Education, quarterly.

Harvey, Mark, *The National Outdoor Leadership School's Wilderness Guide: The Classic Handbook,* New York: Simon & Schuster, 1999.

Heider, John, *The Tao of Leadership,* Atlanta: Humanics Limited, 1985.

Hersey, Paul, Kenneth Blanchard, and Dewey Johnson, *Management of Organizational Behavior: Leading Human Resources,* 8th ed., Upper Saddle River, New Jersey: Prentice Hall, 2001.

Hunt, Jasper S., Jr., *Ethical Issues in Experiential Education,* Dubuque, Iowa: Kendall/Hunt Publishing, 1990.

Johnson, David W., *Reaching Out: Interpersonal Effectiveness and Self-Actualization,* 5th ed., Boston: Allyn and Bacon, 1993.

Johnson, David W., and Frank P. Johnson, *Joining Together: Group Theory and Group Skills,* 7th ed., Boston: Allyn and Bacon, 2000.

Journal of Experiential Education, Boulder, Colorado: Association for Experiential Education, quarterly.

Kalisch, Kenneth R., *The Role of the Instructor in the Outward Bound Educational Process,* Three Lakes, Wisconsin: Author, 1979.

Klein, Gary, *Sources of Power: How People Make Decisions,* Cambridge, Massachusetts: MIT Press, 1998.

Kosseff, Alex, ed., *AMC Risk Management Standards Manual,* Boston: Appalachian Mountain Club, internal publication, 2001.

Kosseff, Alex, and Mark Yerkes, eds., *AMC Outdoor Leader Handbook,* 2nd ed., Boston: Appalachian Mountain Club, 2000.

Krakauer, Jon, *Into Thin Air,* New York: Villard Books, 1997.

Kropp, Goran, and David Lagercrantz, *Ultimate High: My Everest Odyssey,* New York: Discovery Books/Random House, 2000.

Langmuir, Eric, *Mountaincraft and Leadership,* 3rd ed., West Didsbury, England: The Mountain Leader Training Board, 1995.

Lanza, Michael, *The Ultimate Guide to Backcountry Travel,* Boston: Appalachian Mountain Club Books, 1999.

Leave No Trace, *Outdoor Skills & Ethics,* Boulder Colorado: Leave No Trace and National Outdoor Leadership School.

Leemon, Drew, ed., *Adventure Program Risk Management Report,* Vol. III, Boulder, Colorado: The Association for Experiential Education, 2002.

Leemon, Drew, Tod Schimelpfenig, Sky Gray, Shana Tarter, and Jed Williamson, eds., *Adventure Program Risk Management Report: 1998 Edition,* Boulder, Colorado: The Association for Experiential Education, 1998.

Liddle, Jeff, and Steve Storck, eds., *Adventure Program Risk Management Report: 1995 Edition,* Boulder, Colorado: The Association for Experiential Education, 1995.

Luckner, John L., and Reldan S. Nadler, *Processing the Experience: Strategies to Enhance and Generalize Learning,* 2nd ed., Dubuque. Iowa: Kendall/Hunt Publishing, 1997.

Maslow, Abraham, *Motivation and Personality,* 3rd ed. New York: Addison Wesley Longman, 1987.

Maslow, Abraham, *Toward a Psychology of Being,* 3rd ed., New York: John Wiley and Sons, 1999.

McCammon, Ian, "Decision Making for Wilderness Leaders: Strategies, Traps, and Teaching Methods," in *2001 Wilderness Risk Management Conference Proceedings,* Lander, Wyoming: National Outdoor Leadership School, 2001, pp. 16–29.

McClintock, Mary, "Who's in Charge?: Leadership and Decision-Making Among Peers," *Sea Kayaker,* pp. 28–35 (December 2000).

Miles, John C., and Simon Priest, eds., *Adventure Programming,* State College, Pennsylvania: Venture Publishing, 1999.

Mitchell, Richard G., Jr., *Mountain Experience: The Psychology and Sociology of Adventure,* Chicago: University of Chicago Press, 1983.

National Outdoor Leadership School, *NOLS Wilderness Educator Notebook,* Lander, Wyoming: The National Outdoor Leadership School, 1999.

Noddings, Nel, *Caring: A Feminine Approach to Ethics and Moral Education,* Berkeley: University of California Press, 1984.

Peck, M. Scott, *The Different Drum,* New York: Touchstone, 1987.

Petzoldt, Paul, *The New Wilderness Handbook,* New York: W. W. Norton, 1984.

Plous, Scott, *The Psychology of Judgment and Decision Making,* New York: McGraw-Hill, 1993.

Priest, Simon, and Michael Gass, *Effective Leadership in Adventure Programming,* Champaign, Illinois: Human Kinetics, 1997.

Reid, Scott, ed., *The Leave No Trace Training Cookbook,* Boulder, Colorado: Leave No Trace, 2001.

Rogers, Carl R., *On Becoming a Person: A Therapist's View of Psychotherapy,* New York: Houghton Mifflin, 1989.

Rohnke, Karl, and Steve Butler, *Quicksilver,* Dubuque, Iowa: Kendall/Hunt Publishing, 1995.

Satir, Virginia, *The New Peoplemaking,* Mountain View, California: Science and Behavior Books, 1988.

Schiller, Linda Yael, "Stages of Development in Women's Groups: A Relational Model," in *Group Work Practice in a Troubled Society: Problems and Opportunities,* edited by Roselle Kurlan and Robert Salmon, New York: Haworth Press, 1995.

Schimelpfenig, Tod, and Linda Lindsey, *NOLS Wilderness First Aid,* 3rd ed., Mechanicsburg, Pennsylvania: Stackpole Books and National Outdoor Leadership School, 2000.

Schoel, Jim, Dick Prouty, and Paul Radcliffe, *Islands of Healing: A Guide to Adventure Based Counseling,* Hamilton, Massachusetts: Project Adventure, 1988.

Sessoms, H. Douglas, and Jack L. Stevens, *Leadership and Group Dynamics in Recreation Services,* Boston: Allyn and Bacon, 1981.

Slovic, Paul, Baruch Fischhoff, and Sarah Lichtenstein, "Facts versus Fears:

Understanding Perceived Risk," in *Judgment Under Uncertainty: Heuristics and Biases,* edited by Daniel Kahneman, Paul Slovic, and Amos Tversky, Cambridge, England: Cambridge University Press, 1982.

Sugarman, Deborah A., Kathryn L. Doherty, Daniel E. Garvey, and Michael A. Gass, *Reflective Learning: Theory and Practice,* Dubuque, Iowa: Kendall/Hunt Publishing, 2000.

Tannenbaum, Robert, and Warren H. Schmidt, "How to Choose a Leadership Pattern," *Harvard Business Review* 51, no. 3, pp. 162–180 (May–June 1973).

Tilton, Buck, and Frank Hubble, *The Wilderness First Responder: A Text for the Recognition, Treatment, and Prevention of Wilderness Emergencies,* Guilford, Connecticut: Globe Pequot Press, 1998.

———, *Medicine for the Backcountry,* 3rd ed., Guilford, Connecticut: Globe Pequot Press, 1999.

Tuckman, Bruce W., "Developmental Sequence in Small Groups," *Psychological Bulletin* 63, no. 6, pp. 384–99 (1965).

Tuckman, Bruce W., and Mary Ann Jensen, "Stages of Small-Group Development Revisited," *Group & Organization Studies* 2, pp. 419–25 (December 1972).

Tversky, Amos, and Daniel Kahneman, "Judgment Under Uncertainty: Heuristics and Biases," in *Judgment Under Uncertainty: Heuristics and Biases,* edited by Daniel Kahneman, Paul Slovic, and Amos Tversky, Cambridge, England: Cambridge University Press, 1982. Originally published in *Science* 185, pp. 1124–31 (1974).

Useem, Michael, *The Leadership Moment,* New York: Times Books/Random House, 1998.

Wade, Ian, and Mike Fischesser, *The Outward Bound Safety Review Manual,* Garrison, New York: Outward Bound USA.

Warren, Karen, and Sue Tippett, "Teaching Consensus Decision Making," *Journal of Experiential Education* (fall 1998).

Waterman, Laura, and Guy Waterman, *Backwoods Ethics,* 2nd ed., Woodstock, Vermont: Countryman Press, 1993.

———, *Wilderness Ethics,* Woodstock, Vermont: Countryman Press, 1993.

Wilde, Gerald J. S., *Target Risk 2,* 2nd ed., Toronto: PDE Publications, 2001.

Wilderness Risk Managers Conference Proceedings, Lander, Wyoming: National Outdoor Leadership School, annual.

Wilkerson, James A., ed., *Medicine for Mountaineering,* 5th ed., Seattle: Mountaineers, 2001.

Williamson, John E., ed., *Accidents in North American Mountaineering,* Golden, Colorado: American Alpine Club, annual.

Wurdinger, Scott D., and Tom G. Potter, *Controversial Issues in Adventure Education: A Critical Examination,* Dubuque, Iowa: Kendall/Hunt Publishing, 1999.

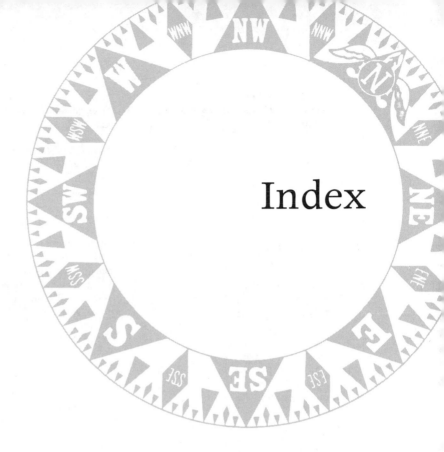

Index